Early Percussion Firearms

Other Books by Lewis Winant:

PEPPERBOX FIREARMS
FIREARMS CURIOSA

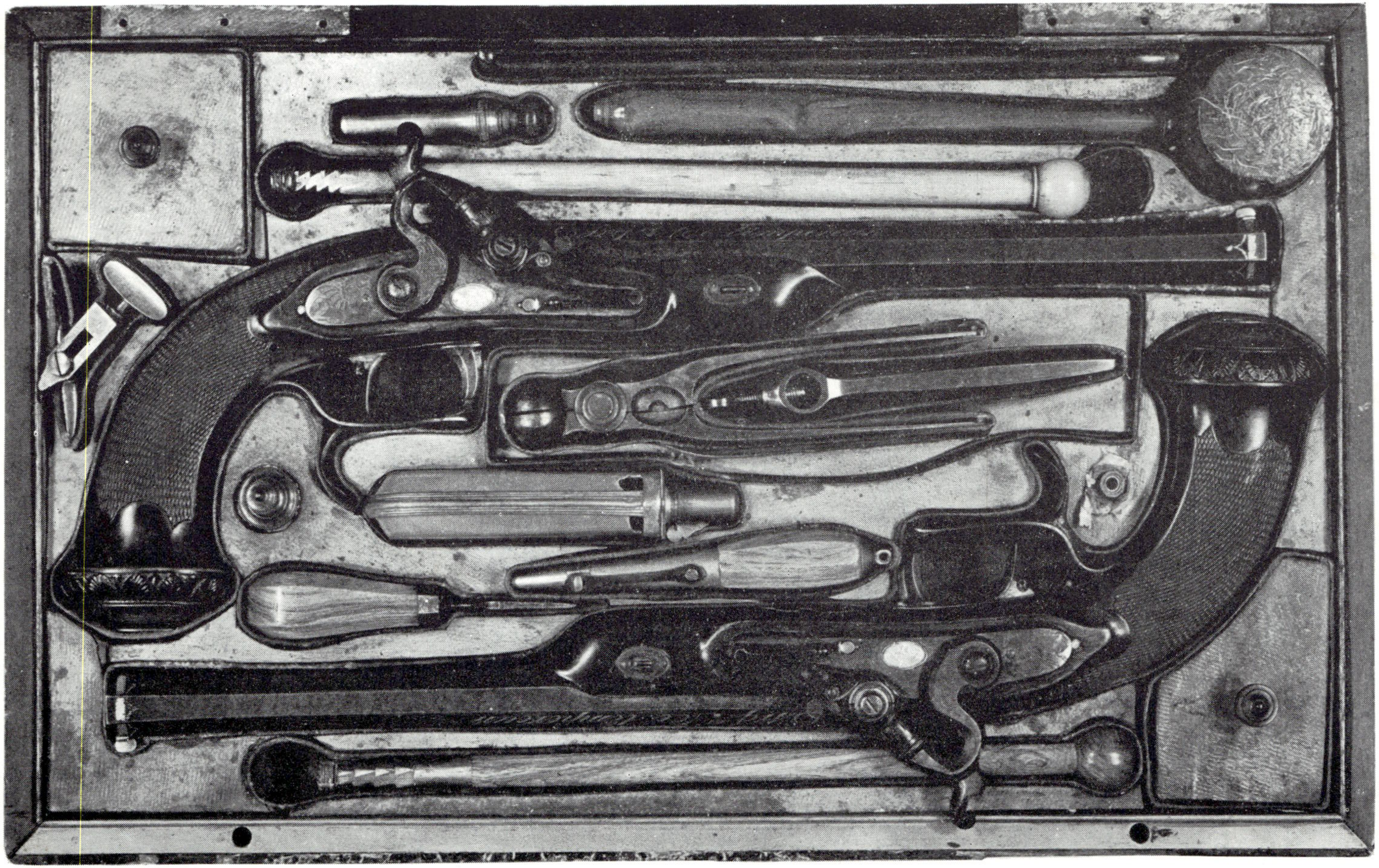

Cased pair of Le Page pistols.
(*New Haven Historical Society Collection. Photograph courtesy of Winchester*)

Early Percussion Firearms

A History of Early Percussion Ignition – from Forsyth to Winchester .44/40

Lewis Winant

Spring Books

London · New York · Sydney · Toronto

First Published in Great Britain by
Herbert Jenkins Ltd.

This edition published 1970 by
The Hamlyn Publishing Group Ltd.
London · New York · Sydney · Toronto
Hamlyn House, Feltham, Middlesex, England

Printed in Great Britain by
Cox & Wyman Ltd., London, Reading and Fakenham

ISBN 0 600 33015 X

Parts of Chapter XI appeared in an article in the August and September, 1955, issues of *The American Rifleman.* Walter J. Howe, editor, kindly gave permission to reprint.

CONTENTS

LIST OF ILLUSTRATIONS

Plates

Plates

Plates

Plates

Plates

Plates

Plates

Diagrams in Text		*Page*
A.	Drawing of Pauly firearms, with tools for loading cartridges	34
B.	Hammer and peg shown on Prelat 1818 patent drawing. (Two of twenty-nine figures.)	44
C.	First page of Joshua Shaw's *A Sketch or History of the Copper Cap, and Percussion Artillery Primer*	47
D.	Affidavit by W. L. Ellsworth supporting Shaw's patent claims	50
E.	Deboubert 1820 patent drawing	54
F.	Nipple, cap, and cap in place on nipple from Prelat 1818 patent drawing	56
G.	Prelat 1810 patent drawing, imitation Forsyth lock	65
H.	Drawing from the *London Journal of Arts and Sciences*	68
I.	Beckwith's percussion gun, for firing with either caps or loose powder	85
J.	Operation of Sharps disk primer	122
K.	Maynard circular	159

ACKNOWLEDGEMENTS

FIRST and foremost in my acknowledgements to men who gave me ungrudging help with this book must be the name of that eminent English authority on firearms, W. Keith Neal. Mr. Neal took many superlative photographs for me of pieces from his distinguished collection which would be difficult, and in some cases impossible, to find elsewhere. He made numerous suggestions of great worth, and he was most kind in giving full answers to my inquiries. Much material which has not previously appeared in book form was supplied by Mr. Neal.

Many Americans—collectors, authorities, students—gave me valuable aid. Mr. Milburn Doss gave me photostatic enlargements of a microfilm of all pages of Henri Roux's *Fusils de Chasse*, of which the only copy I know to exist is in the *Bibliothèque Nationale* in Paris. Dr. W. R. Funderburg put at my disposal his magnificent firearms collection, and sent memoranda which enlightened me on deep problems. Dr. Funderburg sent me for examination and photographing all guns from his collection I asked for, as well as examples of some types I wanted but which I did not know he possessed. To Thomas E. Hall, Firearms Historian of Olin Mathieson Chemical Corporation, and a man of unequalled knowledge in respect of many American and European firearms, I am deeply indebted. Mr. Hall kindly supplied excellent photographs of several guns now in the famous Winchester collection, and he also sent me photostatic copies of relevant matter found in old and rare European works. The Olin Mathieson Museum in New Haven is where every sort of Winchester firearm—including Winchester revolvers—is to be seen, but the museum's vast collection is by no means confined to Winchesters. To George Hyatt go my thanks for letting me have a rare punch-lock Kentucky, and for getting me a photograph of superb quality of a pair of his Butterfield derringers. William Locke sent me rare guns from his exceptional collection to examine and photograph. Henry Stewart furnished photographs of remarkable pieces from his outstanding collection. Mr. Stewart has a great knowledge of old guns, both as to their mechanisms and their histories, and he took time to clear up obscure points. To Paul Westergard I am grateful for much help. Mr. Westergard let me borrow from his fine and diversified collection of guns, and he gave me full access to his notable collection of memorabilia. To my wife, Florence Winant, I wish to acknowledge that her name appears next to last in this grouping only because the names are given in alphabetical order. Were I listing in order those who gave the most important help, her name would lead all the rest. As this listing is alphabetical, Harold Young's name comes last. However, let it be noted for the record that Mr. Young supplied more photographs which are reproduced in illustrations in this book than any one else.

I wish to list names of others—collectors and men interested in the history and development of firearms—who contributed generously, by furnishing photographs, by lending guns or accessories for me to photograph, by supplying conclusive answers to moot questions, by suggestions as to where further exploration could be profitable, and, most important, by criticisms. This additional list of friendly assistants includes both men with private firearms collections and individuals employed by public institutions as well as private establishments that have museums displaying old guns: Mark Aziz; Frank Bivens; Graham Burnside; George Cummings; F. Theodore Dexter; Herbert Green; Louis Hart; John Hintlian; Frank Horner; Paul Janke; Colonel R. C. Kuhn; Harold MacFarland; Robert Marron; Robert McLeod; Henry McMullen; Eugene Miller; Arnott Millett; John Parsons; Eddie Reider; Robert Scurfield; James Serven; Franklin Simmons; Dr. Jack Strassman; John Watson; Leslie White; Dr. Thomas Hoopes, of the City Art Museum of St. Louis; Charles Coles and Mary Chamberlain, of Colt's Patent Fire Arms Manufacturing Company; Stephen Grancsay, Leonard Heinrich, and Randolph Bullock, of the Metropolitan Museum of Art; Mendel Peterson and Craddock Goins, of the Smithsonian Institution; Colonel Frederick Todd and Milton Perry, of the West Point Museum.

There was one time when long search had failed to bring to light a booklet I thought must be in the Archives Building in Washington, and I had given up the search. An hour later, a government custodian of records who had not given up found the document. He then went on a telephone hunt to find me. He located me in the

Patent Office, got me on the phone and told me he had what I was looking for—Joshua Shaw's story of the invention he claimed. That example, along with other instances of friendly, intelligent interest and co-operation, makes me feel I would be remiss if I did not mention the unfailing courtesy of department heads and their staff members in public institutions that do not have firearms collections, such as: the Library of Congress, the National Archives, the Patent Office, the Supreme Court in Washington; the Newark Public Library, in Newark, N.J.; the New York Public Library, in New York; the Franklin Institute, the Historical Society of Pennsylvania, the Pennsylvania Hospital, the Philadelphia Free Library, in Philadelphia.

There are statements in this book which contradict statements made by earlier writers. I had the advantage of being able to unearth, and of being supplied with, fully documented data that were undiscovered by other writers.

LEWIS WINANT
East Camp Walk
Island Heights, N.J.

EARLY PERCUSSION FIREARMS

Now then I'll dwell upon the GUN.
When first this weapon was invented
It had no lock; men were contented,
Or rather were oblig'd, 'tis said,
To use a lighted match instead.

But every age improved it still,
And so, perhaps, the future will.
Remarks on Shooting
W. Watt, London, 1835

CHAPTER I

FORSYTH MUZZLE-LOADING DETONATORS

THIS story of the development of percussion ignition begins with the work of a Scotch clergyman, and ends just before the advent of modern cartridge arms. Our most modern guns are fired by percussion, but in this volume we stop with the guns that immediately preceded the era-opening 1873 model Winchester rifle.

Percussion firearms are fired by a hammer blow that crushes a fulminating mixture. The fulminates are salts, formed by the dissolution of metals in acids, which will explode violently when struck. Who first discovered the explosive properties is not known. The discovery was probably accidental.

A Colt Bisley is called a cartridge revolver; a Colt Dragoon, a percussion-cap revolver; a Manton tube-lock pistol, a detonator. Those guns are properly so called, but they also are all properly called percussion firearms. All are fired by a blow which crushes fulminate. For the Bisley the fulminate is in a cap in the centre of a modern cartridge head, for the Dragoon in a cap set on a nipple, for the Manton in a metal tube pushed in a touch hole.

Black gunpowder, a mechanical mixture of sulphur, saltpetre, and charcoal, under suitable conditions can be made to explode by a blow, as of a heavy hammer on an anvil, but it will not serve in a gunlock as a substitute for a chemical fulminating mixture which may be so compounded as to explode by a light tap.

Fulminates were known and their possibilities examined at least as early as the 17th century, but it was not until after 1800 that successful experiments were carried out in connection with firearms.

A reference to fulminate of gold will be found in any unabridged edition of Pepys's famous diary for November 11, 1663. Fulminating silver was produced in France by Count Berthollet in 1788. That was an extremely sensitive and powerful explosive. Fulminating mercury was produced in England by Howard in 1799 or 1800. That product was somewhat more tractable, but its manufacture was still very risky.

In the late 18th century much experimenting was done in England and on the continent of Europe in the hope of using fulminate as a propellent in a gun barrel, either alone or mixed with gunpowder. As far as is known, no one before the early 1800's did any experimenting with the idea of using a fulminate merely to ignite a powder charge. It may well be that before then some chemist did lay a train of gunpowder, and then lay across it a train of fulminating powder, only to find that when the fulminate was detonated the gunpowder neither exploded nor burned. The gunpowder was merely blown away, and with it perhaps all thought of using fulminate as an igniting agent.

At that time all guns, except matchlocks from an earlier era, used friction ignition. The gunpowder was ignited by sparks resulting from the rubbing of flint against steel in the flintlocks, or steel against flint or pyrites in the wheel locks.

The development of the percussion system of firearms ignition began with the Forsyth invention patented in England in 1807. It progressed to the successful production of a dependable modern centre-fire cartridge in the 1870's. Since the 1870's there have been major improvements and refinements in gunpowder and in fulminating mixtures, as well as in cartridge case and bullet construction, but there has been no basic change in the percussion system of ignition.

The Reverend Alexander John Forsyth, M.A., LL.D., the inventor of the percussion lock, was born at the manse of Belhelvie, a village near Aberdeen, in 1768. He was the son of the Reverend James Forsyth, minister of Belhelvie, When James Forsyth died in 1790, Alexander Forsyth was given the ecclesiastical living. He continued as minister until his death in 1843.

Forsyth diverted himself by hunting waterfowl and by working on chemical and mechanical problems. He kept abreast of scientific developments and knew of the efforts being made to substitute a fulminic acid for the saltpetre in gunpowder. Potassium chlorate was being tried in France; fulminate of mercury in England. Forsyth worked with both preparations and soon learned what earlier experimenters had discovered, that fulminates were unsatisfactory as propellents.

The flint gun was slow. Forsyth had missed birds which dived with the flash of the flintlock and were safely submerged when the shot struck the water. He tried a hood over the lock to conceal the flash, but the device did not content him. He went on to experiment with fulminate as an igniting agent only, not as a propellent. The first experiments involved no more than a substitution of fulminating powder for the fine gunpowder commonly used in the pans of flintlocks. The sparks from the flint would sometimes fire the fulminate in the pan, but the flames were unlikely to pass through the touch hole to explode the gunpowder in the barrel chamber. Forsyth found that better ignition was apt to result when the fulminate in the pan was detonated by a blow rather than inflamed by sparks. However, there were still frequent misfires. The open pan of the flintlock would not suffice for percussion ignition. Forsyth soon apprehended that he could have unfailing discharge of his fowling piece if he could devise a lock that would confine the fulminate in a small space and ensure that flame from the fulminate detonation would be surely directed into the touch hole.

All along in his experimenting with fulminate as an igniting agent, it was Forsyth's thought to use the fulminate finely granulated. Forsyth could hardly have failed to know that more or less successful automatic priming magazines containing fine gunpowder had been developed for use with flint guns. He did much work to devise a magazine that not only would deposit a small carefully gauged amount of priming into a channel leading to the chamber vent, but which would also permit the orifice of the channel to be plugged by the striker at the moment of firing.

The story goes that Forsyth made a successful lock in the spring of 1805, that he fitted the lock to a fowling piece which he used through that season, and that he went to London with the gun in 1806. When he reached London—and that may have been 1805 instead of 1806—the gun was exhibited to Lord Moira, Master General of Ordnance. Lord Moira was so impressed with what Forsyth had accomplished that he asked Forsyth to set up a workshop in the Tower in order to perfect his invention. The lock on Forsyth's fowling piece was probably fragile. Lord Moira wanted a sturdy lock developed, one that would keep priming and powder always dry, that would not break under hard usage and that could be used easily and safely on muskets, and even on cannon.

Lord Moira requested and obtained leave of absence for Forsyth from the Aberdeen Presbytery, and Forsyth then devoted all his time to the production of a lock that would meet Lord Moira's requirements. Forsyth found he had to experiment not only with the lock but also with fulminates to use in it. It seems that after he had worked in the Tower for nearly a year he produced a satisfactory lock for a musket and another for a cannon and that he had compounded a dependable fulminate mixture. But then Lord Moira was succeeded as Master General of Ordnance by John Pitt, the second Earl of Chatham and the brother of William Pitt, the illustrious Prime Minister of England. The Earl of Chatham did not possess his brother's great talents. In fact, history records he had a propensity for making unwise decisions. He peremptorily ordered Forsyth to take himself and his effects from the Tower.

Through the years a handful of improbable stories about Forsyth appeared. Most of them deserve the Scotch verdict, "not proven". The one most frequently repeated deals with an offer said to have been made by Napoleon for Forsyth's invention, and with Forsyth's rejection of the offer. I have no doubt that Forsyth would have curtly refused to deal with Napoleon, but I do have doubt that Napoleon made any offer. Why should Napoleon offer amounts reported to range from $100,000 to $500,000 for an invention he could take without payment? Forsyth guns were available in France directly after they were made in London, and Napoleon had at his command gunmakers such as Boutet, Pauly, Prelat, and Le Page, who could copy and teach others to copy guns like the Forsyth products.

The resistance to change that is in the nature of man is most unmistakable in military thinking. The first issue of percussion muskets to a British regiment was in 1840, and to an American regiment in 1844, yet by 1825 the worst die-hards among the gunmakers gave up trying to convince sportsmen they should stick to flint guns. The sportsmen knew the percussion guns were better and they insisted on having them.

When his invention was rejected by the top brass in the army Forsyth decided there would be a market for his lock among sportsmen. He obtained a patent, set up a shop to make percussion locks and guns, and returned to his parochial duties. James Watt, the inventor of the steam engine, helped him with his patent application, and James Purdey, who later founded the gunmaking firm of that name, served as his gunsmith. They were two extremely able men.

Forsyth's patent was drawn up with great skill, and the high courts ruled it a basic patent. His British patent, 3032 of the year 1807, states: ". . . instead of giving fire to the charge by a lighted match, or by flint and steel, or by any other matter in a state of actual combustion applied to a priming in an open pan. I do close the touch-hole or vent by means of a plug or sliding piece, or other fit piece of metal or suitable material or materials, so as to exclude the open air, and to prevent any sensible escape of the blast or explosive gas or vapour outwards . . ." Referring to the use of fulminate, the patent states: ". . . and as a priming I do make use of some or one of those chemical compounds which are so easily inflammable as to be capable of taking fire and exploding without any actual fire being applied thereto, and merely by a blow, or by any sudden or strong pressure or friction given or applied thereto without extraordinary violence . . ."

Of the Forsyth detonating locks the best known is the one now universally called the scent bottle, because of the shape of the priming magazine. Originally it was called the roller-magazine lock. An example of a pistol with a scent-bottle lock is pictured at the top in Plate 1. In this lock there is a tapered steel plug, about an inch long and nearly a half inch in diameter, having a one-eighth-inch hole drilled lengthwise through its centre. (The tapering is slight, but it is enough to be easily noticed. If the plug appears to be perfectly cylindrical—beware!) This plug is screwed into the barrel breeching from the side. The one-eighth-inch hole in the centre of the plug is a channel, with its outer end sealed, leading directly into the powder chamber in the barrel. When the barrel is loaded and the charge rammed down, gunpowder will enter and fill this channel. Hollowed in the top surface of this plug is a tiny pan, about an eighth of an inch wide and a sixteenth deep. A pin-hole vent leads down from this pan to the powder channel. The scent bottle fits on the steel plug and may be turned around the plug manually through a half circle. The scent bottle has in one end a cavity holding enough priming for perhaps forty shots, and in the other end a firing pin held out by a spiral spring. The scent bottle is held firmly against the plug by means of two setscrews which may be seen in the illustration, one opposite the other. The screws press oil-impregnated packing against the plug.

To prime, the hammer is raised and the scent bottle turned through a half circle until it hits a stop, at which time the priming reservoir is in line with the tiny pan. Enough priming, about an eighth of a grain, falls in the pan to fill it. After priming, the scent bottle is turned back to the firing position shown in Plate 1. It might be better to say the illustration shows the gun in the fired position. The hammer has dropped, driving the firing pin into the pan and detonating the charge.

There is a sliding cover at the reservoir end of the scent bottle, to permit refilling. In the centre of this cover is a little plug of horn, held in place by friction. This plug is a safety feature. In the unlikely event that fulminate in the magazine should be detonated, possibly by the gun being dropped and the magazine struck in the fall, the force of the explosion would pass out through this loosely plugged vent.

This lock had all the essential features needed in a fowling-piece lock. It kept the priming confined so it was not subject to damp and so it would be certain to fire the gunpowder when detonated. It passed the requirements of ease and safety in use. Whether it was simple enough and sturdy enough for an infantryman in the field is uncertain. No official test was made to find out.

As far as is known all the experimental locks made in the Tower by Forsyth for use in hand guns were of the scent-bottle type, with the magazine turning endwise.

Another merit the hunter soon recognized was that Forsyth and all other percussion guns were quicker than flintlock guns. The bullet from a percussion gun gets out of the barrel sooner after the hammer falls. Though a hunter had to revise his ideas about leading birds in shooting flying game, he soon found he had fewer misses with a percussion gun.

It is true the Forsyth detonators were expensive. The lock alone cost as much as a complete flint gun of good quality.

The fulminate powder was sold by Forsyth for ten shillings and sixpence an ounce. That price caused some complaint. It seems costly but it works out at about ten primings for one cent.

The complaints against the price of the fulminate were less important than the complaints made against the fulminate itself. The early fulminating powders deposited undue quantities of corrosive matter. A percussion lock required cleaning after use more promptly than a flintlock. Knowledge of that fact might have had something to do with the unceremonious rejection of Forsyth's invention by the military. In a short time improved fulminating mixtures were worked up. At first the powder was mainly potassium chlorate compounded with small amounts of sulphur and charcoal. In a few years a highly recommended mixture was equal parts of potassium chlorate and antimony, both finely powdered. This was claimed to be unobjectionable and not rust-forming. However, complaints about the corrosive action of fulminating mixtures probably did not die down to a murmur until well in the 1860's. In 1867 Dr. Joseph Goldmark took out a patent, U.S. 69,206, for a fulminating compound that was probably better in all respects than any there had been before. Dr. Goldmark claimed the use of "sulphocyanite of a metal or other base . . . in combination with chlorate of potash." Even the ingredients now used do not make a perfect mixture.

Before leaving the subject of scent-bottle Forsyths it is well to point out that genuine specimens are scarce, valuable, and highly prized by discerning collectors. The Forsyth pistols and locks illustrated in this chapter are unquestionably genuine.

There was a great surge of interest between 1920 and 1930 in detonators bearing the Forsyth name. This had its climax at the end of 1929 when a tablet honouring Forsyth was placed on a wall of the Tower of London. More of that tablet later.

Some may doubt there was no example of a Forsyth gun in the Tower in the early 1920's. However, I have before me two letters written by the late Dr. Paul B. Jenkins, a man intensely interested in anything having to do with Forsyth and his guns, a sometime editor of the Guns and Ammunition Department of *Outdoor Recreation*, later in charge of the Rudolph J. Nunnemacher Collection of Projectile Arms in the Milwaukee Public Museum. Referring to a visit made to England and Scotland a few years before 1926, he wrote, referring to Forsyth arms: "The Tower of London hasn't a single specimen of this type!—which no Englishman will believe. I have had 'em tell me otherwise, in the very Tower itself, until I proved it to them." Again, Dr. Jenkins wrote: "When I personally scoured the Tower for traces of Forsyth and his work, not one person there knew anything about him, and I had to produce to them documentary proof of him and his work as historical realities. Even then they suggested I had better go to Aberdeen to learn something more definite about him!—which I promptly did, and found what I sought too!"

If there still be sceptics, I suggest to them a careful examination of the two large volumes of Charles Ffoulkes's *Inventory and Survey of the Armouries of the Tower of London*, published in 1916. No reference to Forsyth is to be found there.

In the later 1920's, R. W. Reid, Fellow of the Royal College of Surgeons, and grandnephew of Dr. Forsyth, presented examples of Forsyth firearms to the Tower.

Unfortunately, many of the scent-bottle detonators bearing the Forsyth name, guns in which collectors at that time were becoming increasingly interested, are not Forsyth products.

About 1920 an American visitor to England called on a gunsmith who owned a scent-bottle Forsyth. Not only did the American buy the gun at a price higher than the gunsmith had thought would be paid, but he expressed eagerness to buy more of the same kind, as many as could be found. The wretched gunsmith was irresistibly tempted by the prospect of duping collectors and making illicit profits. He proceeded to make quantities of sham scent bottles and hammers, and put them on guns originally fitted with copper-cap locks. Some of the fake scent-bottle Forsyths were made from Forsyth copper-cap guns, but mostly the fakes were made from cap guns of other makes. The Forsyth cap guns were expensive and, anyway, they were not obtainable in sufficient numbers for the counterfeiter's wants. Of course, the easily found and cheaper cap guns of other makes required more alteration. Not only had locks to be changed, but barrel signatures had to be erased and Forsyth signatures substituted. I was surprised when I learned that a name on a barrel could be transformed into another name, inlaid in gold, without difficulty and at little cost.

Please let me digress to make brief comment on the faking of firearms in general. To cover that subject fully and properly a large book would be needed. I greatly doubt that any one man is competent to write it. It may safely be said that an unprincipled present-day faker is not apt to produce a copy of a priceless rarity. Such a gun is not readily available for copying, and the imitation may not sell quickly. A collector too often is interested in buying only a gun like one he has heard about or seen in another collection. The fakers now pretty much confine their activities to the production of well-known and reasonably commonplace revolvers which they can readily sell at towering prices.

Even in the specific case of Forsyths, it is not possible to spell out rules for detecting the spurious guns.

In England as in America it is a serious offence falsely to label a product as patented. The counterfeiter normally avoided engraving that unauthorized certification on a modern reproduction of a scent bottle. Most of the reproductions will have scroll engraving, but not "Patent". However, the first few genuine scent bottles lacked the word "Patent".

It is also true that a lock may be falsely marked with both the Forsyth name and the word "Patent". A lock that was not made by Forsyth and that is unlike any lock made by Forsyth, but which bears the Forsyth name and the word "Patent", will be described in Chapter V.

The wording of either the barrel signature or the lock-plate signature is not alone sufficient to prove whether or not a gun is genuine. Signatures on genuine guns showed slight variations. Usually, but not always, the barrel signatures were plain inscriptions, not gold inlaid.

One thing, however, is sure. If the piece is genuine there will be no crudity in the cutting of the lettering. It should be held in mind that on genuine Forsyths all workmanship, including all lettering and ornamentation, is always of strikingly high quality.

If the lock be taken apart, the steel plug on which the scent bottle revolves should be scrutinized. That plug should be slightly, but definitely tapered. If the plug is cylindrical, if the scent bottle is scroll-engraved and lacks "Patent",—NO!

One form of genuine Forsyth scent bottle that is rarely seen or recognized by collectors is the interchangeable lock. This was developed by Forsyth for the sportsman who wanted flint ignition in reserve if anything happened to his detonator lock, or if he ran out of fulminate. It was a lock that could be easily replaced with an ordinary flintlock in a minute's time with only one tool, a turnscrew. The front and back of one of these rare locks are shown in Plates 2 and 3. The platinum touch hole which lines up with the touch hole of the flint gun can be seen on the inside of the lock. A gun with one of these interchangeable locks can be told from a gun with a non-interchangeable lock by noticing that on the former the scent-bottle magazine is fastened to the lock plate, while on the latter it is fastened to the barrel bearing.

At the bottom in Plate 1 is a pair of folding trigger pistols showing the ultimate development of the Forsyth loose-powder detonator. The priming magazines on these pistols are joined to the hammers by steel couplings, and they move back and forth with the raising and lowering of the hammers. When the hammer is drawn to full cock, as it is on one of the pair, the magazine slides back until it is directly over the small flash pan. The priming then drops from the magazine into the pan. When the trigger is pulled the magazine slides forward out of the way as the hammer comes down. In the nose of the hammer is a screwed-in replaceable firing pin whose point fits with nicety in the small pan, so that as the fulminate is detonated the fire will all be directed to the gunpowder in the barrel.

The screwed-in firing pin can probably be more clearly seen in Plate 4, which shows a very rare early form of the Forsyth sliding magazine. This humpback model, with its retaining spring which was omitted on the late models, was in regular production for a short time only.

It is believed the sliding magazines were the result of an attempt by a competitive gunmaker to infringe the Forsyth patent. Fortunately for Forsyth, the courts looked upon his 1807 patent as a master patent which covered all types of magazine mechanisms designed to dispense fulminating mixtures. Forsyth was free to adapt any sliding magazine to his own gun and to bar its use by anyone else, in England, that is.

Before his patent ran out, Forsyth challenged the Joseph Manton 1818 tube-lock invention, and the courts decided the Manton tube-lock infringed the Forsyth patent. Whether a patent for a copper percussion cap would have been considered by the British courts not to be an infringement will never be known, for no one applied in England for a patent on a gun using a percussion cap until after Forsyth's patent expired in 1821.

The Forsyth detonators were of course made in long guns as well as in pistols, and in double-barrel as well as in single. A fine example of a Forsyth detonator with over-and-under barrels is shown in Plate 5.

The British Government's acknowledgment of the significance of Forsyth's invention was long delayed, but it came a little at a time and finally in very gracious form.

In the late 1830's when British authorities decided to equip the armed forces with percussion guns the newspapers took up the cause of the Reverend Alexander Forsyth. The newspaper campaign was probably started in 1839 by the Aberdeen *Herald*. That paper pointed out that the percussion guns then being adopted for the military forces resulted from Forsyth's invention. It stated that Lord Moira, in order to induce Forsyth to carry on his experiments in the Tower, had proposed that Forsyth's expenses would be paid, as well as the salary of his locum tenens, and that Forsyth should further receive a suitable reward. The article went on to say that Forsyth received his expenses but that he had to pay from his own pocket the salary of the minister who had filled his place in Belhelvie, and that he had received no reward. It ended with, ". . . the only way he can now be rewarded, is by the Government doing what they intended to do before, and by the sporting public taking up the matter with proper spirit. We trust our brethren of the press will aid in obtaining this piece of justice for a quiet unobtrusive, respectable clergyman, who is not more admired for his ingenuity than he is esteemed for his amiable private qualities by all who have the pleasure of knowing him."

In 1840 the matter of suitable remuneration was brought up in the House of Commons. In 1842 the Master General of Ordnance recommended "A gratuity of £200 for remuneration as the original Inventor of percussion for small arms." This amount was paid to

Forsyth shortly before his death. A few months after Forsyth's death the Master General concluded that £200 had been inadequate and proposed an additional payment of £1000 to be distributed among Forsyth's surviving relatives. This further sum was ordered paid, and was apportioned among a niece, a nephew, and a brother-in-law.

Public interest ended with the announcement of the monetary award, and Forsyth and his invention were forgotten history.

Never was a trigger pulled in a modern gun, in sport or in anger, but Forsyth's invention made it possible. None the less, of the millions who were called up from 1914 to 1918 probably not one in a thousand knew that the cartridge he loaded in his rifle was the outcome of that invention.

In 1929 a few students, historians, collectors, and sportsmen decided there should be a memorial to Forsyth that would give him full recognition. When the project was made known, it received support from military and gunmakers' organizations, and from English and Scottish sportsmen. There is now in the Tower of London a handsome tablet in his honour.

The tablet is a work of art in bronze. At the top is a medallion portrait of Forsyth. In the two lower corners are reproductions of two of Forsyth's earliest percussion locks. The inscription on the tablet is:

To the Memory of the Reverend
Alexander John Forsyth
M.A., LL.D.
Minister of Belhelvie
Aberdeenshire
In 1805 he conducted experiments
in the Tower under the Master
General of Ordnance and in 1807
invented the percussion system
which was adopted by the
British Army in 1839

This Tablet was erected
in 1929 by admirers of his
Genius

CHAPTER II

PAULY BREECH-LOADING DETONATORS

THE Merriam-Webster definition of fixed ammunition is "Ammunition in which the projectile is permanently attached to a case which contains the primer and the propellent."

The Pauly breechloader was the first firearm to use fixed ammunition.

Many gunmakers of the 19th century were talented, and a few were geniuses. In the brief list of those inventive geniuses—defining geniuses as those who accomplish what is impossible for the merely talented—Forsyth was first chronologically, but probably Pauly was the most eminent. Forsyth received little acclaim until long after he first invented a percussion lock, but finally he was honoured and his work eulogized. On the other hand, Pauly received high praise from men of science of his day, but later generations have paid him little homage.

Pauly's greatest invention came when Napoleon was conquering Europe. Napoleon wrote, "Inventions coming before their time remain useless until knowledge in general comes to their level." He was not speaking directly of Pauly's invention, but his words applied to it.

The date of Pauly's birth, and the date of his death, both seem lost in the night of time. It is known that Pauly was a Swiss, and that he came to Paris about 1808.

That was a bad time to get recognition in France for any invention. Frenchmen were concerned with the continual wars in which they engaged. Off and on they fought Britain, Austria, Russia, Sweden, Prussia, Spain, and Portugal. It is remarkable that Pauly's breechloader was able to get any favourable attention in such troubled times.

After Waterloo, it took fifty years to revive centre-fire cartridges, the essence of Pauly's invention.

On September 29, 1812, Jean Samuel Pauly was given a French patent for a breech-loading gun that used a self-contained, rimmed, reloadable, centre-fire cartridge.* Pauly's gun, in addition to being the first to use centre-fire cartridges, was the first breechloader to use any form of percussion ignition.

As the salient feature of Pauly's invention was the cartridge, that feature should be described first and in detail.

Plate 6 shows at the bottom three views of reloadable brass cartridges used in Pauly pistols, and two views at the top, with a bullet separating them, of brass rosettes used as heads for the paper case cartridges fired in Pauly rifles and shotguns.

At the bottom right in Illustration A is a drawing, figure 7, of parts of a cartridge ready for assembly. In figures 7, 8, and 9 of this illustration the tools used for hand-loading the paper case cartridges are shown. To understand the making of a cartridge it is perhaps best to refer first to figure 8, which shows a two-purpose punch. When the spindle shown at the far right in figure 8 is inserted in the punch, and the solid end of the punch hit with a mallet while the open end is resting on cardboard, a circular piece will be cut out with a small hole driven through its centre. With the spindle removed, the punch may be used for its second purpose, to cut wads from felt or leather. The wads and the pierced disk being prepared, a piece of paper the length of the cartridge is rolled on the mandrel, figure 7, so as to go about 1½ times around. The overlapping edges are pasted, and at the end of the open cylinder now formed the pierced disk is inserted. The end is covered with thin paper and the whole pasted so as completely to seal the end. After the paste dries, the cylinder is filled with the necessary powder, lead, and wads.

The rosette, which is the head of the cartridge, is of brass and is fitted with a screw. This screw pierces the thin paper and enters the hole in the cardboard end of the cartridge, its threads biting into the cardboard so the rosette is firmly attached.

In the centre of the face of the brass rosette is a little circular steel pan, called a "bassinet" by Pauly, about ⅛ inch across and less than that in depth. There is a fine vent which runs through the centre of this pan and on through the axis of the screw. The end *S* of the priming flask *MS* shown in figure 9 is now placed vertically in the little pan. When the thumb is pressed at point *P* the correct amount of priming powder for one shot is released into the pan.

* French Patents—Series 1, volume 10, page 53, plate 6.

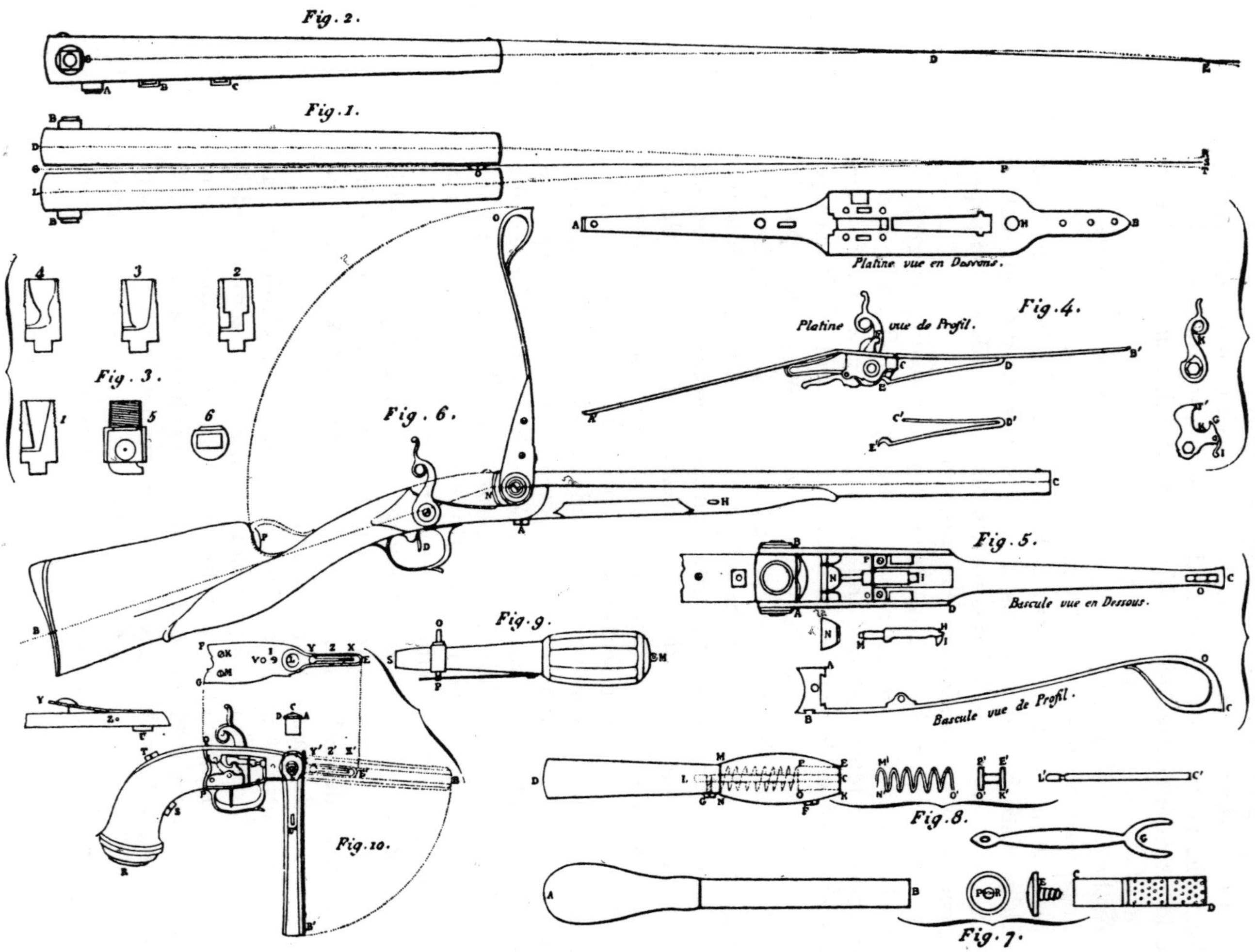

Illustration A. Drawing of Pauly firearms, with tools for loading cartridges

Finally, the piston *O* is used to tamp this priming powder, packing it firmly so it will not be shaken out.

Please note the two-tined fork in the lower right corner of Illustration A, immediately above the cartridge in figure 7. This is a cartridge extractor. The prongs enter a circular groove on the outer face of the rosette and permit easy removal of a fired case. This tool speeded reloading of the gun. A competent man could fire ten to twelve shots a minute from a double-barrel Pauly shotgun like the one in Plates 7, 8 and 9. An expert could do better.

Plate 7 shows the gun with the hinged lever, the bascule, down and the breech closed. In Plates 8 and 9, and in figure 6 of the drawing in Illustration A, the lever is shown raised, with the breech open for loading. When pressed closed the lever is locked by a catch that enters a slot in its looped end. The catch is disengaged by finger pressure when the bascule is raised.

The general idea of breech-loading was old and had been widely used. Pauly's particular method, the use of a hinged lever to open the breech, was not new either, but the action, which employed a long blunt firing pin connected to a cocking lever, was entirely new. As the cocking lever is raised a tumbler turns back through an arc of a circle. A hook on the rear end of the firing pin engages with a slot in the tumbler, and the firing pin is retracted as the cock moves back from repose to half cock to full cock. Then, when the trigger is pulled, a heavy mainspring, which has been compressed by the raising of the cocking lever, turns the tumbler forward and drives the firing pin against the priming powder in the rosette of the cartridge.

The barrels in the shotgun illustrated are chambered. More than that, the chambers are rabbeted to take a rimmed cartridge. Pauly explained there were two reasons for putting a rim on the cartridge head, and for rabbeting the chamber to take the rim. First, the construction gave added assurance that the cartridge would not enter the barrel too far. Second, it was beneficial in preventing escape of gas at the breech.

Some students have been told that the need for an elastic case as an obturator in breechloaders was not recognized until about 1850. In his 1816 British patent Pauly not only referred to the desirability of using a rimmed cartridge to form a gastight joint but he recommended the head of the cartridge to be made of "some plastic or yielding substance, turned or cast in a mould".

The breeches of the barrels are convex, as are the heads of the cartridges. The breeches of the stock are correspondingly concave. The closure is like a ball-and-socket joint.

It should not be thought that the construction of Pauly cartridges completely eliminated gas escape at the barrel breech. There was inevitably a small blowback of gunpowder gas through the tiny hole in the bassinet and from the exposed fulminate in the bassinet. In the top of the bascule of the shotgun illustrated there are two one-eighth-inch-wide hemispherical knobs which on first examination I took to be solid and to serve no purpose other than ornamentation. Each of the hemispheres turned out to be pierced by a tiny vent which permitted gas escape. I think the vents were not really needed, inasmuch as the bascule was raised at every reloading, and each lifting of that lever would result in immediate release of any trapped gas, which would surely be inconsiderable and inconsequential in amount.

At a public meeting of La Société, the association for the encouragement of national industry in France, on July 20, 1814, a report was given on Pauly firearms. This report was made by a commission composed of five men well known in the world of science and art, MM. Bardel, Humblot, Mollard, Regnier, and Brillat-Savarin. Their opinions as to advantages of Pauly guns were that:

"They never hang fire".
"They consume less powder".
"Their barrels cannot be double loaded".
"They are very fast loading and are unloaded and reloaded with great ease".
"Their construction protects against fog and rain".
"They preserve the shooter from the danger he runs, by accident or inattention, in loading with a ramrod".

The conclusion was, "Your Commission thinks the Pauly gun should be given first place among firearms that are known in this day."

The meaning of the statement that the Pauly gun consumed less powder was made clear by its corollary, as stated by Henri Roux, that a projectile from a Pauly would outrange a projectile from a muzzle-loading flintlock, other things being equal.

The fact that Pauly guns could not be double-loaded was a matter of more importance than we can realize now. Muzzle-loading guns could be and often were double-loaded. The records of muzzle-loaders found abandoned on the American Civil War battlefields with two, three, four or more loads in a barrel show the numbers ran into the thousands.

A gun was never double loaded except as a result of human carelessness or inattention. A man in battle, or even a man hunting harmless game, often shows excitement and sometimes handles his gun improperly.

Though the Pauly could never be double-loaded and though it worked beautifully in the hands of a calm, experienced shooter, nevertheless it was no gun for a novice or for anyone who became flurried. It was definitely not for a butterfingers. A heavy mainspring was used, and if the cocking lever were to slip from the fingers when a cartridge was in the barrel there was a possibility of serious accident. Roux cautioned the user: "When a cartridge is in the barrel the gun should always be at either half cock or full cock, never at repose. If the cock is in the repose, the firing pin will press against the priming and may either ignite it or loosen it so it will fall out of the bassinet".

The Pauly was reliable, efficient, and very successful in the hands of anyone who operated it properly and carefully, but it is not surprising the Ministry of War in France rejected it. The Pauly was not rugged enough to take the exercises of the awkward squad. However, the two reasons given by the Ministry for not considering the gun were, first, high cost, and second, the danger in using powder of one composition for propelling the bullet, and powder of a different composition for ignition.

Pauly made rifles, shotguns, and pistols. Any example of a Pauly gun is a rare collector item. Probably a few more pistols than shotguns have survived, and more shotguns than rifles.

A fine Pauly pistol is shown in Plate 10. Another fine Pauly pistol opened for loading, and with a cartridge in the breech, is pictured in Plate 11. Illustration A, figure 10, shows a drawing of a Pauly pistol. An extracted cartridge case is shown in the drawing just above the pistol. That case, like the cartridge in Plate 6, is made entirely of brass and is quickly reloadable. The round bullet was simply squeezed into the mouth of the case after the gunpowder was poured in. Those re-usable metal cases eliminated the trouble of making paper cartridges, but Pauly said: "The paper cartridges are preferable in a pistol being carried by a traveller, to ensure the ball will not loosen and fall, permitting the powder charge to escape".

The Pauly long gun has the barrel, or barrels, immovable. The breech is opened for loading by raising a lever. The Pauly pistol has a barrel that is tipped down for loading when a spring catch on the left of the barrel is released.

The pistols in Plates 10 and 11 do not have a feature I have seen in one Pauly pistol, that is, a small and fragile ejecting rod. This rod, under $\frac{1}{16}$ inch in diameter and hardly one inch in length, was built into the breech of the barrel and held back by a light spring. One end of this short rod rested against the inside of the rim of the cartridge; the other end protruded slightly and diagonally through the outside of the butt of the barrel at the left. Pressure with a finger tip on the rod would start the fired case from the barrel so the case could easily be pulled out with the fingers.

The Pauly pistols in Plates 10 and 11 were designed to use as an extractor, the same sort of two-pronged tool used with the Pauly long guns.

A Pauly pistol with a built-in ejecting rod could be loaded, fired, unloaded, and reloaded even faster than a Pauly long gun. It could be fired nearly as many times in a minute as the most modern single-shot pistol.

The Pauly firearms illustrated in this book bear the Pauly name only, but guns on the Pauly pattern were made by other manufacturers. The collector may come across a gun marked only "Pauly", or "Pauly & Cie" or he may find one marked with the names of both Pauly and one of Pauly's successors, who were Roux, Pichereau, and Lefaucheux in that order.

Forsyth's vital statistics are a matter of record; Pauly's are not. We know Pauly took up gunmaking in Paris in 1808, or perhaps a little earlier. We know he left France and went to England in 1814 and that he was busy in England on one project or another until 1816. In England he used as first names both Jean Samuel and Samuel John. How long he lived in England after 1816 is a question unanswered, as is the question of whether he ever returned to Paris, possibly again to make guns bearing his name. It seems probable Pauly remained in England well after 1816, for Henri Roux, in his *Fusils de Chasse*, published in 1822, mentions in a footnote that Pauly had then been living for several years in England. Hodgson gives evidence, to be cited shortly, that Pauly died before 1828.

Pauly took out several patents in England.

One was for a hollow cannon ball that burst on impact.

Another very interesting patent was one granted jointly to Pauly and to Durs Egg, who like Pauly had been born in Switzerland. This was British patent 3903 of the year 1815. As Durs Egg was, like Pauly, signally famous as a gunmaker, we should fully expect their collaboration to be in the firearms field. Not in this case. The patent granted by King George III on October 24, 1815, to these two distinguished creators of fine guns was for "Certain Aerial Conveyances, and Vessels to be steered by Philosophical or Chemical and Mechanical Means". In 1815 "philosophy" was the word for what we now call physical science and the "certain aerial conveyances" were dirigibles. This Pauly–Egg patent was the first granted in England for an aerial machine.

The inventors had in mind a balloon, shaped like a fish, which supported a "Gondola, boat or car", having a movable tail or rudder. The airship was to have movable "fins, feathers, fans, or wings", devices apparently something like ailerons on modern aeroplane wings. They planned to steer the flying machine up or down, and to the right or left, by warping the ailerons and the rudder by means of machinery which they said was extremely simple and which could be made by any practical mechanic in various ways. They planned to give impulse to the machinery "either by manual or mechanical means using, in the latter case, any first mover which may be applicable to the purpose". As an additional means for guidance and direction of their balloon they recommended a movable weight which would also serve as ballast. This weight was a water-filled barrel, suspended by ropes over pulleys so it could be moved forward or backward. If the barrel were moved forward the head of the craft would nose down, and if moved backward the craft would rise. The water in the barrel would serve as ballast and, by means of a cock, could be discharged as the occasion required.

A device using the principle of the Pauly–Egg movable barrel was employed by Count Zeppelin in his first rigid dirigible. The Pauly–Egg "Fish-Formed Balloon"—after construction began it was named the "Dolphin"—was not a limp craft, one class of which we now call a blimp, as was the Robert Brothers fish-shaped free balloon flown in France in 1783; it was designed to be of the rigid dirigible type as were the Zeppelins.

J. E. Hodgson in his *History of Aeronautics in Great Britain* (London, 1924) tells of the serious attempt made to build one of the patented airships. A shed one hundred feet long and over thirty feet high was built and in it construction of the "Dolphin" was commenced in 1816. A reproduction of figure 117 in Hodgson's book is shown in Plate 13. Within the exterior envelope which was fitted over a wooden frame of what came to be known as "Egg's Folly", was a balloon made of gold-beater's skin in layers—the yield of 70,000 oxen. (The supreme folly in airship building, the R–101, which was intended to be the last word in airships but which turned out to be their deathblow, required more than a million gold-beater's skins, each about three feet by two feet.) Tickets were sold, at a guinea each, entitling the holder to see "one of the [Dolphin] ascensions"—of which none took place. The scheme was said to have cost Egg £10,000.

Given a modern lightweight motor and a propeller, the Pauly–Egg invention might have flown.

Hodgson wrote: "Finally Pauly died before the airship was completed, whereupon the project was abandoned", and added that Durs Egg lived until about 1828. Just when the project was abandoned, or how long Egg survived Pauly, is not stated.

There should be more than passing mention here of two British patents granted to Pauly, 3833 in 1814, and 4026 in 1816, for guns using compressed-air ignition. Of several inventors who took out patents for such guns, Pauly was first.

A compressed-air gun is commonly thought of as one using air as a propellent. A compressed-air-ignition gun uses air to inflame gunpowder. Pauly's theory of compressed-air ignition was sound, and the principle was not altogether new, except as it applied to guns. Pauly's idea was to compress air by means of a piston working in a "syringe", and then force the heated air through a tiny hole in the base of a cartridge, so the "caloric" would ignite the powder in the cartridge.

Pauly suggested that a "small piece of thin paper" be "glued, pasted, or affixed" over the small hole in the base of the compressed-air ignition cartridge, to prevent loss of gunpowder through the hole, but he made no suggestion that a similar piece of paper be placed over the priming which had been tamped in the bassinet in his percussion cartridge.

None of the compressed-air-ignition guns was received with enthusiasm, and none had satisfactory sales. Pauly's ideas were usually well ahead of his time. In this case his idea came too late. If Pauly had thought of it before detonators had been conceived—as anyone might have, inasmuch as the compressed-air system was not based on the percussion system—he, rather than Forsyth, might have been the man who was to make flintlocks antiquated.

Two centre-fire cartridges are shown in Plate 12. The one at the top is a Pauly. The other is a Pottet. The Pottet has sometimes incorrectly been called the first centre-fire cartridge. The fact is the Pottet is merely the first centre-fire cartridge to be produced after the invention of the percussion cap. The Pottet was patented in 1829. The Pauly was patented in 1812 and it was a centre-fire cartridge produced before the percussion cap was invented. A particularly fine Pottet firearm is described in Chapter VII.

Also in Chapter VII there is a description of another Pauly shotgun, a breechloader using percussion-cap ignition.

CHAPTER III

THE INVENTION OF THE PERCUSSION NIPPLE AND CAP

WAS the award made by the 29th Congress to Joshua Shaw for his "invention of the copper percussion cap for firearms" based on an error? The answer is, "Yes".

In passing the "Bill for the Relief of Joshua Shaw", Congress considered and accepted as fact the testimony of F. W. Risque, who stated there was no patent for a percussion cap earlier than Shaw's. Risque, in his search for an earlier patent, simply did not look in the right place.

Did Joshua Shaw get an American patent for a copper cap as early as 1814 or 1816, as many writers have said he did? The answer is, "No".

Joshua Shaw was never in America until after 1816, and American laws prevented his applying for a patent until he had resided in the country for two years.

Was the Joshua Shaw who invented a copper cap an American or an Englishman, a sea captain or an artist? He has been described as an American sea captain, as an American artist, and as an English artist.

The invention, or discovery, of the copper percussion cap was of tremendously far-reaching consequence. In the less than a century and a half since their invention, copper caps have in times of peace set off the shots that have nearly exterminated the elephants in Africa and the buffaloes in the United States. In times of war the flames from caps, or from cartridge primers, which are the same thing, have started billions of bullets on their way to kill millions of men. The copper cap, as used on muzzle-loading guns, became and still remains indispensable to modern high-power ammunition.

As there have been many conflicting statements, of which some were perforce erroneous, about Joshua Shaw and his invention, I shall go to some length to clarify who Joshua Shaw was, when he came to this country, when he obtained a patent for a percussion cap, and who were ahead of him in securing patents for percussion caps. The facts about Joshua Shaw are contained in government records, Philadelphia newspapers of 1817, the treatise written by Shaw himself, *A Sketch or History of the Copper Cap, and Percussion Artillery Primer*—those being primary sources—and in *Journals of the Franklin Institutute*, Philadelphia, and the *Scientific American* of August 7, 1869—those being secondary sources which quote directly from Shaw's writings. Those primary and secondary sources are unimpeachable.

Historical novels have referred to the use of percussion pistols at the battle of Waterloo. It is probable that percussion pistols were carried in small numbers at Waterloo by men on both sides. Such pistols were like the Forsyth detonators of 1807, the Pauly detonators of 1812, or the patch-lock detonators which were the immediate forerunners of the copper-cap guns. There were no copper-cap guns at Waterloo.

Let me point out here that the cap-lock system of ignition was a two-stage invention. The metal cap and the nipple were not invented simultaneously. First there was the nipple. The metal cap came later.

Nipples were used first on patch-lock guns, soon after 1807. Patch primings were made of flattish cakes of fulminate placed between pieces of paper made waterproof by varnishing. Sometimes the primings were called paper caps, and they resembled our modern paper caps used in toy pistols. In use, a patch was pressed fast to the striking nose of the hammer and driven on the nipple by the falling hammer.

The first patch-lock pistols had short stubby nipples integral with the breech; later ones had nipples with screw bases which permitted their removal. The only ones I have seen are British. One having a solid nipple, and made by Cartmell, is shown in Plate 14. Another, having a removable nipple, and made by Samuel Nock, is pictured in Plates 15 and 16.

The perforated anvil on which the hammer fell was commonly called a pivot, a striking peg, or just a peg, but it was a true nipple, or cone, the two words now used to describe the same thing.

The patch-lock pistols shown had quick-detachable striking noses. It was the practice of sportsmen using patch-lock fowling pieces to carry a supply of such ready-primed strikers, just as in later years they carried a supply of copper caps. Plate 17 shows a box of strikers such as a sportsman would have carried with him in the field. Unfired patches, or primings, may be seen in most of the hollows in the pictured striking noses. These have been loosely secured in place by being thrust in with a finger.

It should be noticed that these patch-lock strikers—one is shown detached from the hammer in Plate 16—have solid noses. They look much like the later detachable strikers used in the rare Manton 1816 model pellet lock, but they are not hollow and they do not have any hole in the middle of the striker nose.

The only patent I have come across that mentions a patch lock is one of Prelat's (sometimes incorrectly called "Pulat") French patents. An enlarged reproduction of two figures from that patent is shown in Illustration B. Figure 3 is the hammer, in the head of which the priming was placed. Figure 4 is the peg on which the hammer fell. Prelat says the priming was deposited in the cavity in the hammer nose with the fingers, and he leaves the inference the priming was a bare pellet, not enclosed in paper. I shall have more to say later about Prelat and his patents, but perhaps I should

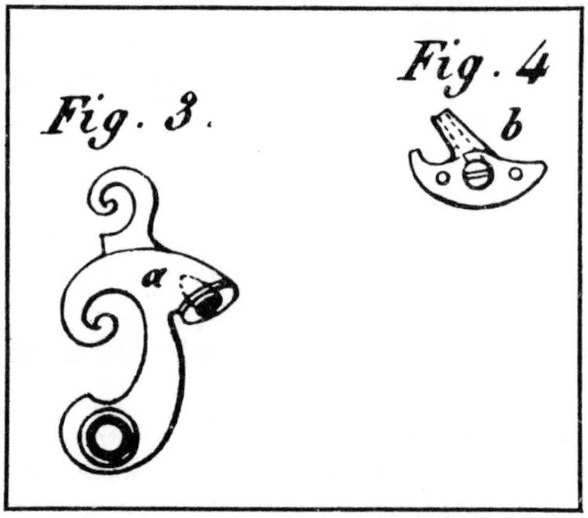

ILLUSTRATION B. Hammer and peg shown on Prelat 1818 patent drawing. (Two of twenty-nine figures.)

mention here that a Prelat patent rarely if ever covered any Prelat invention. It is known the patch lock was created years before Prelat, in 1818, pictured it in a patent drawing, but history is silent as to the creator. I have never heard that any individual ever claimed the patch-lock invention.

Now back to the copper cap and to Joshua Shaw.

Though writers have disagreed both as to Shaw's nationality and his vocation, they have agreed on one point, that Shaw lived for a time in Philadelphia. I went to the Philadelphia Free Library and examined directories for the early years of the 19th century. There were several listings of J. Shaw, and several of Jos. Shaw. The question of whether Jos. stood for Joseph or Joshua was resolved by examination of more directories. The sea captain who lived at 157 South Fifth turned out to be Joseph. The man listed in Kite's Philadelphia Directory for 1814 as "Shaw, Joshua, hatter, 8 South Fourth" posed a minor problem. The 1818 Paxton Directory had a similar listing with the address 100 High Street. (High Street was what is now Market Street.) However, the 1821 M'Carty & Davis Directory listed, in the supplement, "Shaw, Mary, widow of Joshua, hat store, 100 High". I knew I had not found the copper-cap inventor who petitioned Congress in 1846.

I came across "Shaw, Joseph, artist, 570 South Front", as early as 1819. In 1828 I found "Shaw, Joshua, artist, 142 Christian". Was the 1819 Joseph the same as the 1828 Joshua? Fortunately, as we shall find that Joshua Shaw, artist, arrived in Philadelphia before 1819, the answer to the question is of interest only if we wish to establish an address, and Shaw's place of residence is not material to our inquiry.

From the Free Library I went across the street to the Franklin Institute, and there I found proof that the artist, Joshua Shaw, was the inventor of a copper cap.

There is no doubt that Joshua Shaw invented a copper cap and there is no disputing the fact that he obtained an American patent for that cap. However, as we shall see, Shaw appears to have been only one of many inventors, and certainly not the first patentee.

The *Journal of the Franklin Institute* contains numerous articles written by Joshua Shaw. Some deal with painting and artists' problems; some deal with firearms and percussion ignition. In some of the articles Shaw mentions he is both an artist and a maker of percussion caps. One particular instance is his letter of March 20, 1829, regarding fulminates, in which he says he works as an artist. A minor surprise to me, as I had read in a twentieth-century publication that Shaw was a member of the Franklin Institute, was the finding in the *Original Record Book of Members of Franklin Institute*, this notation, "Shaw, Joshua, not a member—1824 through 1831".

In his time Shaw was far better known as an artist than as an inventor. Having found proof that the artist and the patentee in America of the percussion cap were one and the same, I went on to learn much about Shaw's life and his arrival in this country.

Government files contain extensive dry correspondence that passed between Shaw and various officials at the Frankford Arsenal regarding details of Shaw's percussion primer, but that correspondence is surprisingly secretive about who Shaw was and where he came from. The singularly rare book, *A Sketch or History of the Copper Cap, and Percussion Artillery Primer*, the first page of which appears in Illustration C, seems to hide more than it discloses, though that interesting document, written by Shaw himself, gives full support to the revealing autobiographical sketch of his life which was printed in the August 7, 1869 issue of the *Scientific American*. The *Scientific American* article gives prosaic facts interspersed with embittered opinions. Mr. Shaw was dead when the article was printed. He is reported to have died in September, 1860, in Bordentown, New Jersey. The autobiographical material was furnished to the *Scientific American* by John Dickinson, a grandson of Mr. Shaw.

There are a few other factual accounts of Shaw, but, not being first-hand, they lack the convincing qualities of Shaw's own words as reported by the *Scientific American*. William Dunlap's *History of the Rise and Progress of the Arts of Design in the United States*, published in 1834, contains much of what appears in the *Scientific American* memoir. Scharf and Westcott's *History of Philadelphia*, published in 1884, has further sidelights on Shaw's paintings, tells of his activity in forming the Association of American Artists, and states, "he gave up art, and became interested in the sale and improvement of fire-arms".

Shaw's autobiographical narrative in the *Scientific American* sometimes uses first person and sometimes third. After a third-person account setting forth that he was born in Bellingborough, Lincoln County, England, in 1776, and that his father died when he was seven, there is this, "I had from that moment to earn my dinner before I ate it". The article then relates that Shaw's mother remarried and that the stepfather was a plumber and glazier. The first sentence of Shaw's *A Sketch or History of the Coppper Cap* reads: "The Subscriber about the year 1814 or '15, invented the instrument known, and now in general use throughout the civilized world, as the Patent Diamond, used by glaziers for cutting glass". (In Shaw's *Sketch or History* he sometimes uses "I", as he does in the *Scientific American* chronicle, but he usually refers to himself as "the Subscriber".) When Shaw reached the age of fifteen an uncle gave him nine weeks' schooling. He was then apprenticed to a sign painter. As Shaw showed talent in his interview he was accepted without payment of a premium. From house painting and

A SKETCH OR HISTORY

OF THE

COPPER CAP,

AND PERCUSSION ARTILLERY PRIMER.

BY JOSHUA SHAW.

The Subscriber, about the year 1814 or '15, invented the instrument known, and now in general use throughout the civilized world, as the Patent Diamond, used by glaziers for cutting glass. About this time his attention was directed to other objects occupying public notice, and, amongst the rest, the application and use of Percussion, or what is called Fulminating Powders. It was evident that, from the corrosive nature of those experimented upon, they were not suited to the purposes to which they were applied, and that the machinery employed was even yet more objectionable, being extremely dangerous from explosion, by which several lives were lost.

Owing to these objections, and finding the whole affair was about to be lost sight of, the subscriber was induced to investigate the properties of the different compositions, and his first step was to originate, through chemical means and manipulations, an entirely new material, perfectly free from the corrosive properties of those in use at the time. This was the first point to gain, without which the most perfect machinery for applying it as a means of discharging fire-arms, could prove of no real value.

The next object to be accomplished was one of great difficulty. There was a new combination of elements, chemical and mechanical, to be rendered subservient to each other, requiring experience and some practice in both departments, little thought of when viewing the insignificant loooking copper cap, as it is now prepared and applied. Percussion powder in the grain, was inseparable from danger, applied in any way. The magazine lock was the most approved means of applying it, but from its dangerous tendencies had been given up, and the whole affair was being lost sight of.

After a thousand considerations had been bestowed upon the whole matter, the first movement with the powder was to reduce the grains, by mixing them with water, and forming them into a paste, being satisfied that in grains

A

Illustration C. First page of Joshua Shaw's *A Sketch or History of the Copper Cap, and Percussion Artillery Primer*

sign painting he went to work on canvas. His work, particularly as a landscape painter, was well received. He lived in Manchester, Bath, and London, and apparently was successful in the sale of his paintings.

Shaw became the friend of the famous Benjamin West. If that friendship had not existed I might not have been able to learn the day of Shaw's arrival in this country.

I wish to quote from the *Scientific American* report the part that tells why Shaw left England, and also about his statements regarding the invention of the copper cap.

> He next returned to London, where he enjoyed considerable popularity and received many commissions; but being so unfortunate as to differ in politics from the aristocratic directors of the British Institution, he was subject to persecution, and the prize awarded to his painting of the deluge, by that institution, was with-held. This and other subsequent events disgusted him with England, and he resolved to come to America. He had previously, however, made the acquaintance and secured the warm personal friendship of Benjamin West, then President of the Royal Academy, who urged him to canvass for a membership in that institution, but he refused to stoop to what he considered a degradation, the begging for honours to which he considered his merits entitled him.
>
> He, therefore, after obtaining introductory letters from West to many distinguished men of the time in the United States, came to Philadelphia, where he permanently established himself. He was the bearer of West's celebrated picture of "Christ Healing the Sick", a present to the Philadelphia Hospital, where he placed it appropriately, and where it still hangs.
>
> In 1814 he invented the copper percussion cap. He, however, kept the discovery secret until his arrival in America, when he sought to obtain a patent for it, but was refused on the ground of his being an alien, the law at that time denying a patent to aliens unless they had resided two years in this country.

The 1869 article said West's famous painting was then hanging in the Philadelphia Hospital. It is still hanging, in what is now the Pennsylvania Hospital. It is a large painting, and an impressive sight.

From the Franklin Institute I went to the Pennsylvania Hospital, and there I saw the picture, but I was unable to learn there exactly when it was brought to Philadelphia in the care of Shaw. A visit to the nearby Historical Society of Pennsylvania gave me the answer.

The October 13, 1817, issue of *Poulson's American Daily Advertiser* reported the arrival on that day of the *Electra*, and announced that the painting, "Christ Healing the Sick", came on that ship. A report some days later in the same paper said the picture was put on display November 3, 1817.

It is proved that the Joshua Shaw who invented a percussion cap was an English artist, that he came to this country in 1817, and that he could not have obtained an American patent as early as 1816.

It is not surprising that the writer of a gun book published in 1920, said, speaking of the invention of the copper cap, "Many inventors claimed it. Priority, however, seems to rest with Joshua Shaw, an English artist living in this country, who applied in 1814 for a United States patent. Not having been a resident in this country for two years, it was refused". That exactly quoted statement is factually incorrect, but its author did no more than go slightly too far in his assumptions. Let's see what he had to go on. He, presumably, had heard that Congress had recorded that Joshua Shaw had obtained a patent for a percussion cap. He, presumably, had no idea that Congress had been led up the garden path. He must have known that all records of the texts of all Shaw's American patents had been destroyed in the 1836 Patent Office fire, and that the patents had not been restored. He probably had read the *Scientific American* report, and he mentioned what Henry Wilkinson had written, in 1841, in *Engines of War*, that Shaw had invented an iron cap in 1814, a pewter cap in 1815, and a copper cap in 1816.

Wilkinson was repeating what Shaw had told him. Wilkinson, in his book, does not say when the conversation with Shaw took place, but it may well have been in 1833, when Shaw made a return visit to England. Wilkinson was convinced Shaw was the inventor. He says that Shaw "made application for a patent in England, but the solicitor to whom it was referred decided it could not be obtained without infringing Forsyth's patent then in force". Mr. Wilkinson believed that Joseph Egg bought the invention from a gunmaker named Roantree, who in turn had obtained it from a workman employed by Joshua Shaw.

Though there is no record in the Patent Office of patents taken out by Shaw prior to 1836, other than a bare listing of titles and dates, there is an affidavit in the Government Archives Building which reads: "This certifies that Joshua Shaw of Philadelphia obtained a patent for percussion caps of guns on the 19th of June, 1822, and one also for percussion Lock of Cannon in October 24,

1828, and one for percussion primers for Cannon in Dec. 3, 1832". This document is reproduced in Illustration D. It is signed by W. L. Ellsworth, Commissioner of Patents, and bears the seal of the Patent Office.

Not even the title or date of the 1822 Shaw patent appears in the Patent Office records, though the bare titles and dates of six other patents taken out by Shaw between October 24, 1828, and March 17, 1834, are to be found recorded under what are called

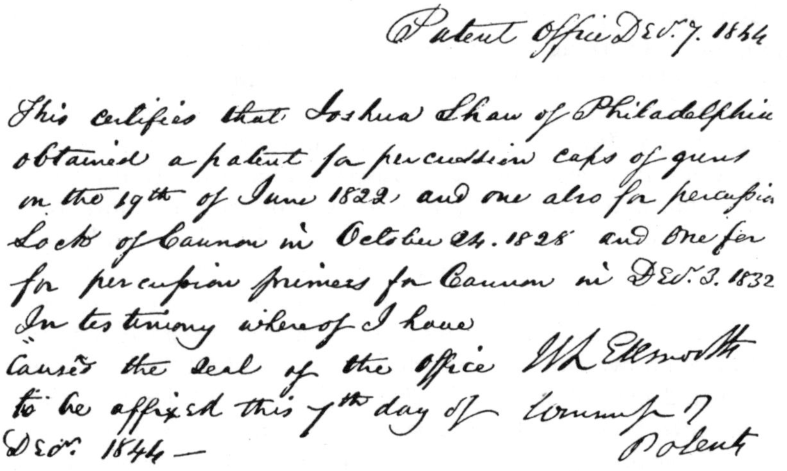
Patent Office Dec. 7. 1844

This certifies that Joshua Shaw of Philadelphia obtained a patent for percussion caps of guns on the 19th of June 1822, and one also for percussion Lock of Cannon in October 24. 1828 and one for for percussion primers for Cannon in Dec. 3. 1832
In testimony whereof I have caused the seal of the office to be affixed this 7th day of Dec. 1844 —

H L Ellsworth
Commr of Patent

ILLUSTRATION D. Affidavit by W. L. Ellsworth supporting Shaw's patent claims

the "X patents". The reason for the omission of all record of the 1822 patent may be found in the following quotation from the 1829 *Journal of the Franklin Institute* where in a listing of patents there is the following, "For an improvement in Guns and Fire-arms, which improvement consists in a priming head and cap applied to guns and fire-arms, for the purpose of priming and giving them fire, by the means of percussion, fulminating or detonating powders; Joshua Shaw, Philadelphia. First issued June 19th, 1822, surrendered for the purpose of correcting the specification, and re-issued May 7 [1829]". The practice of the Patent Office, at least before 1836, was to destroy all records of patents that were issued and later surrendered.

The reason there is no copy to be found in the Patent Office of any early Shaw patent is because Shaw was either too apathetic or too disinterested to comply with the Patent Office pleas that he supply information that would permit restoration.

Joshua Shaw may have been the first to experiment with a metal percussion cap. However, neither his own claim to being the first inventor, nor Wilkinson's support of his claim, are sufficient to warrant unqualified confirmation by unbiased judges. There is too much to be said for other men who surely also made copper caps. It would be wearisome, and impossible, to detail all the claims made by every man who professed to be the true first inventor. W. W. Greener wrote, in *The Gun and Its Development:* "In England the inventors of the copper cap were as numerous as the gunmakers —nearly every armourer, London and provincial, laying claim to the invention".

In editions after the fifth, of *Instructions to Young Sportsmen,* Colonel Peter Hawker said—I quote from the sixth edition, published in 1830—"When Joe first brought out his detonators, in Davies-street (those which were discarded from giving so much trouble), he made me the most perfect gun I ever saw; and, doubting whether such another could be got, I set my wits to work in order to simplify the invention. At last the plan of a perforated nipple, and the detonating powder in the crown of a small cap, occurred to me. I made a drawing of it, which I took to Joe. After having this explained, he said he would show me something in a few weeks' time; when, low and behold! there was a rough gun altered precisely on my own plan! . . . Thus Joe, who led the fashion for all the world, sent out a few copper-cap guns, and I know with some degree of reluctance".

Joseph Manton's troublesome detonators, to which Hawker referred, were those made on Manton's 1816 pellet-lock patent, not on his 1818 tube-lock patent.

It will be seen that Hawker had a strong claim to the invention.

The fifth edition of Hawker's *Instructions to Young Sportsmen* appeared in 1826, long after—perhaps ten years after—Colonel Hawker showed his sketch to Manton. Why did not the story appear in the fifth edition, as several writers have mistakenly said it did? It seems most likely that it was not until the sixth edition was in preparation that Hawker attached importance to the wrangling that had been going on as to who was first with a copper cap. The fact is, Hawker, in the same sixth edition, said, "I do not mean to say I was the inventor of it—very probably not". Then he went on to say, "But if Mr. this and Mr. that have any fancy to claim the invention, they may safely fire their ammunition into all the periodicals they please, as I shall not indulge them with any paper-war on the subject".

Captain Lacy, in 1842, in *The Modern Shooter*, wrote: "Although the copper cap be a diminutive, yet there have been as many claimants to the honour of the invention, as, of old, there were contending cities for the honour of having given birth to Homer". Lacy mentioned the strength of the claims of Hawker, of Egg, and of Purdey. He did not mention Shaw. Lacy said, "Mr. Egg indisputably laid the earliest claim to the invention", and added that Egg had assured him many years before that the first copper cap "was made out of an old penny-piece". Lacy said Purdey told him of producing a brass cap, made from the tag of an old umbrella, "which was handed about for some time, and, a year or two afterwards, 'Mr. Egg brought out the copper cap!' "

It is to be noticed that both Wilkinson and Lacy implied that Egg was the first prominent gunmaker to put out a copper-cap gun.

Purdey said the idea came to him while he was talking about the trouble there was in wet weather with the detonating patches which "were then in vogue". The genesis of Purdey's metal-cap invention was his contemplation of an inverted tumbler. Of the birth of Shaw's metal-cap invention let us see what Shaw himself has to say in his *A Sketch or History of the Copper Cap*.

After the first sentence regarding the invention, "about the year 1814 or '15", of the "Patent Diamond", Shaw wrote: "About this time his attention was directed to other objects occupying public notice, and, amongst the rest, the application and use of Percussion, or what is called Fulminating Powders". A little farther on he said: "After a thousand considerations had been bestowed upon the whole matter, the first movement with the powder was to reduce the grains, by mixing them with water, and forming them into a paste, being satisfied that in grains it would never become a safe and convenient material for the discharge of firearms. In this way it was applied in various forms, but still the particles were liable to friction by contact, and it was evident that they must be separated to be rendered safe. At length it was determined upon to divide their parts, and a piece of steel wire was procured, about three-sixteenths of an inch in diameter, and cut into short lengths, about three-eighths of an inch each, in which holes were drilled at one end, about half or three parts through, and in cavity the paste was deposited for safe keeping, beyond which little was dreamed of". Then, the statement continued, one of these "bits of steel"—Shaw's first cap was of steel—happened by accident to become fixed on the ivory tip of an artist's pencil lying on the desk. The fulminate-filled container was hit a smart blow, and there was a small explosion which shattered the pencil. The thought came then of placing the cap on a nipple.

Why did Shaw write *A Sketch or History of the Copper Cap*? He did it to back up his memorial to Congress in which he asked for compensation for our Government's use of what he claimed was his invention. Shaw had always felt he had not been paid adequately for his work at Frankford Arsenal. That was his primary reason. The culminating reason was given by Shaw in the postscript to his *Sketch or History*. He there stated he "was induced to make this statement from reading" the account of the discovery of the percussion cap in Wilkinson's *Engines of War*.

Shaw's paper-bound treatise has printed on the last page the line, "Bordentown, N.J., March 4th, 1847". The booklet bears no publisher's name. However, its similarity in format to a booklet printed in Washington in 1847 by J. & G. S. Gideon makes it seem probable the "Sketch" was also printed by the Gideon firm.

A petition was made to Congress (House of Representatives, Bills and Resolutions, 29th Congress, 1st session, H.R. 206, Feb. 10, 1846) asking that Shaw be remunerated for his invention. A committee investigated the merits of Shaw's claim with considerable thoroughness. That committee looked at the previously mentioned affidavit made by the Commissioner of Patents to show that on June 19, 1822, Shaw was granted a patent for a percussion cap. The members examined a report contained in an 1847 letter written by F. W. Risque to Colonel Talcott, which says, "No patent has ever been obtained in England for a percussion copper cap, nor has any ever been obtained in France, or any of the European Governments so far as I have been able to discover".

The committee recommended to Congress that the "Bill for the Relief of Joshua Shaw" be approved. The bill was passed. Congress left the amount of compensation to the Secretary of War, but stipulated the sum was not to be in excess of $25,000. Secretary of War Marcy asked for advice from the Ordnance office. Lt.-Col. Talcott, of that office wrote Marcy, April 3, 1847, that he thought a sum from $10,000 to $12,500 was ample. Marcy had the final decision, and on May 3, 1847, he wrote to the Second Auditor of the Treasury, regarding Shaw, "I have found due to him, upon principles of justice and equity, from the United States, the sum of Eighteen thousand Dollars, as a full compensation for the past and future use of his invention". On the following day Shaw signed a receipt for a requisition for $18,000 from the Treasury.

On December 11, 1854, Shaw petitioned for an additional $7,000, unsuccessfully. In 1860 Shaw's daughter petitioned for $7,000, again unsuccessfully.

Shaw's patent for a copper cap was dated 1822. Two patents for a copper cap in combination with a nipple were obtained in France earlier than that. In one of those patents, Deboubert's, September 20, 1820, a lock utilizing a copper cap and a nipple was the sole invention claimed. In the other and earlier patent, Prelat's, July 29, 1818,* a cap and a nipple are shown as parts of a claim for the

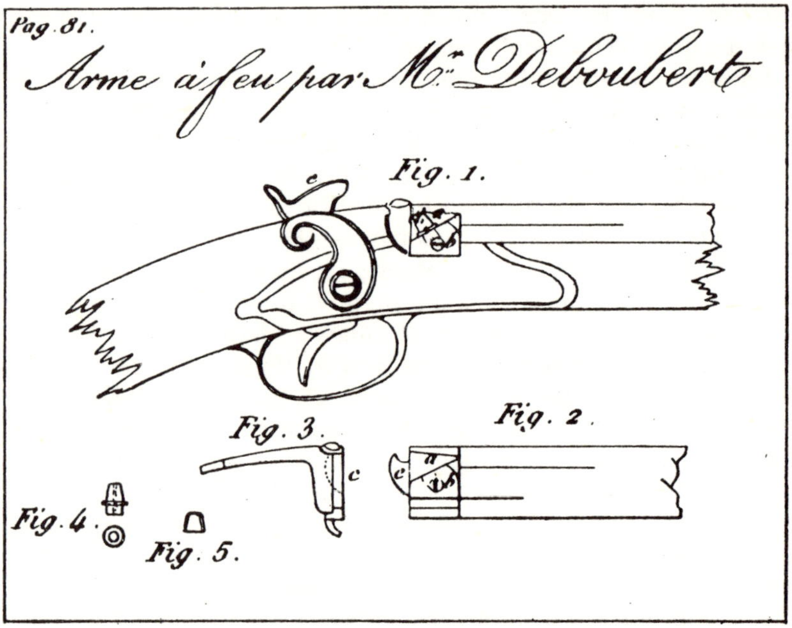

ILLUSTRATION E. Deboubert 1820 patent drawing

invention of five different forms of percussion ignition. No English patent containing a claim for the invention of a percussion cap was ever granted. The earliest English patent to show a percussion cap was granted to Sampson Davis in 1822.

I think it unlikely any researcher will come up with a still earlier patent for a percussion cap, but I do not deny there is a possibility that I, like Mr. Risque, did not look in the right place, and that some German, Russian, or other European, was the first patentee.

A reproduction of the Deboubert patent drawing is shown in Illustration E. Figure 4 of the drawing is the "little cone or nipple

* See the footnote on p. 56.

of steel" (*petit cône ou bouton d'acier*). Figure 5 is the "hat of copper serving to cover or to be put on the cone" (*chapeau en cuivre, servant à couvrir ou coiffer le cône*). The Deboubert specification also states that the copper cap contains fulminate of silver in the bottom, and that the steel cone is pierced in the centre by a hole which connects with the touch hole of the barrel.

In regard to Prelat's 1818 patent it should be stressed that the fact Prelat obtained a patent is not acceptable as evidence that Prelat invented a copper cap, or that he ever made one. Prelat's patent simply indicates that someone had invented a copper cap as early as 1818, though in that year copper caps had not come to the notice of sportsmen. In support of that last statement let me point out that T. B. Johnson, in the first edition of *The Shooter's Companion*, published in 1819, gave generous space to detonators, particularly to those made by Forsyth and Manton, but that he gave not the slightest indication he had ever heard of a metal percussion cap. In the second edition, published in 1823, Johnson wrote enthusiastically of copper caps and said, "Copper cap guns will unquestionably become general".

The reason we cannot consider Prelat as the true inventor of the copper cap is because it was well known Prelat made a business of importing guns from England and then taking out French patents for new features he found.* Prelat was active during and slightly after the Napoleonic Wars, when there were no restrictions on the appropriation of the enemy's inventions, patented or not. Examination of the text of the 1818 Prelat patent leads the reader to conclude Prelat's vague specifications were based partly on what he had seen and partly on what he had heard. As early as 1810 Prelat obtained a patent for a loose powder detonator that was a faithful copy of the lock Forsyth patented in 1807. The 1818 Prelat patent makes clear how far Prelat was willing to go in copying the invention of others. That 1818 patent embraces five different means of detonating fulminate. One is a patch lock, with the priming in the hammer nose; a second is for pellets in the touch-hole mouth as in the American punch locks; a third is for pellets in a sliding magazine, as in the late Forsyth locks; a fourth is for fulminate in a "sausage", with the illustration showing a typical Manton tube lock; a fifth is for a copper cap of the top-hat variety and its accompanying nipple.

To show the complete patent drawing on one page here would require overmuch reduction in the size of the figures. Illustration

* *Armurerie*, Paulin-Désormeaux, M. A. O., Paris, 1852.

F shows an enlargement of all the figures in the drawing that relate to a copper cap and nipple. The enlargement appears in the original plate in an area less than one inch by one half inch. I can see how Risque could have overlooked these small figures when he searched for a French patent that would antedate Shaw's, but I do not understand his missing the Deboubert 1820 patent. That should have been easy to spot as a patent for a copper cap, and as earlier than Shaw's.

It would appear that the French examiners of patents may also have overlooked Prelat's 1818 patent when Deboubert's application came before them.*

Figure 15 in Illustration F is the nipple; figure 14 is the cap; figure 16 is the cap in place on the nipple.

ILLUSTRATION F. Nipple, cap, and cap in place on nipple from Prelat 1818 patent drawing

It is abundantly clear from the text that the Prelat patent covered a cap made of copper. It is also apparent that Mr. Prelat's concept of the construction and functioning of a copper cap was different from the idea held by such men as Egg, Hawker, Purdey, and Shaw. Those men realized a cap should have a malleable crown that would flatten but not shatter under the hammer blow. Prelat said the cap should be made of very thin copper foil (*d'une feuille de cuivre rouge très-mince*) that would tear and go to pieces (*qui se déchire et tombe ensuite par fragments*) under the drop of the hammer. Could Mr. Prelat have witnessed the detonation of a faulty cap and assumed the breaking of the cap was intended?

Prelat was vague about the priming used in copper caps. He merely said the fulminating powder was prepared expressly for copper caps and could not be used for anything else. He offered

* *Footnote.* An index of French patents—the A.D. 1826 *Catalogue des specifications . . . des Brevets d'Invention*—gives rise to some uncertainty as to the exact date to be assigned to the Prelat patent for a percussion cap. The Catalogue states that the part of the patent which includes the claim for the nipple and cap was dated July 28, 1820. It is to be noted, however, that the A.D. 1825 *Description . . . les Brevets d'Invention* which contains a complete transcript of the Prelat patent in question, gives July 29, 1818, as the patent date, with no exception. Moreover, there is nothing in the accompanying plate, which illustrates the nipple and cap as well as all of the other items described in the text, to indicate the date is other than July 29, 1818. In any event, it is clear that Deboubert's specification for a cap, dated September 20, 1820, was later than Prelat's.

no explanation of the difference between the priming used in copper caps and that used in paper caps or patches.

Who first *patented* a copper cap? Almost certainly it was Prelat, in France. Who first experimentally *placed* a metal cap on a nipple? Probably no one will ever know.

CHAPTER IV

AMERICAN PUNCH LOCKS AND ONE AMERICAN TUBE LOCK

MOST improvements in firearms were inventions of men whose lifework was directly concerned with firearms. However, some outstanding firearms inventions were supplied by professional men whose callings were quite unconnected with firearms.

The Scotsman, Forsyth, who invented the percussion system of ignition, was a minister of the gospel. The American, Guthrie, who first developed the American punch lock, was a doctor of medicine.

The name "punch lock" was used only in the United States and only when percussion locks were first made in this country, in the late 1820's. After a few years the punch lock came to be generally known as the pill lock.

The punch lock was the only form of early detonator made in this country as early as 1830, except the copper-cap lock. Loose-powder detonator guns, guns with patch locks, guns using waxed primings, were never produced here. If any were used here, they came from Europe.

The punch-locks discussed in this chapter have simple uncomplicated locks that required the shooter to prime the touch holes manually. American guns having magazines which fed the pills mechanically are found in Chapter IX.

The American punch lock had near counterparts in some European pill locks, but the American lock seems to have been independently invented and developed in New York State. A few gun-makers in Pennsylvania, Ohio, and New England occasionally fitted a gun with the now-called pill-lock ignition, but nearly all examples the collector will come across will bear names of makers in towns and cities in central, western, and northern New York. American punch-lock guns were never numerous, and they are now lamentably scarce. The locks were used chiefly on long guns, and but rarely on pistols.

Dr. Samuel Guthrie, a surgeon of the War of 1812, has claim to lasting fame, first because he was one of three men, the other two being Liebig of Germany and Soubeiran of France, who independently discovered chloroform in 1831, and secondly because he was the American inventor of fulminate in the form of pills. Dr. Guthrie's non-medical pills were made of potassium chlorate mixed with gum arabic. He secured permission to attempt to fire the sunset gun at a military post with his pills, and there the name "punch lock" was born. He placed a pill in the vent of the cannon, set a blacksmith's punch on the pill, and hit the punch with a hammer. The experiment was successful in firing the gun, but a witness pointed out that soldiers could not be expected to carry around a punch and a hammer.

Dr. Guthrie returned home and altered the lock on a flint gun so it would fire his percussion pills. He discarded the frizzen, made the pan so small it would confine a single pill, and clamped in the jaws of the cock a pointed iron punch in place of the flint.

This was in Sackets Harbor, New York, about 1826. The exact date of Guthrie's punch-lock gun is uncertain. It is certain that Guthrie had been experimenting with fulminates, and getting himself burned and disfigured by untoward explosions, for several years before 1826. I have seen a reproduction of a photograph of a distillery which bears the printed description, "Old mill where percussion caps & chloriform [sic] were first made in the year 1813. Sacket Harbor, N.Y." The description is wrong on two counts: (1) The date 1813 is four years before Dr. Guthrie settled in Sackets Harbor; (2) Dr. Guthrie never had anything to do with the invention or manufacture of percussion caps. In fact, when he began manufacturing his percussion pills, he inveighed against copper caps, claiming caps were less efficient, not so sure-fire, and not so safe, being apt to fly into fragments.

Dr. Guthrie in a short time developed in western New York a market for his fulminate pills, which he distributed through merchants in the area. It is not known that Dr. Guthrie made any attempt to market any punch locks, or punch-lock guns. The demand for guns to use Dr. Guthrie's pills was met by the regional gunsmiths.

Any gunsmith who was competent to convert a flint gun to percussion cap could convert a flint gun to pill lock. The simplest method of conversion from flint to percussion was by screwing a vented cylindrical plug into the side of the barrel where the flint touch hole was. This "side-plug" could be fitted with a nipple to hold a cap, or a cavity to hold a pill. The gunsmith could use the original flint cock with an iron striker substituted for the flint, or he could fashion a complete new percussion hammer. If a gunsmith were commissioned to make a completely new pill-lock gun, he would often make the new lock just as if he were making a side-lock conversion with a new percussion hammer.

The first successful punch-lock firearm to get other than local acclaim was produced by William A. Hart of Fredonia, New York. One of the Hart pistols is shown in Plate 18. The lock was patented by Mr. Hart on February 20, 1827. This screw-barrel pistol has a centre hammer with the cavity for the fulminate pill located at the top rather than on the side. The ingenious feature of the Hart mechanism is the sliding cover that may be pushed over the vent after the gun has been loaded and primed. The hammer can be let down to rest on the cover, as shown, and then the loaded gun can be carried safely in the pocket. Cocking the hammer automatically draws back the sliding cover so that a touch on the trigger will drive the hammer downwards to detonate the fulminate pellet. There are only three moving parts in the firing assembly; the hammer, the mainspring, and a part which is a combination trigger and sear and acts as a spring for both.

Another punch-lock pistol which is scarce but not so infrequently heard of as the Hart is the Rogers & Heart. A Rogers & Heart is shown in Plate 19. Several of the old Bannerman catalogues—the 1920 catalogue, page 106, for instance—picture a similar pistol and give the name as Rogers & Hearst [*sic*]. Those catalogues say the pistol was "evidently changed from flintlock". It is my opinion the pistol was never converted from flintlock. The lock is of the back-action type and it would seem the pistol could never have had any room for a frizzen. Several others have also mistakenly given the name as Rogers & Hearst, but Stephen Van Rensselaer, in his *American Firearms* correctly lists "Rogers & Heart, Utica, N.Y." His accompanying description of a pistol by that maker is: "Percussion pistol, calibre ·36, length 11½ inches, altered to pill-lock". I assume Mr. Van Rensselaer meant "altered from percussion cap", and that he did not mean, "altered from flintlock". The pistol shown here has the common type of cylindrical side-plug used to convert flint guns to percussion, but this pistol is clearly not a conversion from flint. It is debatable whether it was made as it is now, or was originally designed for copper caps.

William Hart of Fredonia, New York, was the earliest American maker of pill locks whose name has come down to us. He started manufacturing the guns commercially in 1827, and his name as a maker of locks is the only name mentioned in the *Shooter's Manual*, published that year in Philadelphia. That book is considered to be the first comprehensive American treatise on guns and shooting. Rogers & Heart, of Utica, New York, was probably the last manufacturer to produce pill locks commercially and that firm went out of business in 1861.

An early Kentucky rifle with punch-lock ignition is shown in Plate 20. (In case there is a reader who thinks all Kentucky rifles came from Pennsylvania, let me point out that many Kentuckies were also made in Ohio and in New York. A few were made in other states, even including Kentucky.) This rifle was presumably made in Rochester, New York. It is marked on the lock plate "E. Gilbert patent, Rochester, N.Y." Ephraim Gilbert obtained his patent April 3, 1829. This rifle is stocked to the muzzle and has a long patch box but in several other respects it is different from most Kentuckies. The wood is walnut, whereas most Kentuckies are stocked with maple. The patch-box cover is hinged on the side, whereas most covers are hinged at the top. The two decidedly unusual features are: (1) the lock is a mule-ear punch lock, (2) the stock is take-down. To take the gun apart it is necessary only to withdraw the ramrod and the rearmost barrel wedge, after the hammer has been placed at half cock. As the gun has a hinged breech, the barrel can then be lifted out of the stock. It is necessary to cock the hammer when taking the gun apart, because the pointed striking nose rests in the touch hole when the hammer is down. The illustration shows the gun taken apart, but with the ramrod pushed back through the thimbles.

The mule-ear, or side-slapping, punch lock, with its hammer nose entering a vent in the side of the barrel, would seem to be the simplest possible method of converting a flint gun to percussion. The original flint touch hole could be shaped to hold the pill and receive the punchlike nose of the hammer. However, though mule-ear percussion-cap guns turn up from time to time, mule-ear pill-lock guns are almost never seen. Of course, it may be that many long guns were converted from flint to mule-ear pill lock and then to mule-ear copper cap. The second alteration might be impossible to detect, if a new percussion cap hammer were fitted.

The most celebrated maker of pill-lock guns was William Billinghurst of Rochester, New York. Billinghurst guns of the 1830's,

1840's, and 1850's were the most finely made American guns of their day. Billinghurst was the only American maker whose guns were conceded to be the equal in quality of the British "best" guns of the period, and the only one whose products were sought by wealthy sportsmen of South America and India. Billinghurst was best known overseas for his double rifles and his revolving rifles. In this country his fame came more from his superbly accurate bench guns.

The pill-lock gun in Plate 21 is a combination of a 7-shot rifle and a shotgun. The shotgun barrel takes the place of the conventional centre pin and the cylinder revolves around the shotgun barrel. The cylinder is turned manually. A catch under the barrel ensures perfect alignment of each chamber with the barrel. The chambers themselves have rifling to coincide with the barrel rifling. The lock has two hammers and two triggers, one combination of hammer and trigger for the rifle, the other for the shotgun. Each hammer has the typically pointed nose designed to go into the cavity where the fulminate pill awaits the blow that will detonate it.

A pill-lock revolver that was never in quantity production and which may have been produced only experimentally is shown in Plate 22. This is a late pill-lock gun and not a New York product. It was patented by Henry S. North of Middletown, Connecticut, and Chauncey D. Skinner of Haddam, Connecticut, United States patent 8982, dated June 1, 1852. The North & Skinner revolver is known to collectors as a pill-lock arm, but the pills were quite different from the pellets made by Guthrie. The pills were more like the paper caps used in the much earlier European patch-lock guns but they were not held in the hammer nose and driven on a nipple as were the European paper caps. To quote from the patent specification: "On the periphery and near the back end of the rotating breech are six recesses, in which are made the touch-holes leading to the chambers of the rotating breech. The said recesses are made to receive each a disk, one side of which is covered with percussion-powder. The said disks are to be pressed into the recesses with the side on which the percussion-powder is placed to come in contact with the touch-holes for the purpose of priming." I assume the disks were non-metallic, because the patentees assert that the rotating breech will not be clogged by the disks as they say it might be with copper fragments from detonated caps. The use of the fulminate-coated disks was not claimed in the patent. What was claimed was the simultaneous revolving of the cylinder and the cocking of the hammer by the act of pressing the trigger guard down and then back.

The Billinghurst guns and the North & Skinner guns had the primings inserted directly into hollows in the cylinders. In a punch-lock revolving gun, not illustrated, made in Springfield, Massachusetts, by James Warner, pills were inserted in wide-mouthed replaceable nipples screwed in the cylinder.

A breech-loading American tube lock is shown in Plate 23. The photograph shows the breech after being opened by the throwing forward of an underneath lever. The tube primer is smashed when the blunt-nosed hammer drives down on the sharp-nosed plunger which rests on the fulminate-filled tube. The lock functions much as does the earlier Austrian Tinderschloss, which along with other European tube locks is discussed in the next chapter.

The gun is marked, "Designed by E. J. Gerdom 1860". The date is late for a tube lock. I know nothing about Mr. Gerdom. It is rumoured the gun was built in Albany, New York. The odds are long against any collector's finding another example.

CHAPTER V

EUROPEAN FOLLOWERS OF FORSYTH

IN America, no percussion gun of any type was made until after the invention of the copper percussion cap.

In Europe, after Forsyth's momentous invention of the percussion system but before the copper percussion cap was known, there were in use in muzzle-loading guns four different types of percussion ignition:

1. Loose fulminating powder in small grains.
2. Fulminate in flattish paper patches.
3. Fulminate in pellets, varnished or waxed.
4. Fulminate in metal tubes.

In addition to these four types for muzzle-loaders, there was the tamped powder ignition used in Pauly breech-loading cartridges.

The Forsyth and the Pauly detonators have already been described. So have two pistols, a Cartmell and a Nock, that used paper patches.

The four percussion types listed above were made not only before metallic percussion caps were in use, but after, and consequently guns described in this chapter, though not including any that detonated metallic percussion caps, will not be limited to guns made before such caps were invented.

(Other early percussion firearms, i.e. percussion-cap guns and still other types that were followers of the percussion-cap guns, are found in succeeding chapters.)

Those followers of Forsyth whose guns had locks equipped with turning or sliding magazines designed to supply multiple priming charges sometimes had the magazines filled with fulminate in the form of loose powder, sometimes in the form of small pellets. In the case of some of those guns, even after the reading of patent specifications, it is impossible to determine whether the maker intended to have grains of loose powder used, or small pellets.

Some of the followers were no more than copyists, both of the Forsyth principle and the Forsyth construction. Others, like Joseph Manton, for instance, followed Forsyth's basic principle but developed radically different, and at times improved, construction.

Perhaps the most slavish imitation of a Forsyth lock is the one for which Prelat obtained a patent in France in 1810. The patent drawing is shown in Illustration G.

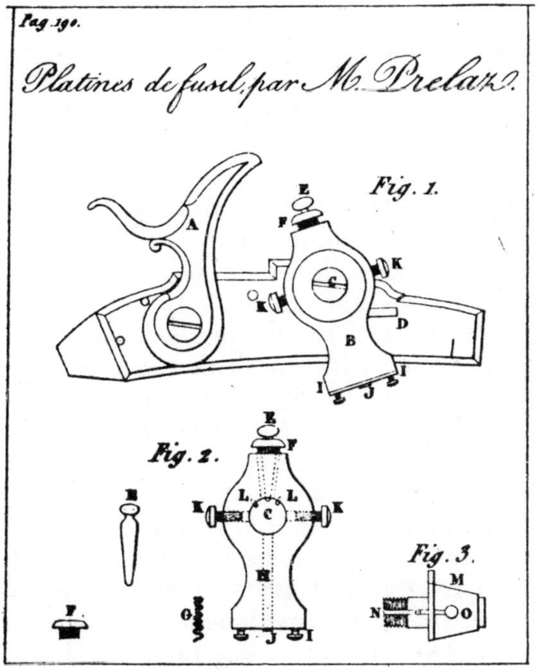

ILLUSTRATION G. Prelat 1810 patent drawing, imitation Forsyth lock

A well-known fake Forsyth lock, which has been pictured at various times as genuine, is pictured in Plate 24. Two reasons for denying its genuineness are: (1) the engraving of the name has a slovenliness quite foreign to true Forsyth engraving; (2) the construction is that of the scarce J. Jones & Co. lock, which is shown in the next illustration. Actually, this spurious lock is a Jones lock from which the Jones name has been erased and the Forsyth name substituted. This faking was done in the early years of the present century.

What is probably the only example in existence of an undefiled J. Jones & Co. lock is shown in Plate 25. Comparison of it with the twentieth-century "Forsyth" in the preceding illustration exposes the deception.

Examination of this illustration of the Jones "Improved Percussion" lock may cause the observer to surmise it is a conversion from flint. It is not a conversion; it originated as a true loose-powder detonator early in the percussion era. It does work like a flintlock, in that the hammer knocks back the magazine, just as in a flint gun the hammer knocks back the frizzen. When the magazine is let down, as in the illustration, a spring bolt opens a small hole in the base of the magazine to let a minute quantity of fulminate drop into a pan. The little hole in the magazine base is closed by the spring the moment the falling hammer throws back the magazine.

An interesting unmarked but certainly British pistol is shown in Plates 26 and 27. This self-priming detonator has a bronze magazine, for loose-powder fulminate, which turns sideways, as a door opens and closes. Plate 26 shows the magazine turned to deposit fulminate at the mouth of the vent leading to the chamber in the barrel. Plate 27 shows it turned with the firing pin receiving the hammer blow. My examination of the pistol gave me no hint as to the name of the maker. The hammer, which appears to be a Forsyth product, is a replacement. One hundred and fifty years ago hammers broke as frequently as eye-glasses and watch-crystals fifty years ago. A replaced hammer on a rare old gun is accepted without demur by a discriminating collector. Perhaps I should mention that I know that in the last four years at least three publications have pictured this pistol and stated it was a first-model Forsyth.

British patent 6675 was granted in 1834 to "Henry Shrapnel, of Salisbury, Wilts, Major General in the Army and Colonel in the Royal Artillery", for the self-priming lock shown in Plate 28. This Henry Shrapnel was the same man who invented the bursting artillery shell which bears his name. Millions of rounds of shrapnel have been produced and fired, but probably only a few of the Shrapnel locks were produced. Examples of a gun with a Shrapnel lock are extremely scarce. This gun was made well after percussion caps were in common use. We know the fulminate was in the form of pellets, rather than loose powder. In his patent General Shrapnel stated the fulminate was in the form of "detonating balls", released one only for each shot. The round magazine which has a screw top to permit refilling is moved manually back and forth. When fully back with the hammer raised, the magazine pushes away the pan cover and permits a "detonating ball" to enter the ventlike pan. When the magazine is pushed forward, the pan cover returns to its protective position, where it is held lightly by spring pressure. When the gun is fired, the falling hammer gets the pivoted pan cover out of the way in time to let the hammer nose hit the fulminate.

Plate 29 shows the first type of detonator produced by the famous Westley Richards firm. This has a magazine for loose-powder fulminate. A British patent, 4611 of the year 1821, was issued to Richards. The patent drawing itself gave no indication that Richards contemplated the use of fulminate in any form other than loose powder in a magazine. However, in Volume 3 of the *London Journal of Arts and Sciences*, which was printed soon after the invention was patented, there is the statement on page 226: "In the event of the magazine breaking, the cover, figure 6, may be substituted. In this construction a patch or pellet is used." The *Journal*'s illustration referred to is reproduced in Illustration H. "Figure 6" is in the lower right corner.

The oscillating lever, which appears in figures 1, 2, and 3, and by itself in figure 4, was called "the slider or propelling bar", and was the feature of the invention. When the hammer fell, it drove the rear end of the lever down and caused the front end to throw the magazine, or the cover, whichever was in use, up and away from the pan. Figures 1 and 2 of the illustration show the action.

There is a difference between the priming magazine shown in the *London Journal of Arts and Sciences* illustration of a lock, and the priming magazine on the actual gun in Plate 29. When the magazine is turned down, as in figure 1 of the London periodical's representation, a wedge on the side of the pan forces back a spring so that a sliding bar, within the magazine and attached to the spring, is withdrawn sufficiently to allow a pinch of priming powder to enter the pan. In the case of the real gun in Plate 29 the control of the fulminate is managed manually by turning the two little projecting handles. A half-circle turn opens or closes the hole in the base of the magazine.

Most of these early Westley Richards detonators now in existence have the small pan cover for use with pellets, rather than the

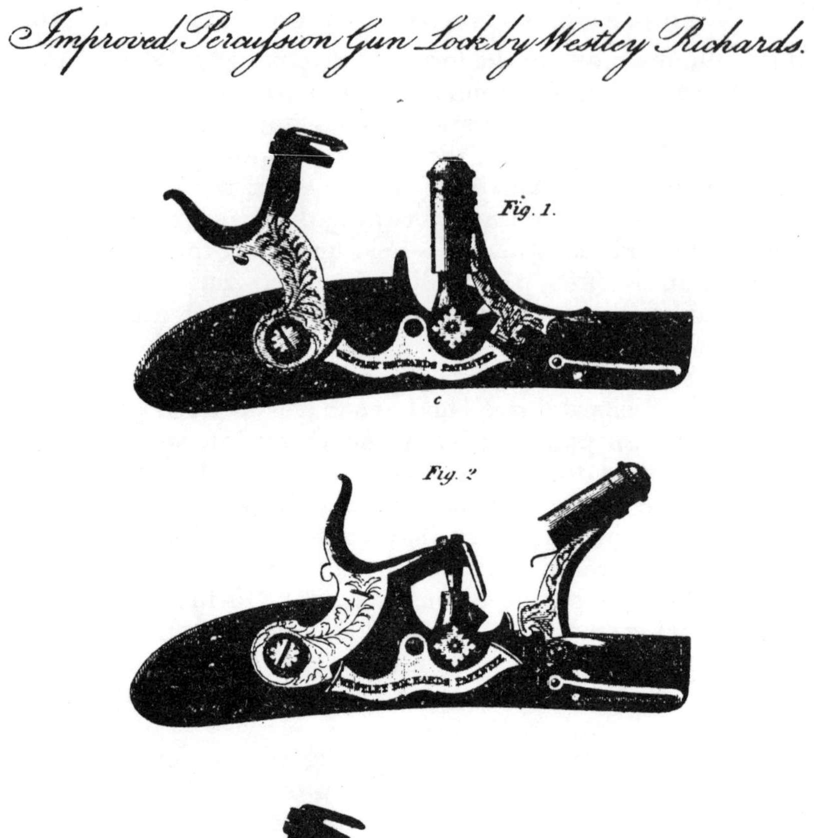

Illustration H. Drawing from the *London Journal of Arts and Sciences*

magazine for use with loose powder. How many have been converted it is not possible to say. A change-over required simply the substitution of a figure 6 cover for a figure 5 magazine, and such a substitution normally should defy detection. My guess is that the great majority of the Richards locks with simple covers were originally so made. For one thing, many sportsmen opposed all self-priming guns, fearing the magazine would blow up.

We come now to the scarce Egg self-priming guns. The statement was recently published that "it is doubtful if any examples survive" of guns with the priming mechanism patented in England by Joseph Egg in 1822. Plates 30 to 33 are of such guns that have survived in fine condition. These patented Egg guns are of two types, both having priming magazines supplying fulminate in pellets. In both types the force of gravity is relied upon to bring the pellets close to the pan so a perforated slide attached to the hammer will pick up and carry a pellet into the pan each time the hammer is raised.

Of the two types, the first, shown in Plates 30 and 31, was a failure. This had pellets in channels back of the breakoff of the breech and held in place by a hinged cover which can be seen partly raised in Plate 30. To utilize gravity's force, the muzzles had to be lowered.

The successful type, known as the "improved model", is shown in Plates 32 and 33. This had the pellets in tubular magazines lying alongside the centre rib. In this type the muzzles had to be raised during the act of cocking to permit gravity feeding.

In both types the slide covering the pellet in the pan is automatically withdrawn when the trigger is pulled.

According to Mr. Scurfield, an English collector and student, it is probable that only about twenty Brown Bess muskets were made of the type shown in Plates 34 and 35. Numerous marks on the gun identify it as a Brown Bess. When the musket was in England some years ago it was catalogued as having an Egg lock. As I own the gun, I have more than an academic interest in attributing the lock to that master gunmaker, Joseph Egg, but I must agree with English students that it was not made by Egg. The lock's construction conforms to Egg's specification in his British patent 4727 of 1822, which applied to ". . . a priming chamber attached to the barrel or barrels of any description of fire-arms, either as shown in the Drawing or varied in any other form, place or position contiguous to the barrel, and in the necessary shield or sliding guard, which also may be varied in shape and position for the purpose of admitting the priming to the touch hole when the piece is loaded and of cutting of the communication between the chamber and the touch hole when the piece is discharging." The illustrations show a tubular "priming chamber" contiguous to the barrel. When the hammer is down, as in Plate 34, a small pan in the "sliding guard" is in line with the priming magazine, and receives the fulminate. When, as in Plate 35, the gun is cocked, the "sliding guard" rises until the pellet of fulminate is in line with the touch hole, and in rising cuts "communication between the chamber and the touch hole". In addition to the usual "Tower", broad arrow, and "G R" under a crown, the lock plate carries the name "Hayward". Glendenning, in his *British Pistols and Guns*, reports that the 1834 directory of Kipling's "sleepy Chester"* lists a William Hayward as being then in the gun business. It is probable William Hayward made the lock; it is equally probable that William Hayward, who was a contemporary of Joseph Egg, was at least strongly influenced by Egg's patented construction.

It is held by some that a Brown Bess is always a firelock—a gun with flint ignition—of the type used by British infantry through the 1700's up to the adoption by the Board of Ordnance of the East India Company's Pattern Musket. I prefer to class this Hayward gun also as a Brown Bess, and even the later Rousseau self-capper that is described in Chapter IX.

The reason the famous flintlock musket that was the primary infantry weapon used by both the British and the American forces in the American Revolution has always been called the Brown Bess is often not understood.

Some collectors mistakenly believe the barrels of all Brown Bess muskets were originally brown. From that assumption comes part of the misconception. Actually, new Brown Bess muskets were "as bright as hands can make them",† at least up to the late 1750's when some of the muskets issued to the British Light Infantry had barrels stained brown. Barrels of British muskets were, in general, not browned until 1800 or later. The "Brown" in "Brown" Bess comes wholly from the lovely colour of the wood stocks.

A few people think the "Bess" part of the name has some relation to Good Queen Bess. The black-painted guns of the time of the first Queen Elizabeth were quite unlike the Brown Bess muskets, which first appeared during the reign of George I. The "Bess" is derived from the German or Danish "bus", which, in words like

* *The Grave of the Hundred Head*, by Rudyard Kipling.

† Robert Scurfield, "British Military Smooth-Bore Firearms", *Journal of the Society for Army Historical Research*, Vol. XXXIII *et seq.*

arquebus and blunderbuss, means gun. "Brown Bess" means simply "Brown Gun". It should be remembered that the Four Georges who were kings of England from 1714 to 1830 were likewise rulers of the German sovereign state of Hanover, and that the first issue of Brown Bess muskets may have been to German subjects of George I.

The Forsyth patent had expired some five or ten years before the double-barrelled pistol shown in Plates 36 and 37 was produced by one of the several men named William Green who were gunsmiths in London at various times. Mr. Green used a magazine that turns in a vertical plane, and has a spring-backed plunger in its top like the Forsyth scent bottle. The pictures show how meshing of teeth on the cock with teeth on the magazine causes the magazine to turn as the cock is raised and lowered.

Another detonator pistol which, like the William Green, has a magazine that is put in charging position by cocking the hammer, is the Lewis & Tomes, shown in Plates 38 and 39. A bar connects the hammer and the magazine. One illustration shows the magazine in priming position; the other shows the magazine turned out of the way by the hammer's downward movement.

A pistol unlike any that has gone before is shown in Plate 40. It is marked "Towlson" on the lock plates, and "Towlson, Marlboro & Newbury" on the rib between the barrels. Towlson is the maker's name; Marlboro and Newbury are two towns. Each hammer has built in it a magazine holding six fulminate pellets. To prime, the magazine is turned manually, for each shot, through one sixth of a circle.

Another, and less scarce, pellet-lock pistol having a priming magazine built in the hammer is shown in Plate 41. It was made by the London gunmaker, Charles Moore. There is some resemblance to the earlier Westley Richards and probably later General Shrapnel construction, both guns previously mentioned, in that a projection on the breast of the hammer moves a pivoted lever to let the pin in the nose of the hammer drive into the priming.

Before a description of a few continental loose-powder or pellet detonators is given, two more unusual pieces by famous English makers will be shown.

Plate 42 pictures a little-known gun patented by the well-known Westley Richards in 1841, British patent 9177. The fulminate was contained in a flat, wedge-shaped papier-mâché primer which was pushed sideways over the touch hole where it was gripped by two curved bits of metal. The advantage claimed over the copper cap which was then in general use was that the flat primer was firmly anchored, whereas the cap was not. A second feature—both features were unique—was the use of a striking plug made hollow and with a perforation through its side for the purpose of letting out smoke and gas after the ignition of the charge. This striking plug looks exactly like a nipple, except for the little hole in its side, and is screwed into the nose of the hammer. A replacement is kept in a hole bored in the underneath part of the stock.

Plate 43 shows a pellet lock patented by Joseph Manton in 1816. Joseph Manton was known to sportsmen of his day as "The King of the Gunmakers", and guns equipped with this, his first percussion lock, were certainly produced in considerable numbers, but the lock here pictured is probably one of only two such locks that now exist. This lock was made to be interchangeable with a flintlock.

An easily detachable plug fitted into the hammer. A hole, drilled the length of the plug, contained both a fulminate pellet and a floating firing pin to detonate the fulminate. The illustration shows three of the plugs, one in the hammer, one with the firing pin in it, and one with the firing pin withdrawn.

Plate 45 shows a box partly filled with detachable plugs for an 1816 model Joseph Manton gun. If you will compare this picture with Plate 17, you will notice the Manton strikers have holes in their centres, whereas the strikers for the patch locks are solid. When the Manton hammer came down, the hole in the centre of the striker connected with the vent in the anvil, so the flame would pass to the powder charge. It will be noticed the anvil is in the form of an inclined plane, unlike the pegs on patch locks.

The extreme scarcity of examples of 1816 Joseph Manton locks has two causes. First, Forsyth brought a successful action for patent infringement, and that put a stop to the sale of the guns. Second, the locks on the whole were not well received, and most of the guns were eventually converted to percussion cap.

A pair of the best known of the continental European detonators is the Le Page pair in Plate 44. These pistols are not self-priming. They were primed for each shot by powder from a flask which threw one centigramme of fulminate into the vent which may be seen in the lug screwed into the barrel breech in Plate 46.

The detonation of the fulminating powder was accomplished by the hammer driving a plunger through a housing. The illustration showing the two pistols has the pistol at the top with the housing turned so the hammer drives the plunger into the vent. The lower pistol has the lock ready for priming.

Both pistols are dated 1812 inside the lock plates and under the barrels. Le Page guns with locks like those on these pistols were tested before April 28, 1810. On that date a committee submitted a lengthy report on two such guns to the Society for the Encouragement of National Industry. Le Page had made the guns available on July 29th of the previous year. The report stated that Mr. Le Page had set out to overcome difficulties that had confronted Mr. Prelat when the latter imitated the Forsyth scent-bottle lock. The report's reference to the Prelat copy was, "Some time ago Mr. Prelat made a new gunlock, based on a model imported from England". (See Illustration G, this chapter, of the Prelat copy.) The highly favourable report said that three hundred and three shots were fired through each Le Page gun, with no mishap and no misfire.

The members of the committee were worried about the possibility of explosions of the fulminating powder when it was carried in flasks or other containers. When earlier experiments were conducted with fulminates for use as propellents, particularly in France and Spain, there had been heavy property damage and much loss of life. Mr. Le Page assured the committee members that with his improved powder the danger could be eliminated "by avoiding very *strong* blows struck by very *hard* objects". (The italics are the committee's.) The report went on, "To support this contention, he put 130 grams of the same powder in a cask having a capacity of around one cubic decimeter, attached the cask to a board to which were nailed crosswise four cleats, and to the board tied a very long cord, by means of which a young man pulled the board swiftly over very rough ground for a distance of around 600 meters. The same test was repeated after adding twelve lead balls weighing about 17 grams each to the powder. Finally, the cask, loaded with the same balls, was dropped twice from a height of around 12 meters upon a very hard surface. In none of these experiments did the powder fire". With commendable scepticism the committee tested the roughly handled powder in the locks of the Le Page guns, to see if it would work perfectly. It did.

A little more should be said about this French pair of Le Page pistols. They are certainly among the first, and possibly the very first, detonating pistols to be imported into the United States. These beautifully made, finely engraved and gold inlaid pistols are in a case with many accessories, such as a flask for gunpowder and another for priming powder, a bullet mould, a wrench, a screw-driver, loading and cleaning rods, et cetera. The cased set belonged to Colonel David Humphreys of Derby, Connecticut. Colonel Humphreys was an American Revolutionary officer, sometime aide-de-camp on the staff of His Excellency, General Washington. Humphreys was later United States minister to Spain. He was born in 1752 and died in 1818. The frontispiece pictures these pistols in their case with accessories.

Let's leave that simple and meritorious detonator produced in quantity by a well-known French maker and turn to a complicated and frail detonator produced probably in small numbers by a little-known French maker. This gun, Plates 47 and 48, shows by markings on the barrels it was made in St. Etienne by Cessier. The photograph, taken from the side, shows the magazines fitted with hinged covers that may be snapped up when the magazines need refilling. The construction of the locks make it appear the fulminate was in the form of small pellets, as it would be if the detonating mixture had been moistened with spirits of wine or vinegar and pressed through a sieve. Cocking the firing pins is done by turning the side levers, best seen in the photograph taken from above. With the gun cocked, if a button on the side is pressed, a sliding member slides out sharply, impelled by the long spring alongside the barrel, and fulminate passes from the magazine to the touch hole. The sliding piece must be pushed in before the trigger is pulled, to allow the firing pin to get through to the fulminate. I think this gun has the most ill-contrived lock I ever came across, but the gun should interest most collectors because of its oddity.

An unusual, unsigned, but more sensible French detonator is shown in Plate 49. There is a side magazine for pellets of fulminate. When the hammer is raised an attached link forces fulminate from the magazine into the pan and then closes the pan. As the hammer falls an attached chain opens the pan.

The French pistol (Plates 50 and 51) is, like the one just described, by an unknown maker. This is a rarely found type. Most detonators had small-nosed hammers which crushed hard pellets about the size of mustard seeds. A few, like this one, had large-nosed hammers which crushed less hard pellets coated with wax and about the size of peas. Guns that required use of wax-coated pellets were not popular, and for that reason are extremely scarce. The unpopularity arose from the fact the wax would soften on a hot day, or even from body heat.

The large pan is a circular well with its touch hole directly in line with the centre of the barrel bore. This centre-fire pistol employs a bent hammer which is perforated to allow escape of the blown-back gas, which must have been considerable.

Another French detonator, this one signed "J. J. Rissack", is pictured in Plate 52. This was readily, but not quickly, primed. In firing, the hammer struck down on the floating firing pin centred in a round screw-in plug. After each firing it was necessary to turn out the plug, insert fulminate, and then screw in the plug.

I should have mentioned at the outset that the early European detonators pictured here—those using patches, loose powder, or pellets—represent only a small fraction of the many makes produced. Hundreds of gunmakers in England, and other hundreds on the continent, struggled with the problems of giving their customers safe, efficient detonators. There were many failures. Some resulted from poor design or construction, others from lack of good publicity or financial backing. Early detonators are much scarcer than flintlock or even wheel-lock guns, though nearly all the friction-ignition guns are much older. The explanation is, the friction-ignition guns were steadily manufactured for a period of years ten times the short run of early detonators.

Let's look at a few detonators from other European countries.

The gun that more than any other has misled gun collectors interested in the development of firearms ignition is the Spanish piece shown in Plate 53. This gun was made by Joseph Gutierez, an early nineteenth—repeat, *nineteenth*—century gunmaker of Seville. The lock is much like the second model Forsyth in operation.

One reason for the bewilderment in collectors' minds is the fact that when the gun was sold at auction on April 1, 1923, by Sotheby, Wilkinson & Hodge, the catalogue description included, "This is believed to be the earliest example of a gun fired on the detonating principle, the lock being inscribed 'Seville 1720' " and "Previous to the discovery of this gun Forsyth was the accepted inventor of the detonating lock in 1807". My priced copy of the Sotheby catalogue shows the gun fetched £63. That was a tidy sum in the days when United States paper money was redeemable for gold, and a British pound was equal to $4.86, but I think the price would have been much higher if bidders had not mistrusted that 1720 date. The bidders at the auction were also probably struck by the fact the gun was half-stocked and had a trigger guard of a shape consistent with early nineteenth-century design but not with early eighteenth-century. The second reason for the perplexity was the surprising fact that Herbert Jackson, in his large and beautifully illustrated *European*

Hand Firearms of the Sixteenth, Seventeenth and Eighteenth Centuries, devoted the larger part of a chapter to his supposition, based wholly on this gun, that detonating locks had existed long before Forsyth.

The date on the loose-powder magazine is 1820, but, perhaps merely as a result of ordinary wear, or perhaps because of rubbing, the 8 looks like a 7.

Mr. Neal's *Spanish Guns and Pistols* makes it clear Forsyth detonators were well established before this Gutierez gun was made.

I was once offered a Spanish double-barrelled shotgun with fine tube locks and the date 1796 in large letters in gold on the barrels. Buyers of Spanish guns should remember that fine old barrels were often re-installed on later guns. A Spanish gun with barrels by a famous maker who flourished in 1750, furniture by another famous maker of 1800, and locks by an 1850 maker is not unimaginable. The tube-lock gun offered me was simply a gun originally flintlock with locks converted to tube ignition long after 1796.

Another Spanish lock which, like the Gutierez, has the outside mainspring and the sear working through the lock plate, typical features of miquelet locks, and which, also like the Gutierez, has an engagingly unconventional hammer is shown in Plate 54. The pan, with a pivoted and side-swinging cover which is fitted with a floating striker, is manually primed for each shot with a pellet of fulminate.

The multiformity of detonators is amazing. A pair of unsigned Belgian pellet-lock pistols unlike any pistol that has gone before is pictured in Plate 55. To prime one of these pistols a pellet of fulminate is placed in the hole that shows up after the large-headed screw in front of the trigger guard is turned out. When the screw is then turned in, the fulminate will rest between the end of the screw, which acts as an anvil, and a floating firing pin.

Many fine detonators were manufactured in Austria by Joseph Contriner. One of a pair of beautifully made Contriner detonators, in very fine condition, is shown in Plate 56. The priming magazine, which has a tight-fitting snap cover, slides on a bar. The magazine is linked to the hammer so that when the hammer is brought to full cock, fulminate will drop into the vent. As the hammer falls, the rod linking the hammer to the magazine pushes the magazine forward along the bar and out of the way of the striking plug screwed into the hammer nose.

At the beginning of this chapter four early types of percussion ignition were listed. The fourth one was fulminate in metal tubes.

Tube-lock ignition never became as generally popular as copper-cap ignition, but, in Europe, its popularity was greater and lasted longer than any other early percussion system, always excepting the copper cap. A young aristocrat making the prescribed Grand Tour in the 1820's could probably have found tube-lock guns in all the countries he visited, just as he could have found loose-powder or pellet detonators if he had been determined to hunt them out.

Sportsmen who used big-bore shotguns for wildfowling, and particularly those who used punt guns, preferred tube locks. They liked the sure ignition of heavy coarse powder charges under all weather conditions.

The tube primer was a small cylinder of thin copper, often no larger than a pencil lead and less than an inch long, usually open at both ends, filled with fulminate. Most of these tube primers were detonated by a hammer striking across the middle. However, some were detonated by a blow on the end. In the last chapter of this book several forms of tube primers will be illustrated. Some of the type made to be crushed across the middle have one end closed and hooded. This umbrella-like end protected from blast and discomfiture anyone who might be close alongside the lock when the gun was fired, and it also made easier the removal of a fired tube that had not been blown clear by the explosion.

Joseph Manton, the English inventor of the tube lock, patented it in 1818, British 4285. His 1816 pellet lock, British patent 3985, was one of his few failures, but this 1818 tube lock was one of his many successes.

A tube used in a Manton gun had both ends open. When one end was pushed in the touch hole, the tube rested on an anvil attached to the lock plate. A snap cover was let down to secure the tube. The cover had an opening which let the hammer nose through to crush the middle of the tube. The detonation of the fulminate was sure to fire the gunpowder charge. Sometimes the explosion also sent the empty copper tube to the side with such violence as to injure a shooter's companion. Plate 57 shows a gun made by the famous London gunsmith, John Blanch, having a lock, with the small cover raised, identical in design to a Manton lock.

The 1818 Manton patent tube lock was judged an infringement of the basic Forsyth patent, but, as the Forsyth patent had not long to run, tube locks were soon being sold by many gunmakers.

A gun having a different method of holding a tube primer is shown in Plate 58. This was made by George Fuller, a London gunmaker. The tube is gripped by a nipper spring instead of being held by a snap cover.

Two views of a tube lock which requires neither a clamp nor a snap cover to hold the tube are pictured in Plates 59 and 60. This bears the name of Charles Lancaster, London. One view shows the large touch hole ready to receive the tube primer. The other view shows an umbrella-type primer inserted with the hammer striking it across the middle. Colonel Peter Hawker strongly commended this Lancaster lock.

Another tube lock highly praised by the celebrated Hawker is shown in Plate 61. This, patented in 1831, British 6071, was one more of the Westley Richards inventions. In the ninth, and best, edition of *Instructions to Young Sportsmen*, Hawker, commenting on this Richards primer, said: "I have tried it repeatedly, and never yet knew it to fail; and my son, of the 74th regiment, shot with it for a whole season, and never had a miss-fire. The next season he accompanied me to the coast, where we had heavy seas and much wet weather; and while my copper caps were missing about two shots out of ten, his primer never failed once". The tube was thrust down into a nipple similar to a nipple on which common caps were placed, except that the hole in it was of much greater diameter. The tube was detonated by a blow on the end. Descriptions of such tubes will be found in the last chapter.

A Wilkinson underhammer musket, which used the same sort of tube, has the nipple with its large hole centralized in Plate 62.

A continental European pistol which also had a tube primer detonated by a blow on its end is shown in Plates 63 and 64. This was made in Germany by Guntermann. It will be noticed there is a lever attached to a circular plate which has a hole in it. A bullet is rammed down the barrel until stopped against a shoulder. When the lever is put in a vertical position, as in Plate 63, the mouth of the powder chamber is tilted up to receive a charge of gunpowder. Then, when the lever is turned forward and down, as in Plate 64, the chamber mouth is aligned with the barrel bore, with the charge kept in place by the bullet. Also, when the lever is down, the tube inserted in the hole in the circular plate is under the hammer.

The other continental tube locks now to be described all have the tube crushed in the middle, rather than hit on the end.

Plates 65 and 66 are of an Austrian gun converted from flint to tube lock. This form of tube lock was invented by Giuseppe Console. According to *Deane's Manual of the History and Science of Fire-arms*,

Console was an employee "in the imperial Austrian service at Milan" at the time the lock was invented, in 1835 according to Deane. Plate 65 shows a pivoted arm tipped back against the spring that once controlled a flintlock's frizzen. With the hammer cocked, the lock is ready for insertion of a tube in the touch hole. To fire the gun, the pivoted arm is first let down, so that a prong on the underside will rest against the tube, keeping it firmly against the anvil which replaces the original flintlock pan. Then the trigger is pulled and the hammer nose drives the arm hard against the tube, crushing it.

Of the curiously few printed references to this lock, all I have seen had the spelling "Consol". A glance at the finely engraved lock in Plate 67 will explain my reason for spelling the inventor's name, "Console". I think the reproduction of the photograph will clearly show the final "e" in the gold-inlaid name.

The tube lock most frequently found in gun collections is often incorrectly referred to as a pill lock. The misunderstanding is largely due to the fact that several gun dealers who should know better have catalogued such guns as "pill locks". One 1907 catalogue stated these "pill locks" were of "1790 period", a date at least fifty years too early. The lock is another Austrian invention. It has a pivoted arm—something like the one on the Console—that is thrown back when a tube is to be inserted in the touch hole. An important difference is that this arm, or cover for the tube, is a solid piece on the Console, whereas on the pistol shown in Plate 68 the arm is fitted with a large circular floating striker, having a sharp edge on the underside. Muskets and cadet guns, as well as pistols, having this form of tube lock, have been widely sold in America. Of the old guns imported since World War II by antique dealers these Austrian pieces comprise almost the only examples of early detonators, except, of course, the copper-cap guns. American dealers travelling in Europe in search of antiques will still find the Austrian tube locks offered at prices they will pay, but they will rarely find other early rare detonators at any price.

Austrian tube-lock muskets were bought both by the North and the South in the American Civil War, but it is probable most of them were changed over to percussion cap.

Colonel Lewis in his *Small Arms and Ammunition in the United States Service* reports on tube primers for Austrian muskets. It seems the Austrian tube was similar to a Manton tube, except that it had a copper wire attached to one end, to make handling easier.

An especially fine French gun having a lock with a feature not found on other tube locks is shown in Plate 69. This gun was made in Langres by Sauvain. The feature is a spring cover which when snapped shut retains the tube in the touch hole and prevents its being blown out. The picture shows the cover pressed down and the touch hole open to receive the tube.

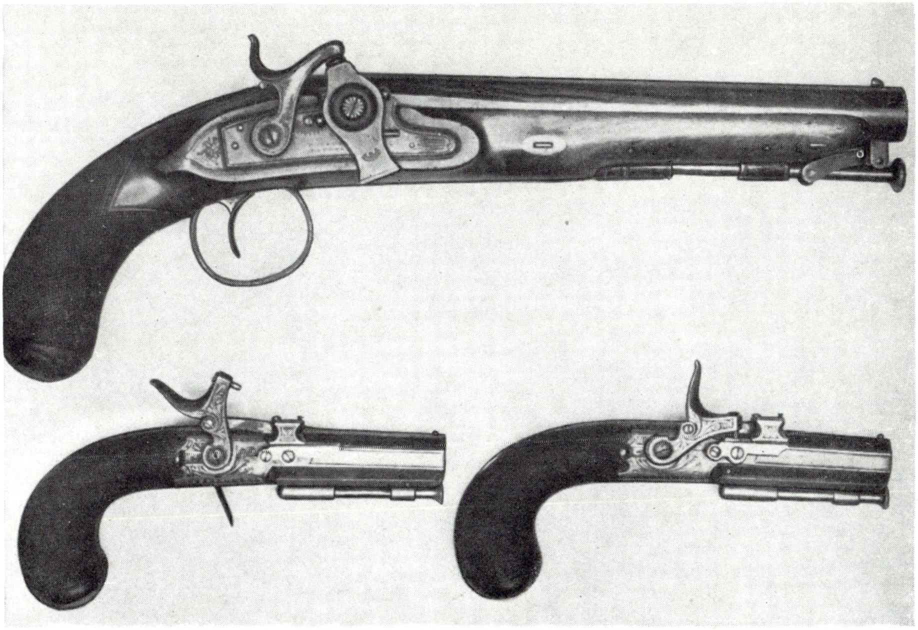

1 Forsyth scent-bottle pistol (*top*); Forsyth folding-trigger pistols with sliding priming magazines (*Collection: Henry M. Stewart*)

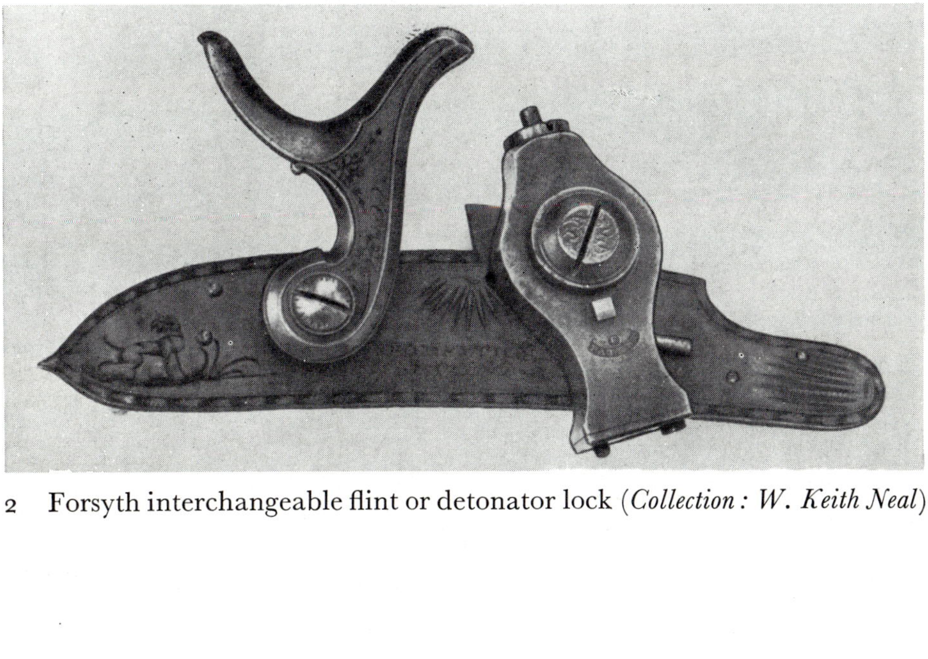

2 Forsyth interchangeable flint or detonator lock (*Collection: W. Keith Neal*)

3 Forsyth interchangeable flint or detonator lock (*Collection: W. Keith Neal*)

4 Forsyth sliding-magazine pistol showing screwed-in firing pin (*Collection W. Keith Neal*)

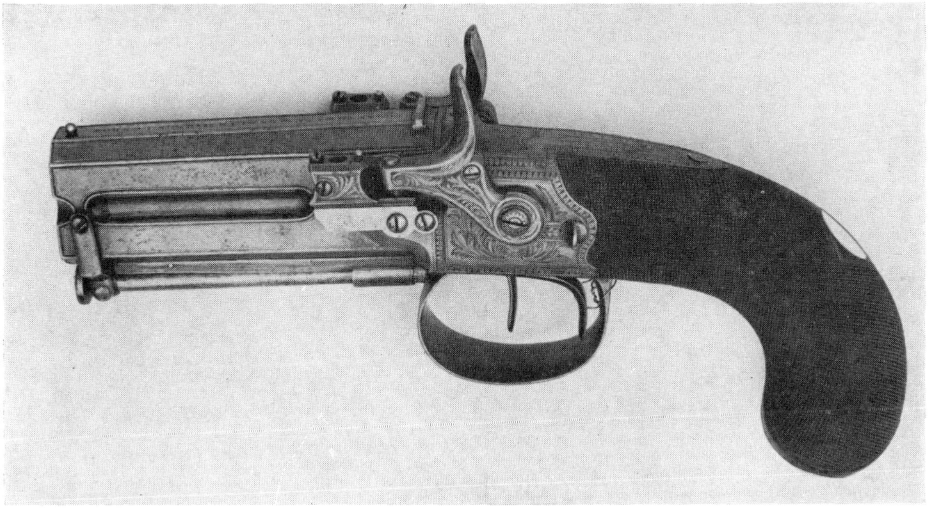

5 Forsyth over-and-under pistol (*Collection: The Metropolitan Museum of Art*)

6 Pauly cartridges and components (*Collection: Dr. W. R. Funderburg*)

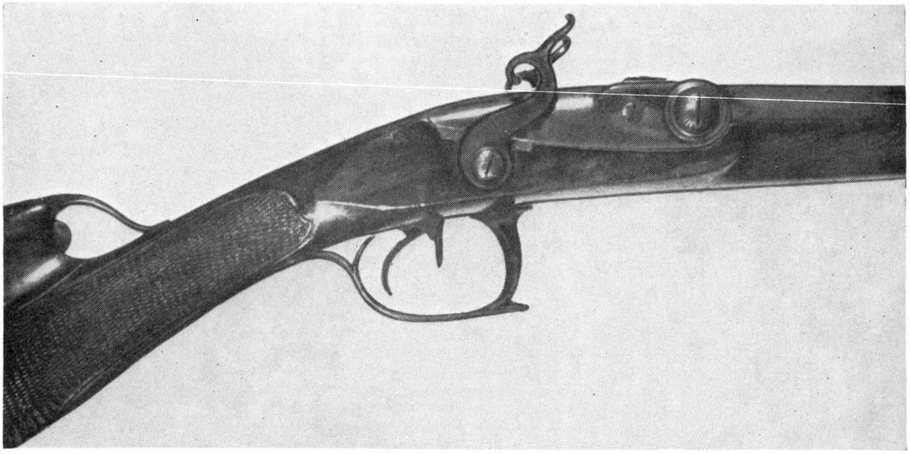

7 Pauly shotgun with breech closed (*Collection: Lewis Winant*)

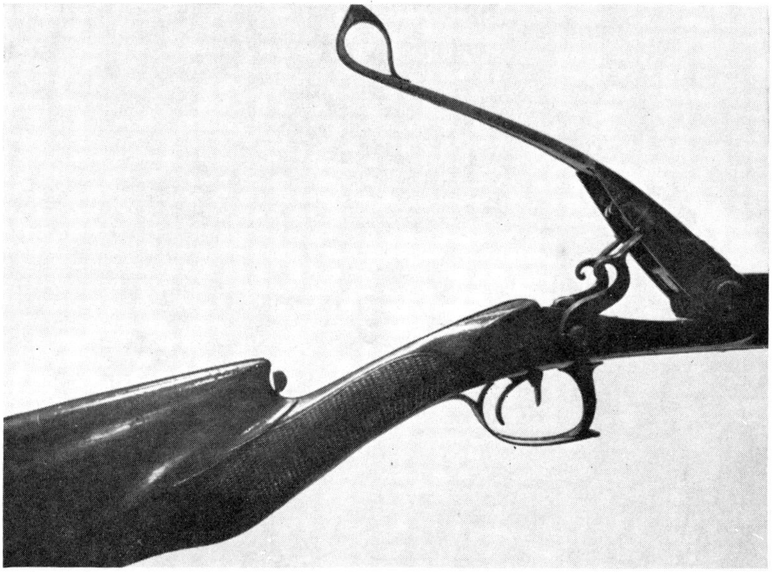

8 Pauly shotgun with breech open (*Collection: Lewis Winant*)

9 Pauly shotgun with breech open (*Collection: Lewis Winant*)

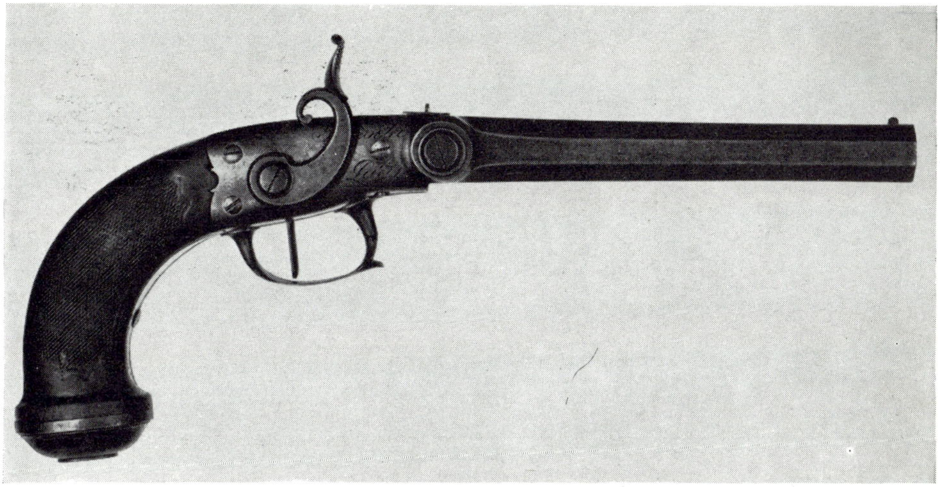

10 Pauly pistol with breech closed
(*The Winchester Collection*)

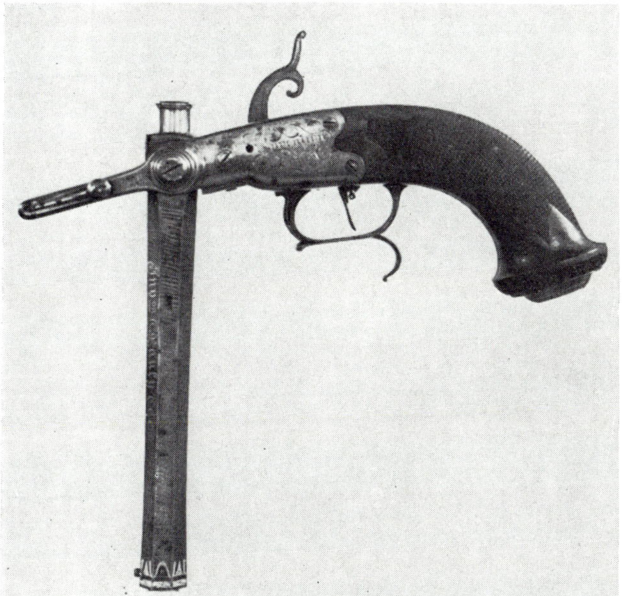

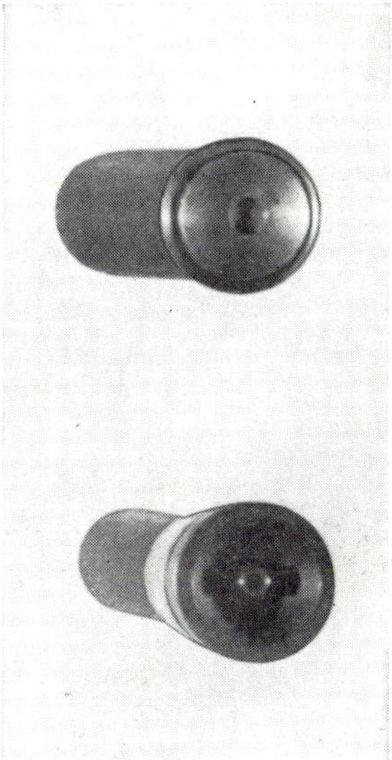

11 (*left*) Pauly pistol with breech open and cartridge inserted
(*Collection: Dr. W. R. Funderburg*)

12 (*right*) Pauly cartridge (*top*); and Pottet cartridge (*bottom*)

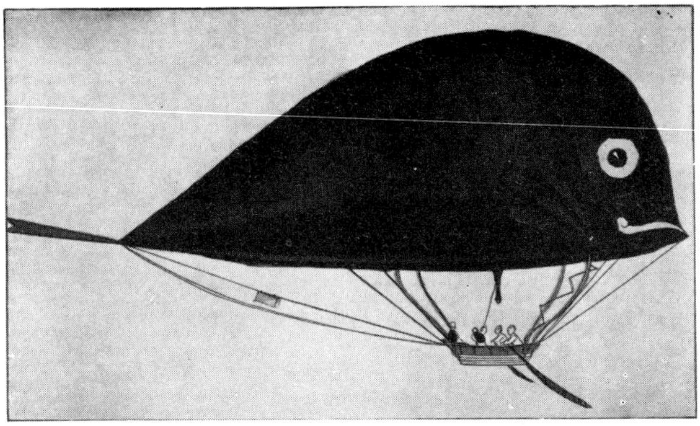

13 Pauly and Egg's Dolphin or Fish-formed Balloon. 1816 (*J. Hodgson's* The History of Aeronautics in Great Britain)

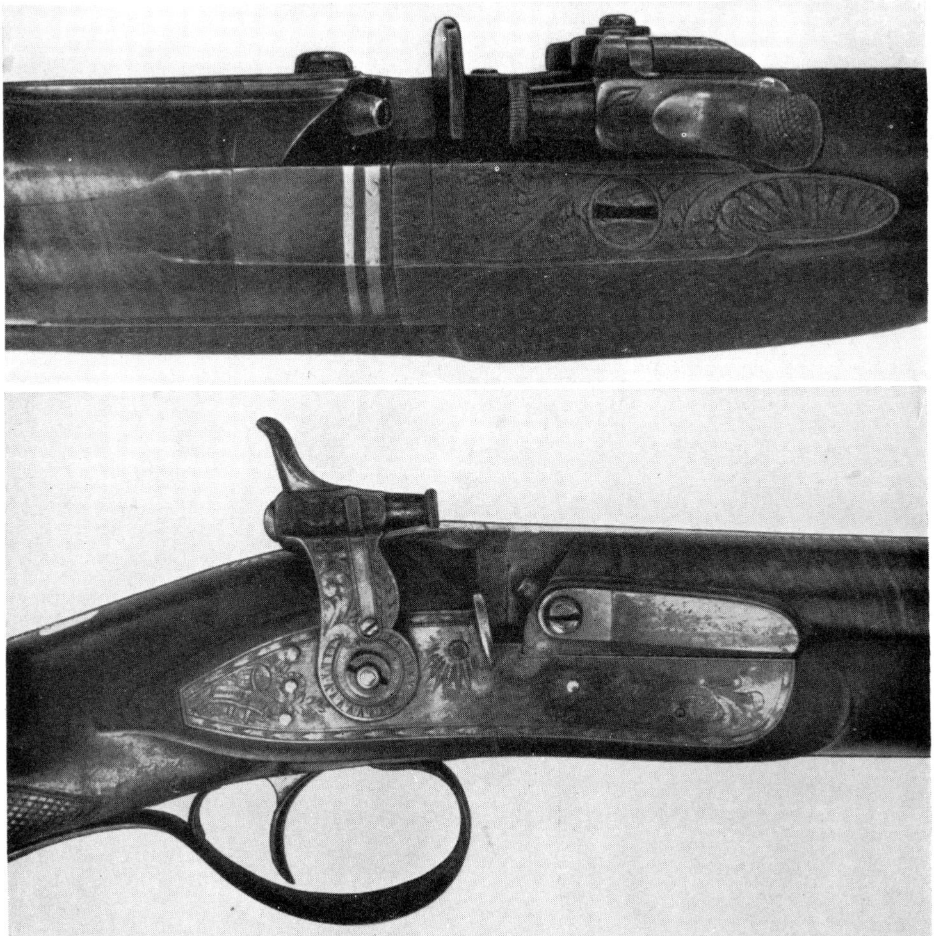

14 Cartmell patch-lock, top and side view (*Collection: W. Keith Neal*)

15 Nock patch-lock pistol (*Collection: Paul C. Janke*)

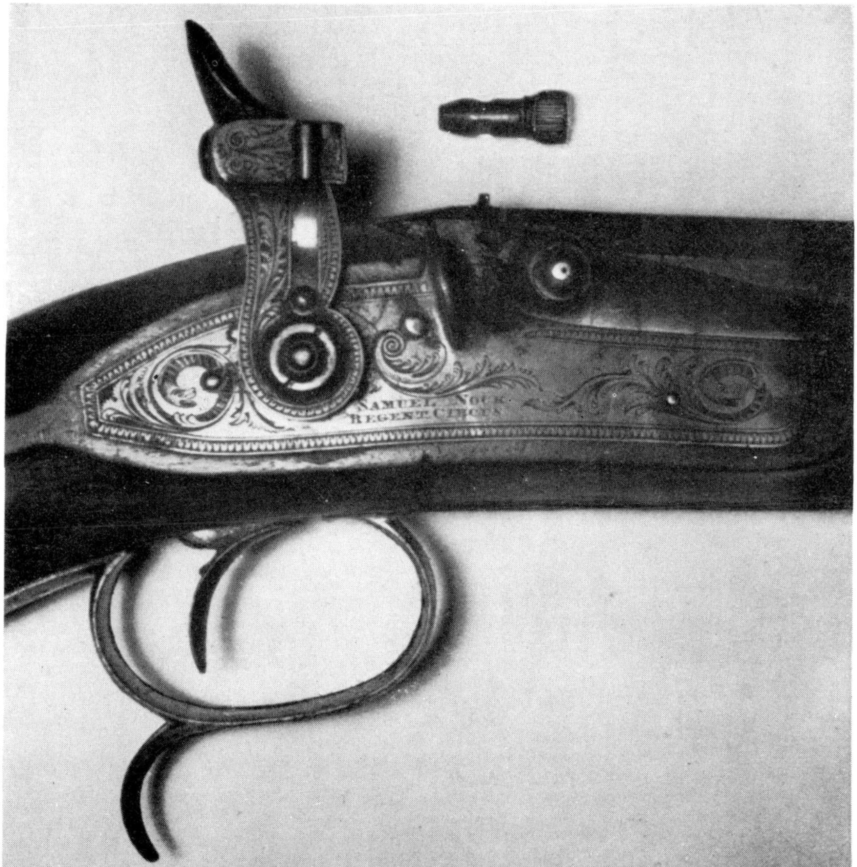

16. Detail of Nock patch-lock pistol with removable striker (*Collection: Paul C. Janke*)

17 Patch-lock strikers (*Collection: W. Keith Neal*)

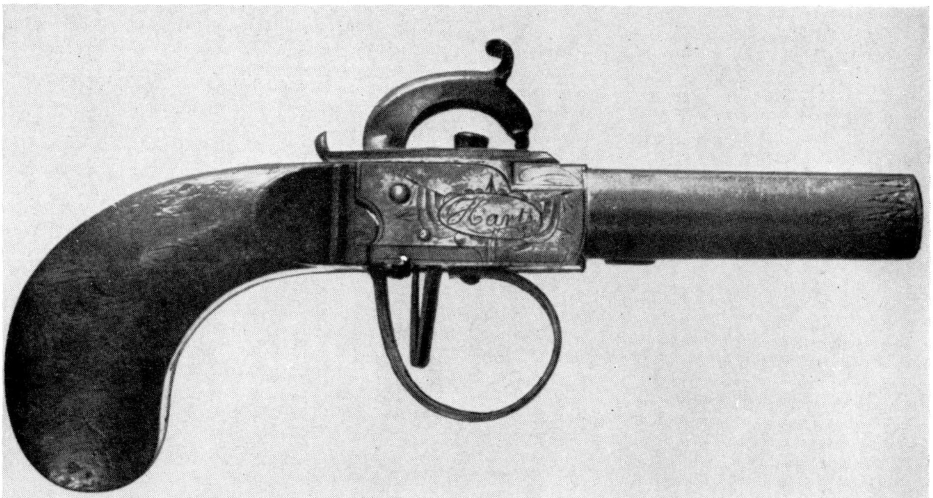

18 Hart punch-lock pistol (*Collection: Lewis Winant*)

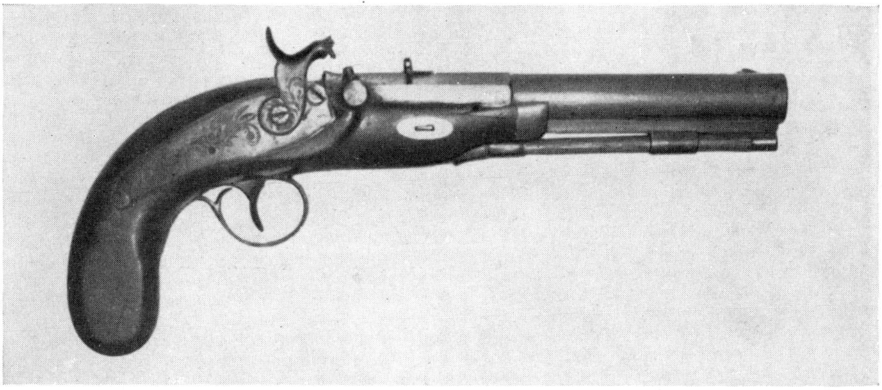

19 Rogers & Heart punch-lock pistol (*Collection: Lewis Winant*)

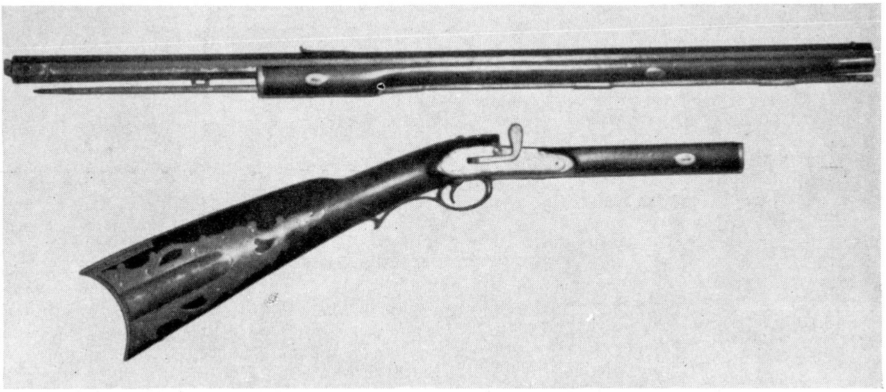

20 Gilbert punch-lock rifle (*Collection: Lewis Winant*)

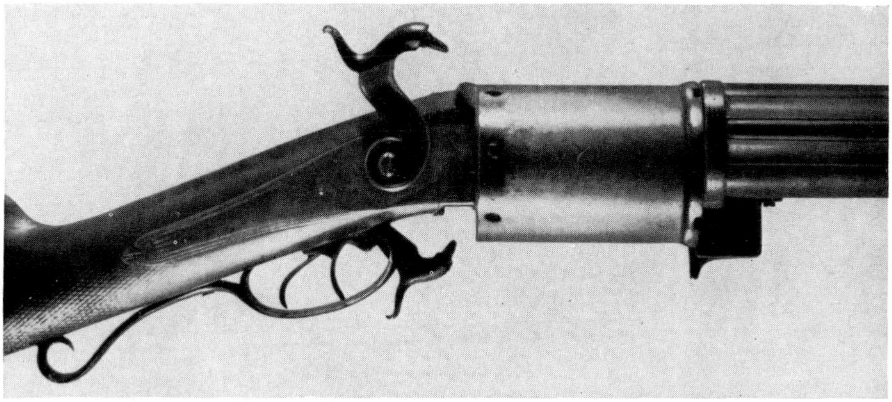

21 Billinghurst pill-lock combination rifle and shotgun (*Collection: Mark Aziz*)

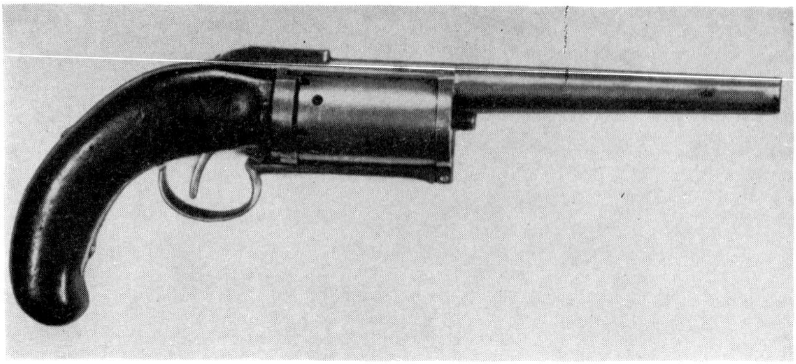

22 North & Skinner pill-lock revolver (*Collection: Smithsonian Institution*)

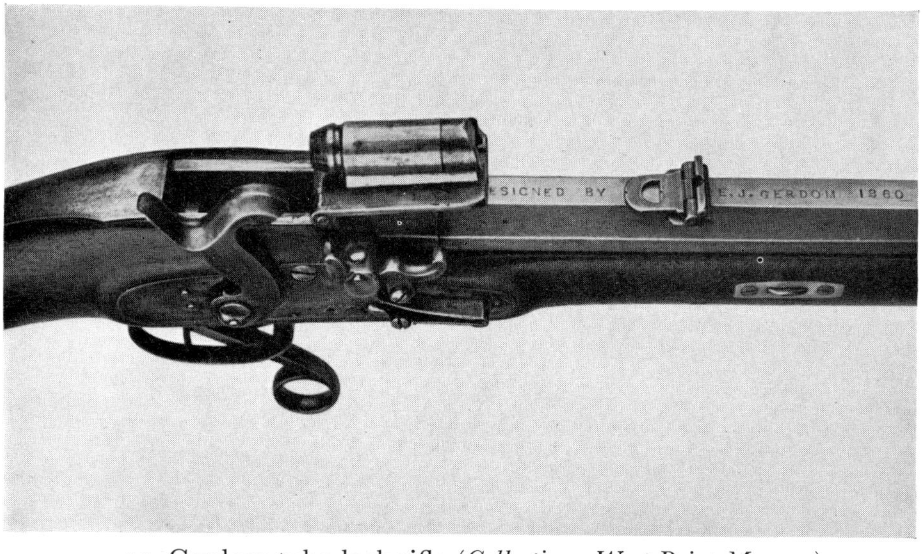

23 Gerdom tube-lock rifle (*Collection: West Point Museum*)

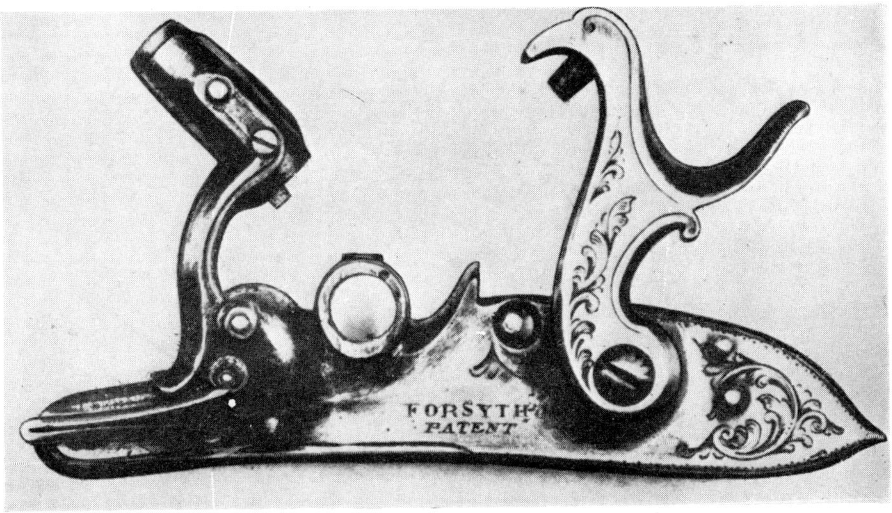

24 Lock fraudulently labelled Forsyth

25 J. Jones & Co. lock (*Collection: W. Keith Neal*)

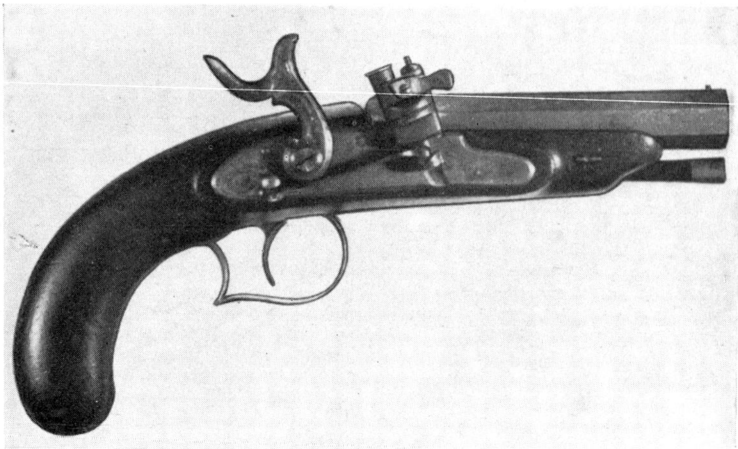

26 Unsigned British pistol with magazine in priming position (*Collection: Franklin B. Simmons*)

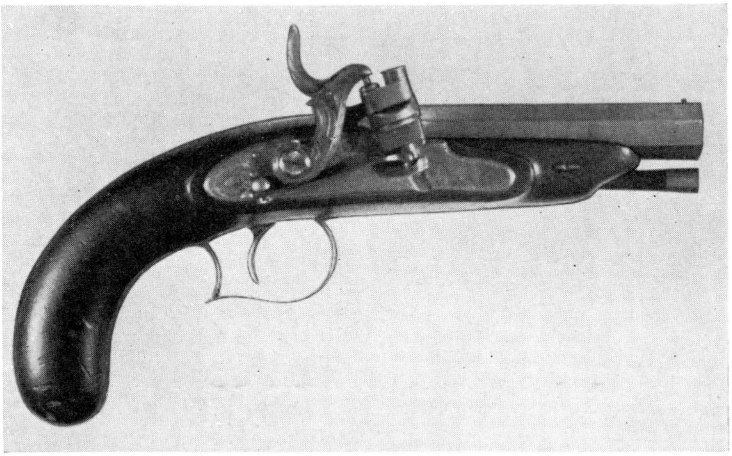

27 Unsigned British pistol with the magazine in firing position (*Collection: Franklin B. Simmons*)

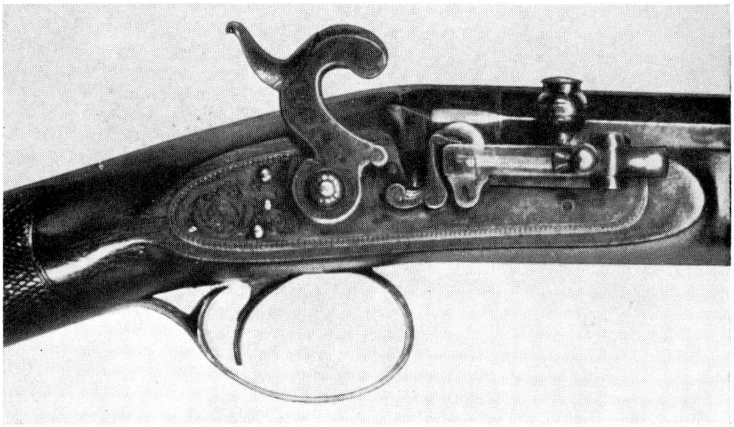

28 Shrapnel shotgun (*Collection Lewis Winant*)

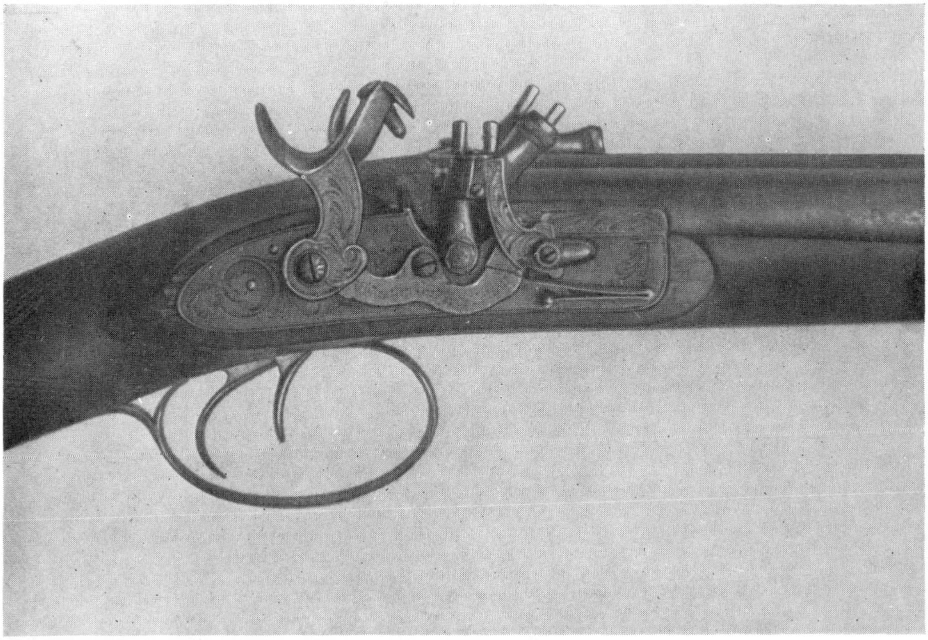

29 First Westley Richards detonator (*Formerly in the Harrod Collection*)

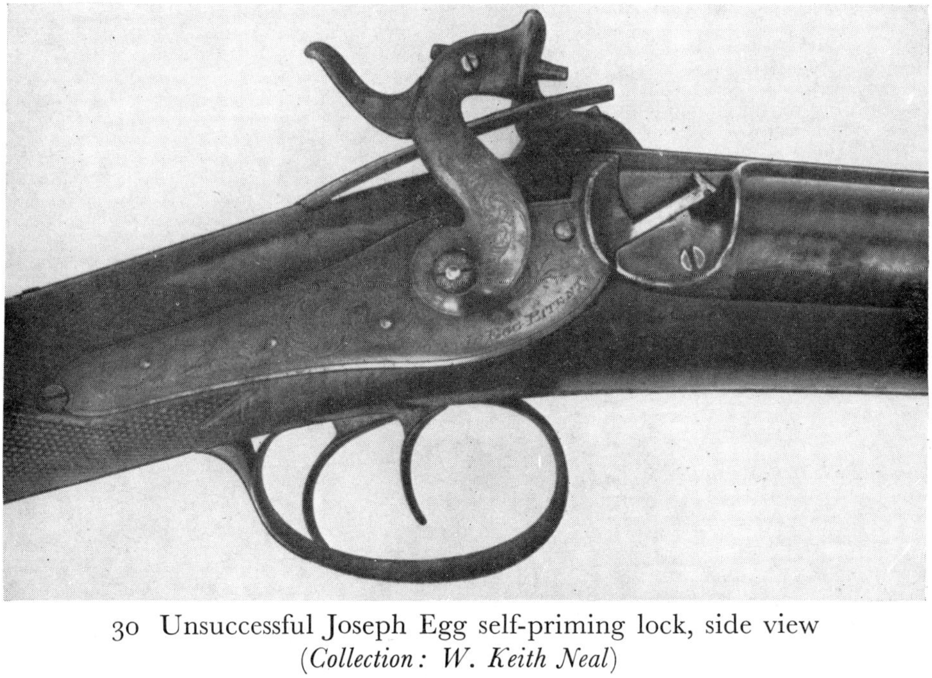

30 Unsuccessful Joseph Egg self-priming lock, side view
(*Collection: W. Keith Neal*)

31 Unsuccessful Joseph Egg self-priming lock, top view
(*Collection: W. Keith Neal*)

32 Joseph Egg "improved model", side view (*Collection: W. Keith Neal*)

33 Joseph Egg "improved model", top view (*Collection: W. Keith Neal*)

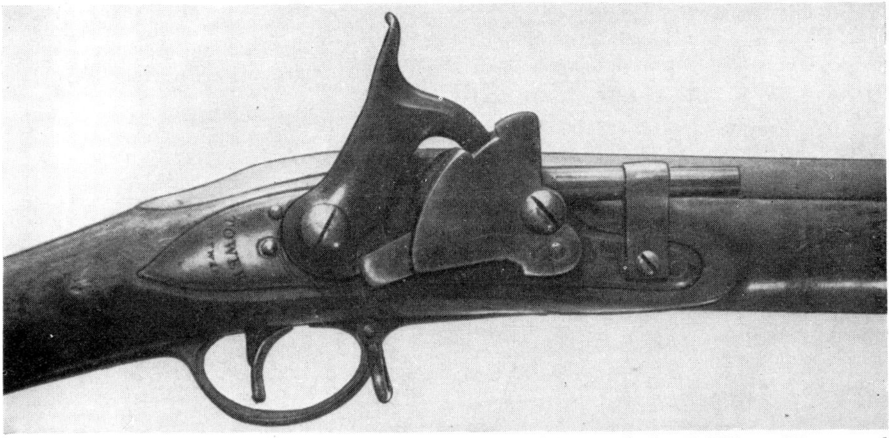

34 Brown Bess musket with Egg-type lock, possibly made by William Hayward, hammer down (*Collection: Lewis Winant*)

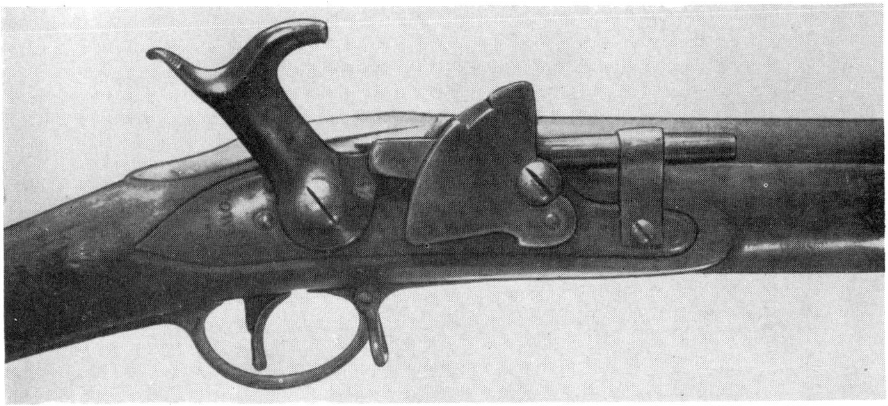

35 Brown Bess musket with Egg-type lock, possibly made by William Hayward, hammer up (*Collection: Lewis Winant*)

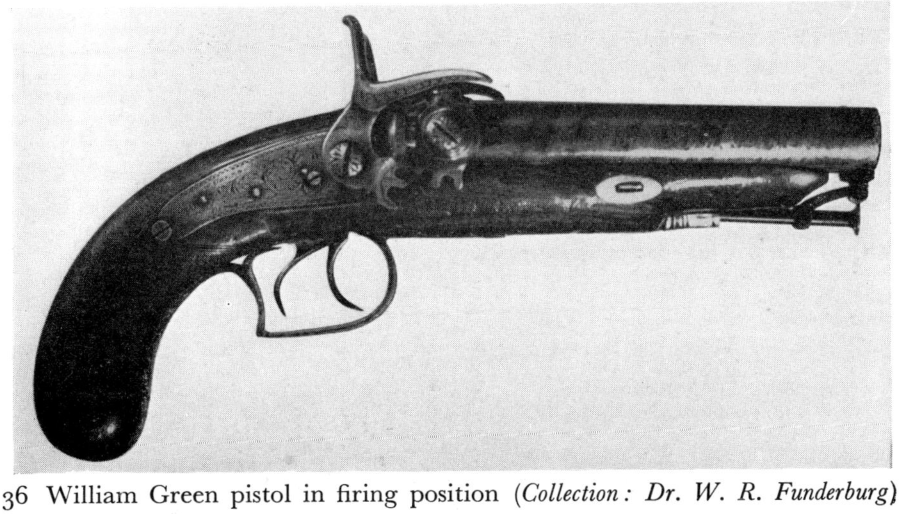

36 William Green pistol in firing position (*Collection: Dr. W. R. Funderburg*)

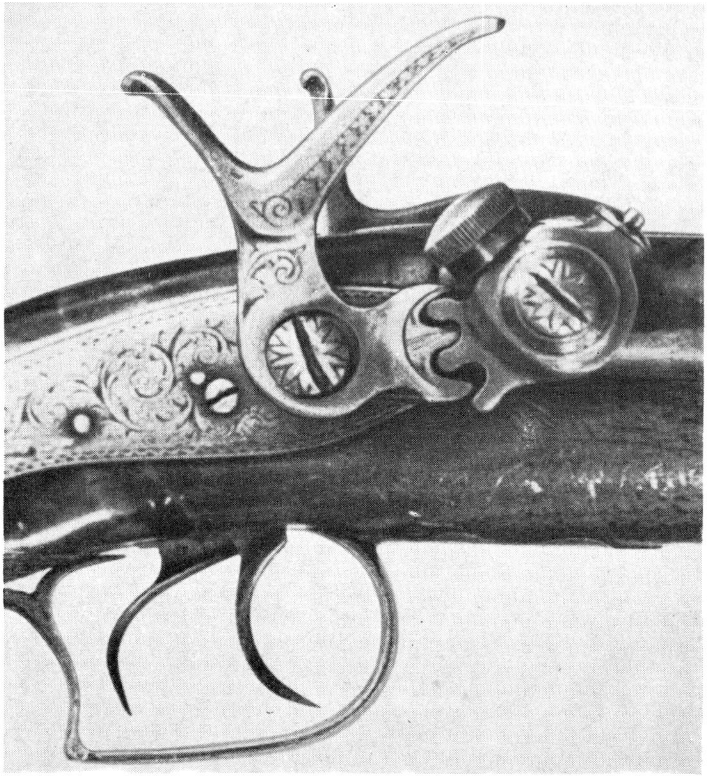

37 William Green pistol in cocked, charging position
(*Collection: Dr. W. R. Funderburg*)

38 Lewis & Tomes pistol, cocked, in priming position
(*Collection: Dr. W. R. Funderburg*)

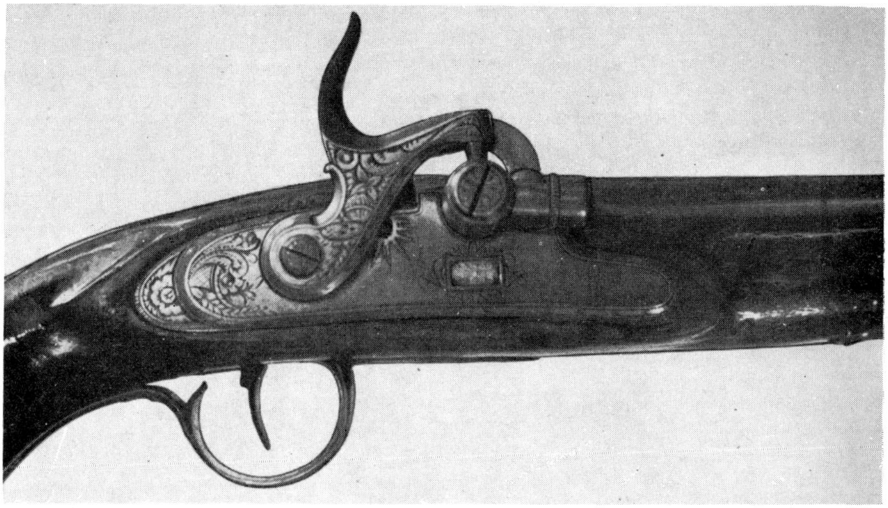

39 Lewis & Tomes pistol, in firing position (*Collection: Dr. W. R. Funderburg*)

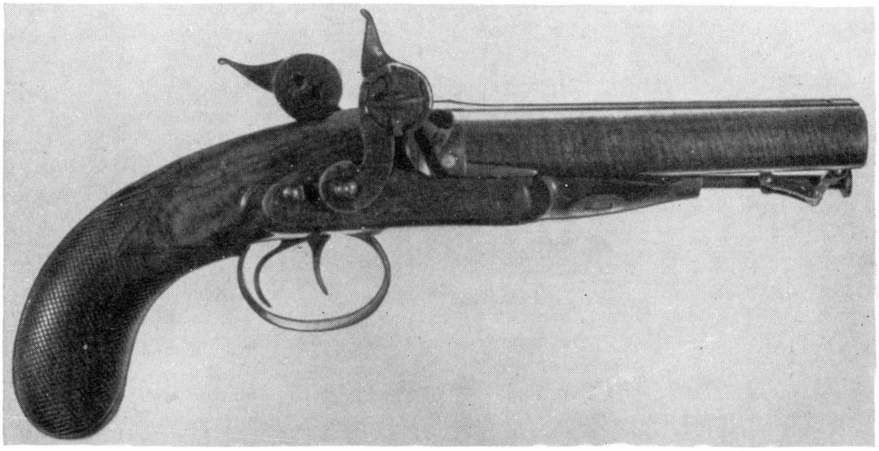

40 Towlson pistol with priming magazine built into hammer (*Collection: Dr. Jack Strassman*)

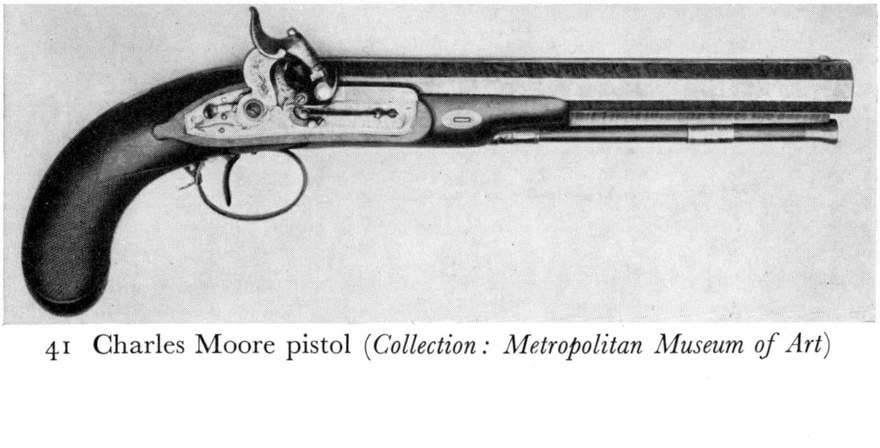

41 Charles Moore pistol (*Collection: Metropolitan Museum of Art*)

42 Westley Richards gun using papier-mâché primer
(*Collection: Lewis Winant*)

43 Joseph Manton lock with firing pins and plugs (*Collection: W. Keith Neal*)

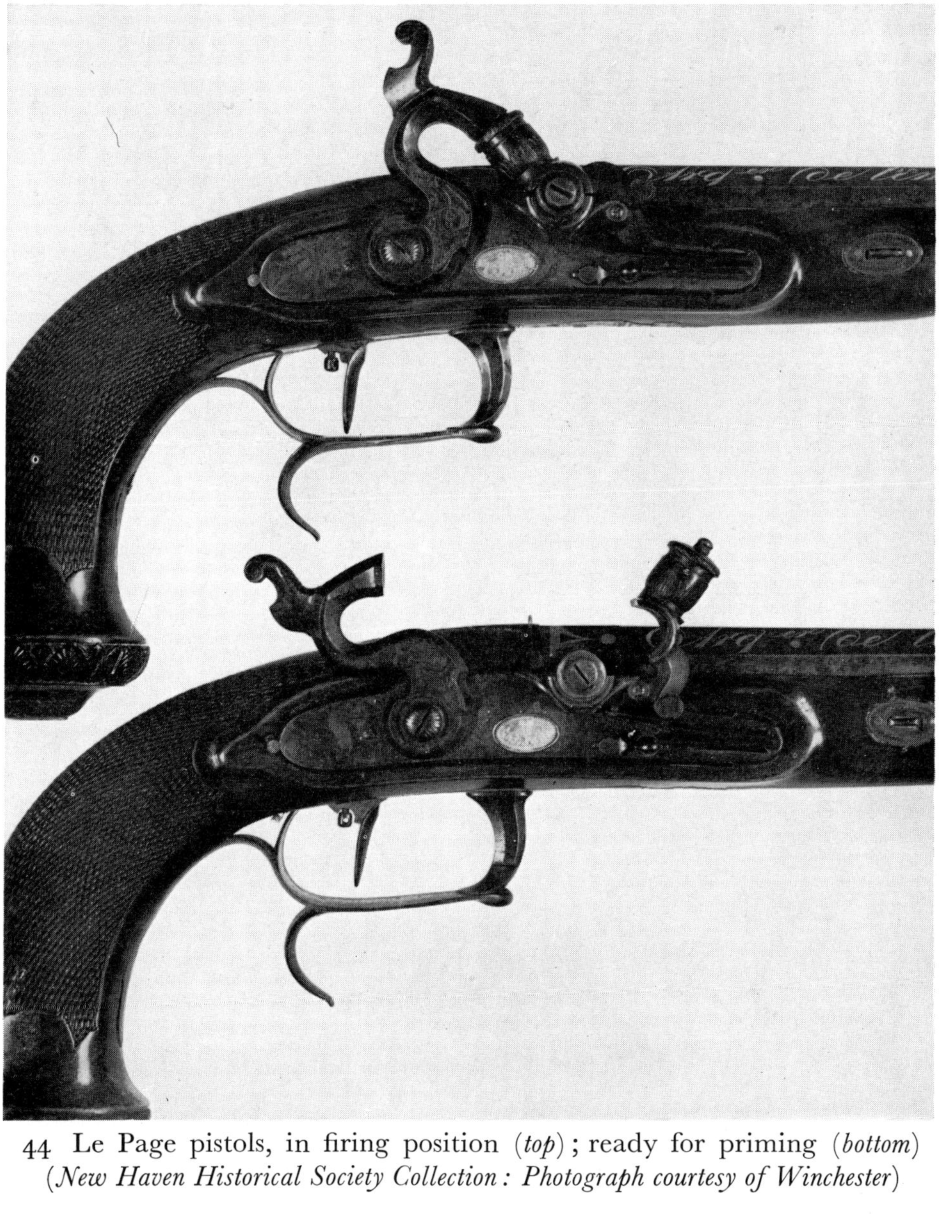

44 Le Page pistols, in firing position (*top*); ready for priming (*bottom*) (*New Haven Historical Society Collection: Photograph courtesy of Winchester*)

45 Plugs for 1816 Manton lock (*Collection: W. Keith Neal*)

46 Le Page pistol, top view (*Collection: New Haven Historical Society Photograph by courtesy of Winchester*)

47 Cessier gun, side view (*Collection: Robert Marron*)

48 Cessier gun, top view (*Collection: Robert Marron*)

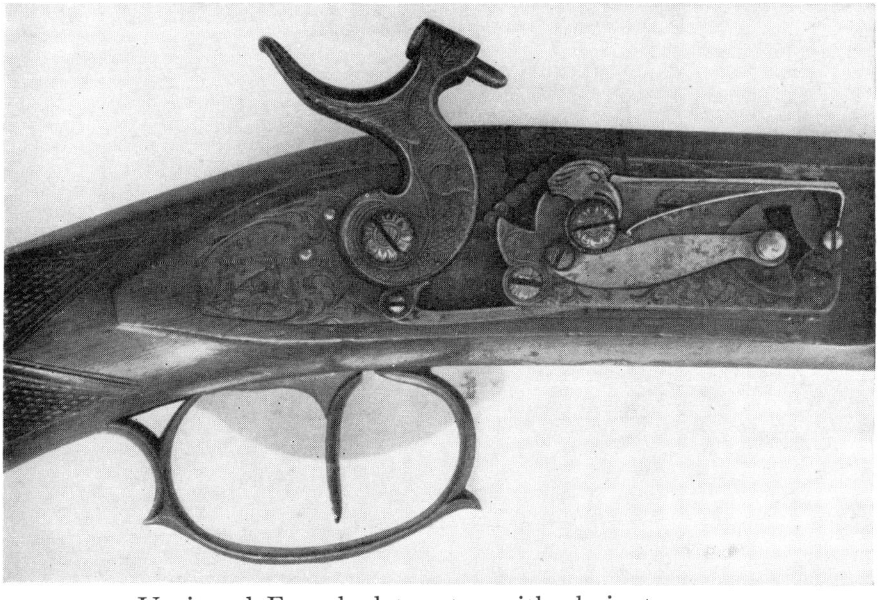

49 Unsigned French detonator with chain to open pan
(*Collection: W. Keith Neal*)

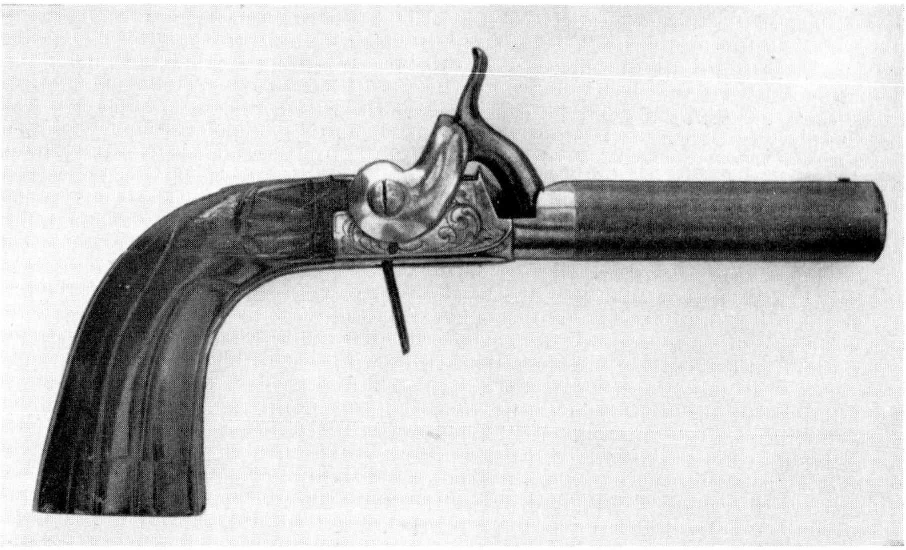

50 Unsigned French detonator with large-nosed hammer, side view
(*Collection: W. Keith Neal*)

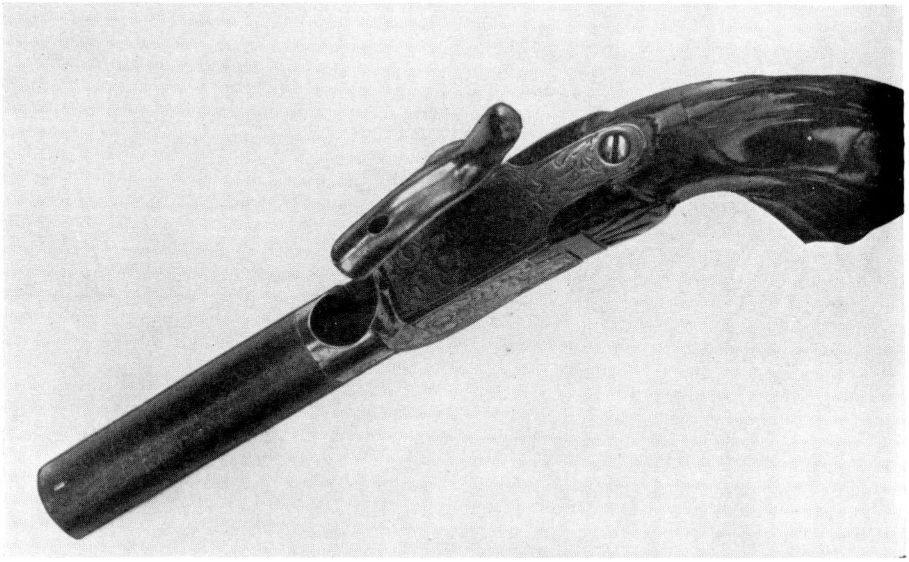

51 Unsigned French detonator with large-nosed, hammer, top view
(*Collection: W. Keith Neal*)

52 Rissack pistol (*Collection: Metropolitan Museum of Art*)

53 Spanish Gutierez lock (*Collection: W. Keith Neal*)

54 Unsigned Spanish lock (*Collection: W. Keith Neal*)

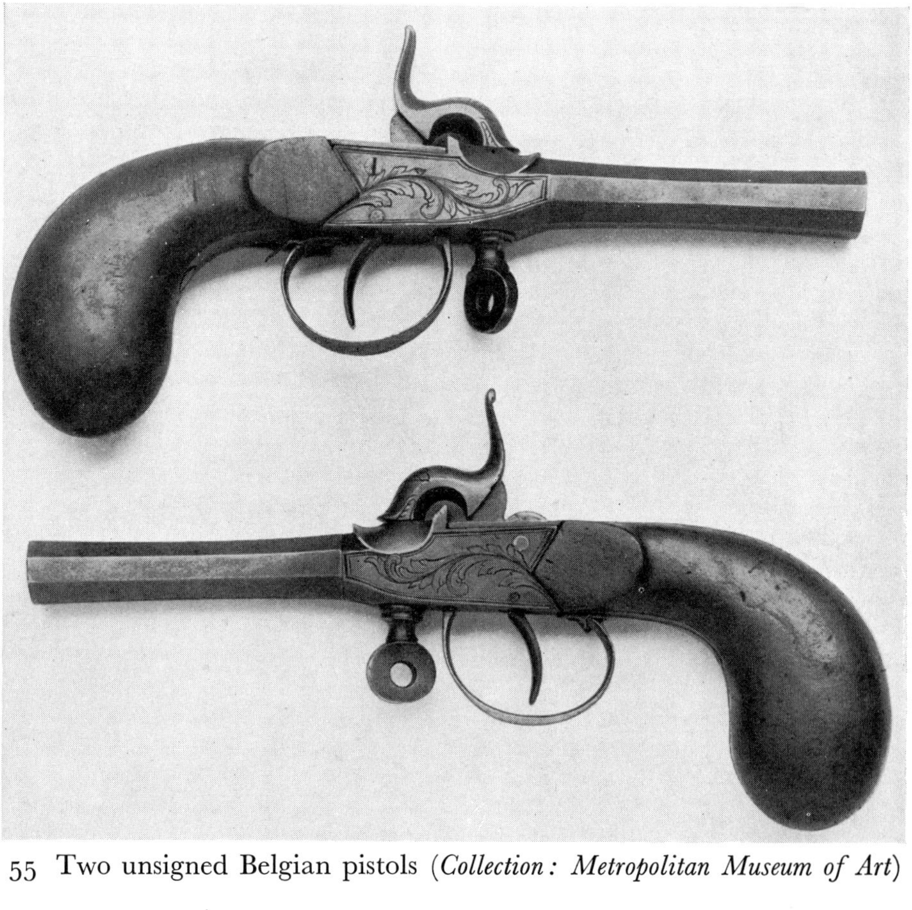

55 Two unsigned Belgian pistols (*Collection: Metropolitan Museum of Art*)

56 Contriner lock pistol (*Collection: Dr. W. R. Funderburg*)

57 Blanch gun, using a tube lock identical to a Manton lock (*Collection: Lewis Winant*)

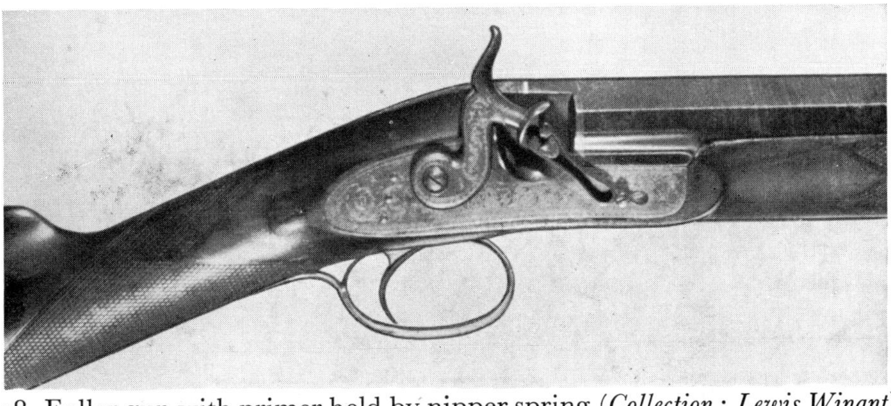

58 Fuller gun with primer held by nipper spring (*Collection: Lewis Winant*)

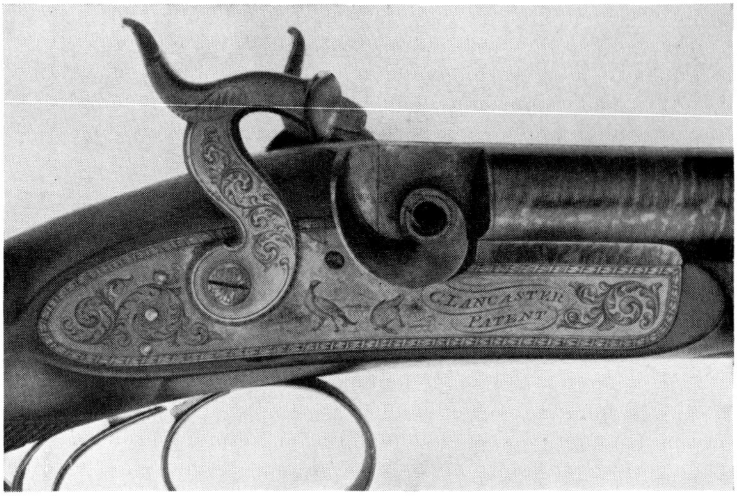

59 Lancaster lock cocked, with touch hole empty (*Collection: W. Keith Neal*)

60 Lancaster lock with tube primer in place in firing position (*Collection: W. Keith Neal*)

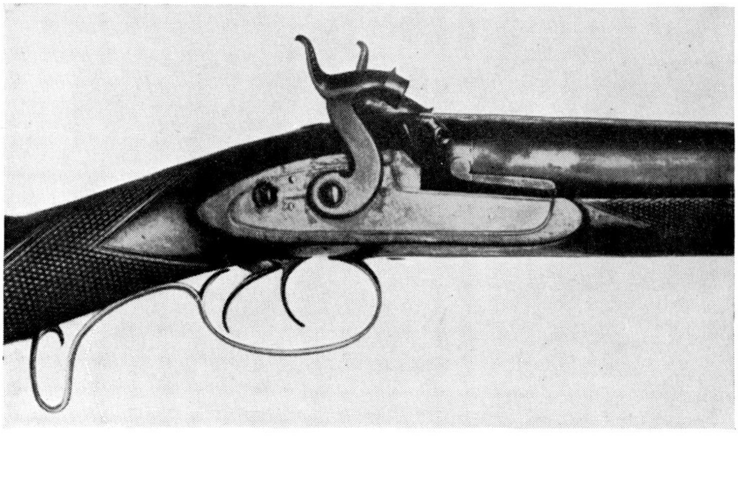

61 Westley Richards tube-lock gun (*Formerly in the Harrod Collection*)

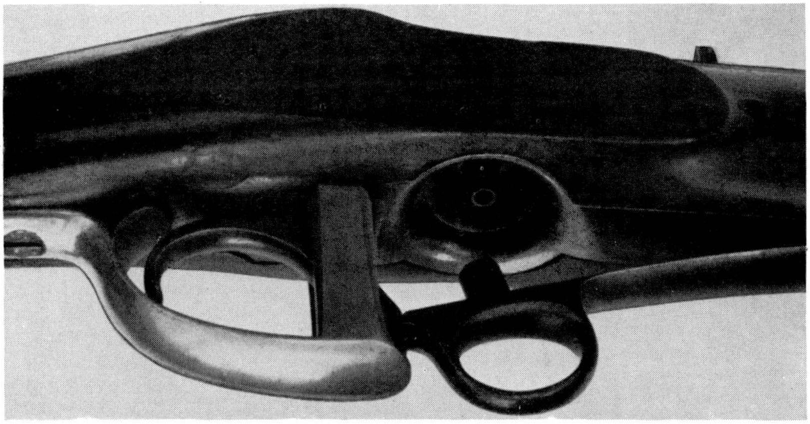

62 Wilkinson underhammer musket using a tube lock
(*Collection: W. Keith Neal*)

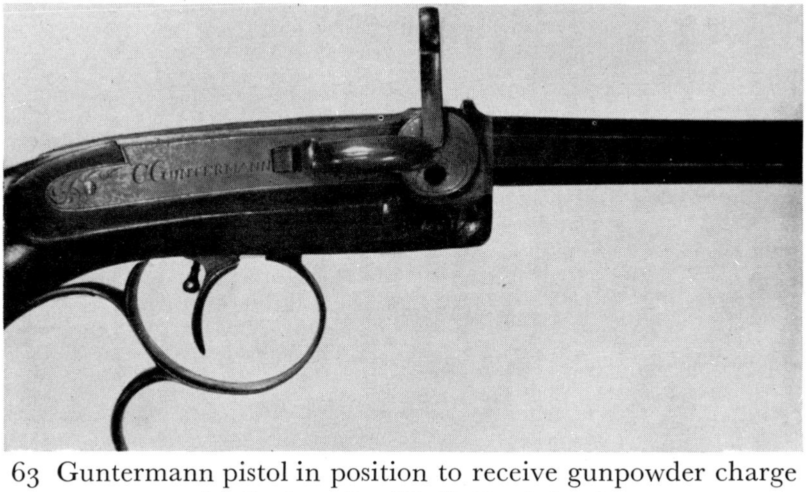

63 Guntermann pistol in position to receive gunpowder charge
(*Collection: Dr. W. R. Funderburg*)

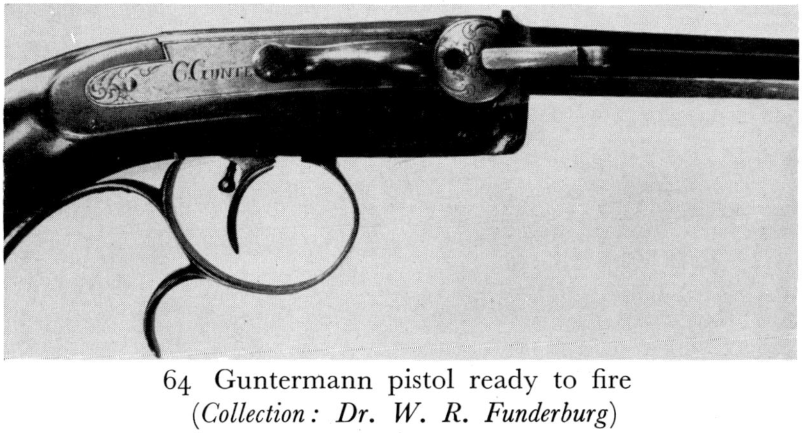

64 Guntermann pistol ready to fire
(*Collection: Dr. W. R. Funderburg*)

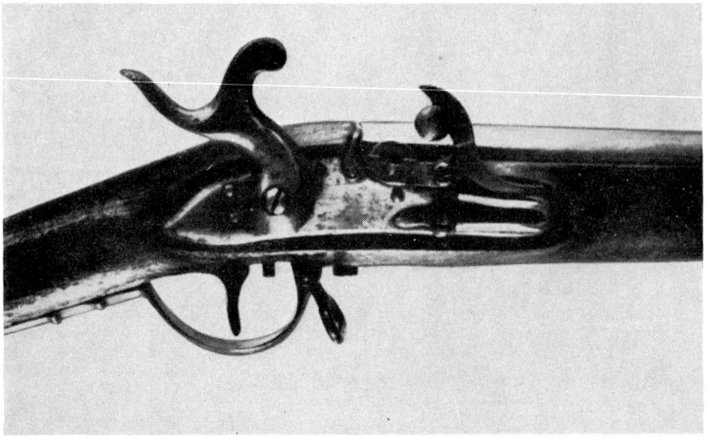

65 Austrian flint gun converted to Console-style tube lock, cocked (*Collection: Lewis Winant*)

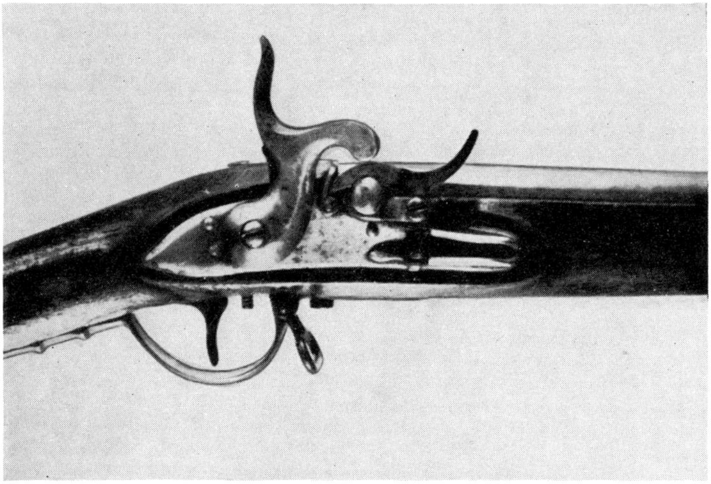

66 Austrian flint gun, converted to Console-style tube lock, in firing position (*Collection: Lewis Winant*)

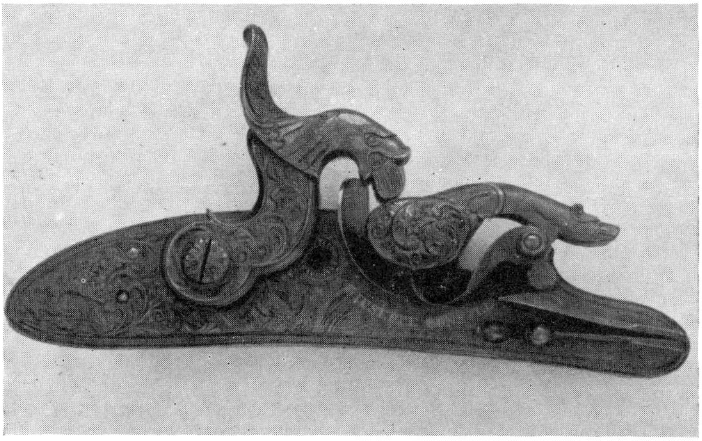

67 Console tube lock (*Collection: W. Keith Neal*)

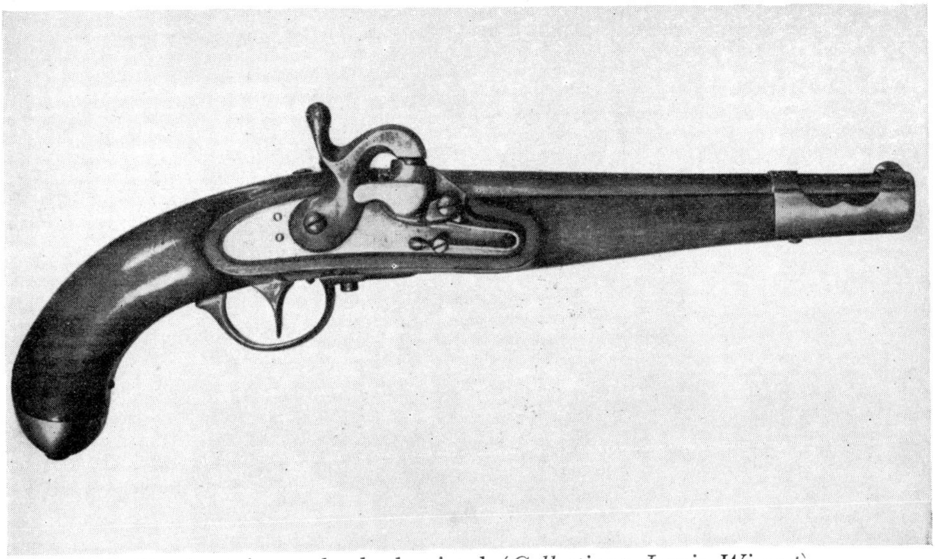

68 Austrian tube-lock pistol (*Collection: Lewis Winant*)

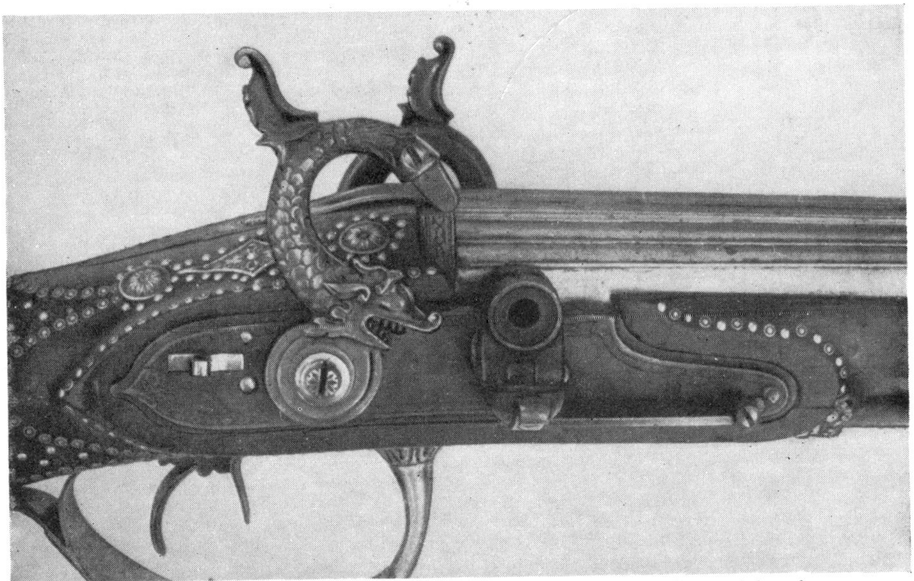

69 Sauvain lock with spring cap to prevent tube from blowing out when fired (*Collection: W. Keith Neal*)

70 Davis Devolving Pan lock (*Collection: W. Keith Neal*)

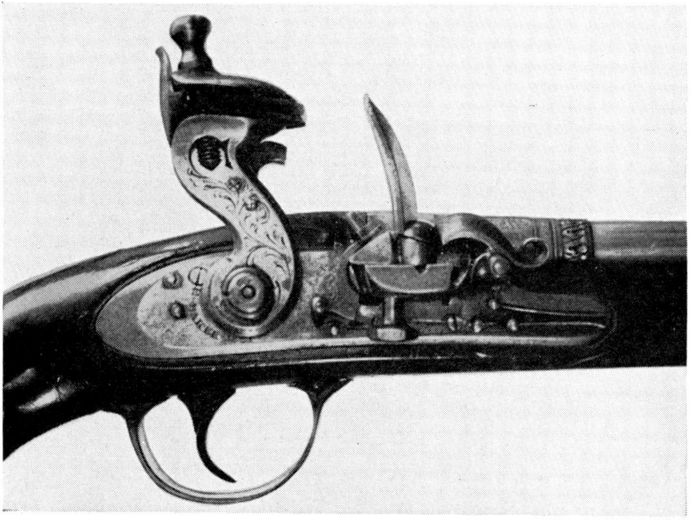

71 Baker combination flint and percussion pistol, ready to fire by flint (*Collection: Dr. W.R. Funderburg*)

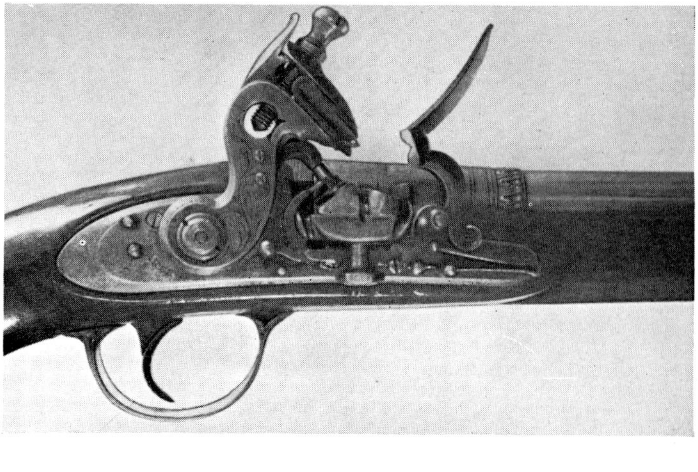

72 Baker combination flint and percussion pistol, having fired by percussion (*Collection: Dr. W. R. Funderburg*)

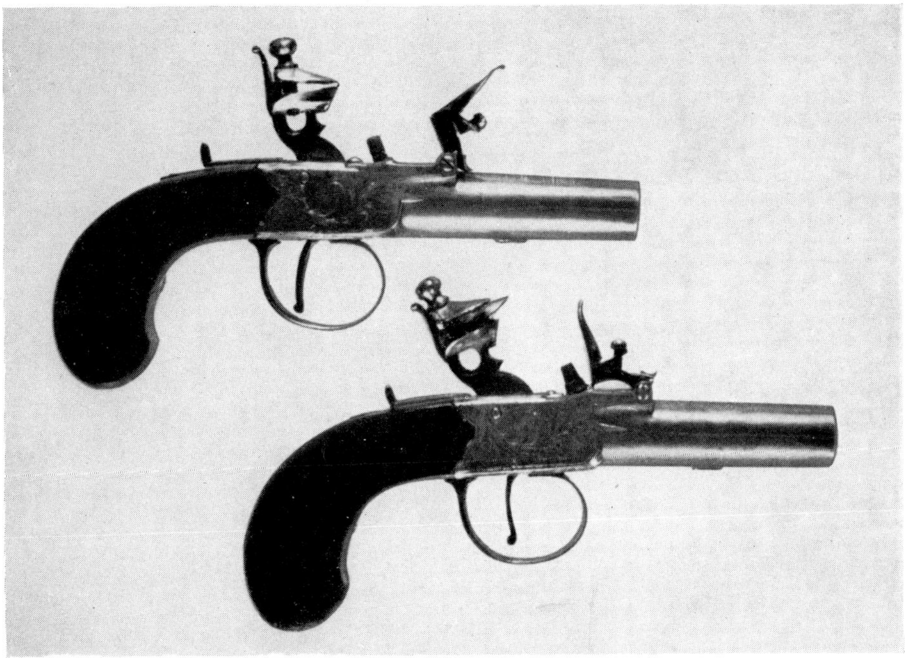

73 Mabson, Labron & Mabson combination pistols. Top pistol ready to fire by percussion, bottom by flint (*Collection: Eddie Reider*)

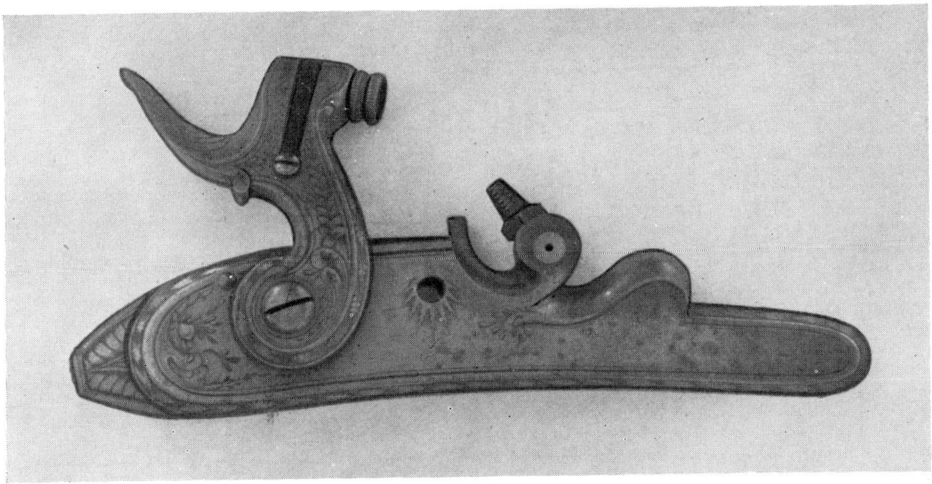

74 Interchangeable lock (*Collection: W. Keith Neal*)

75 Jackson copper-cap pistol (*Collection: Lewis Winant*)

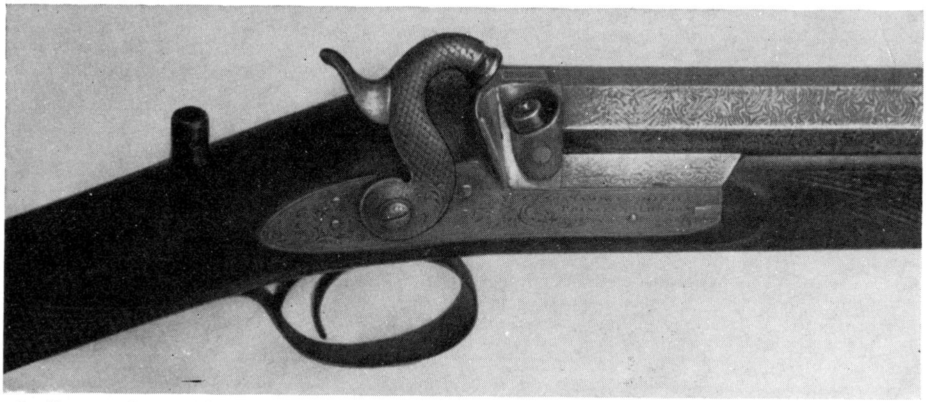

76 Samuel & Charles Smith gun, using "Smith's Patent Imperial Cap" (*Formerly in the Harrod Collection*)

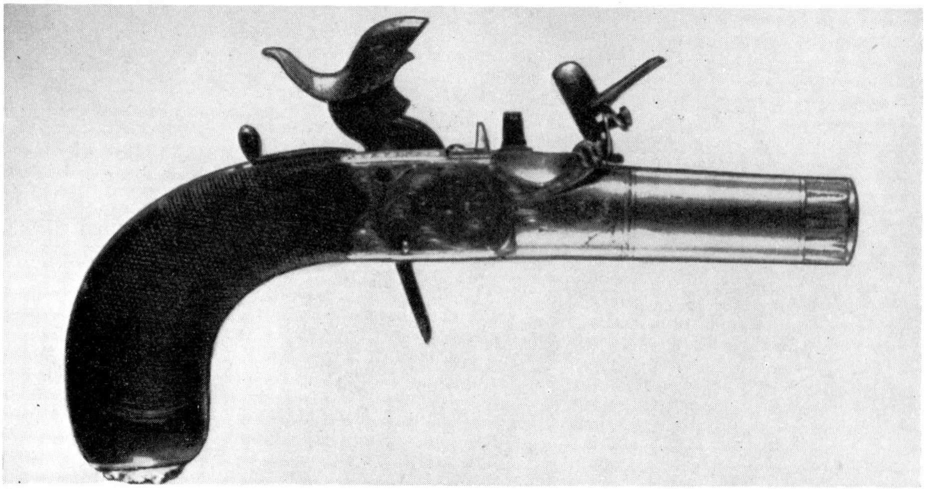

77 Fisher pistol with hinged guard up (*Collection: Paul Westergard*)

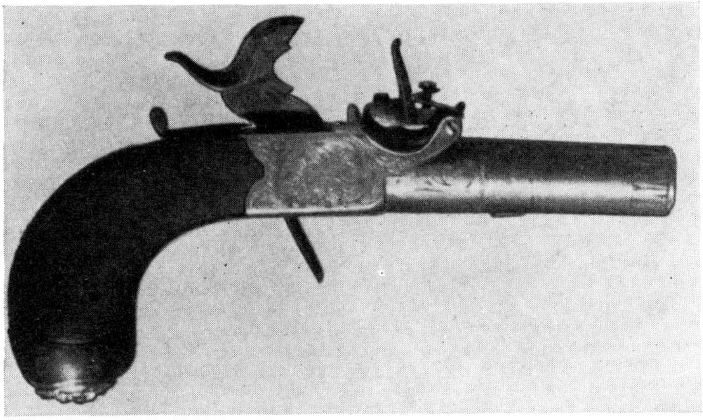

78 Fisher pistol with hinged guard in down position ready to fire (*Collection: Paul Westergard*)

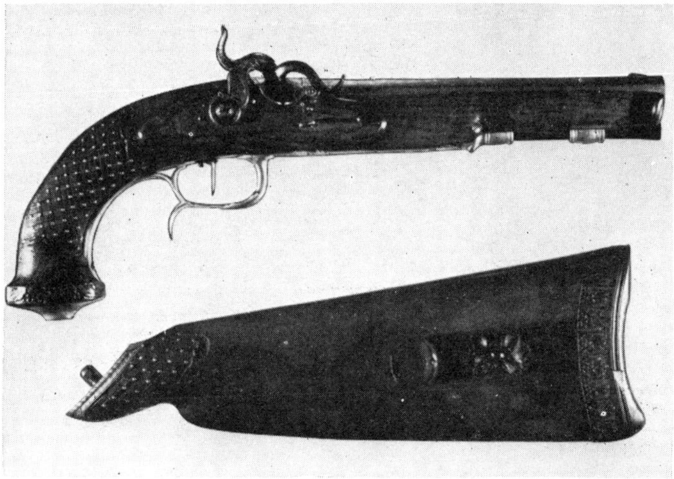

79 German pistol with shoulder stock and nipple guard (*Collection: Lewis Winant*)

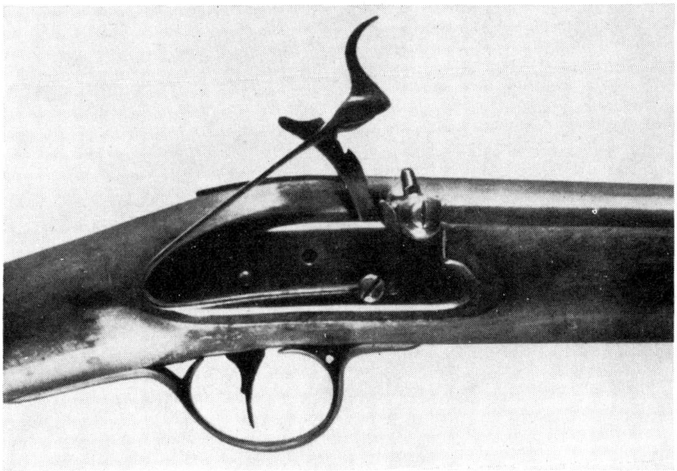

80 Lacy & Davis gun (*Collection: Lewis Winant*)

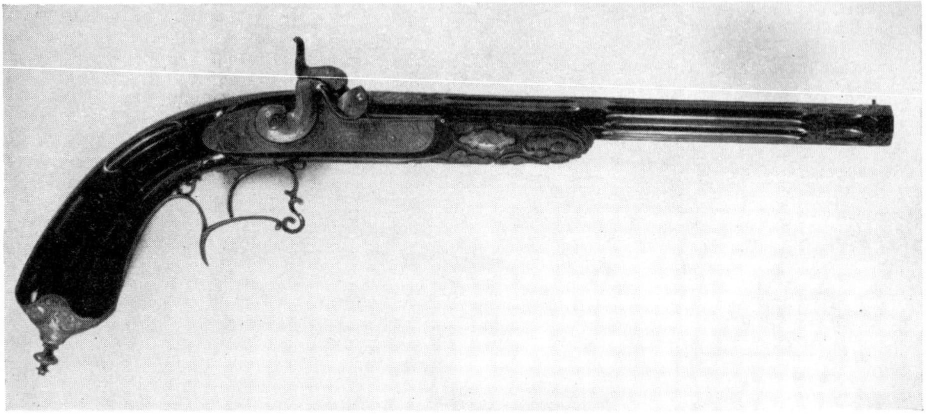

81 Julian pistol engraved by Potgisser (*Collection: Lewis Winant*)

82 Underhammer bootleg pistols (*Collection: Lewis Winant*)

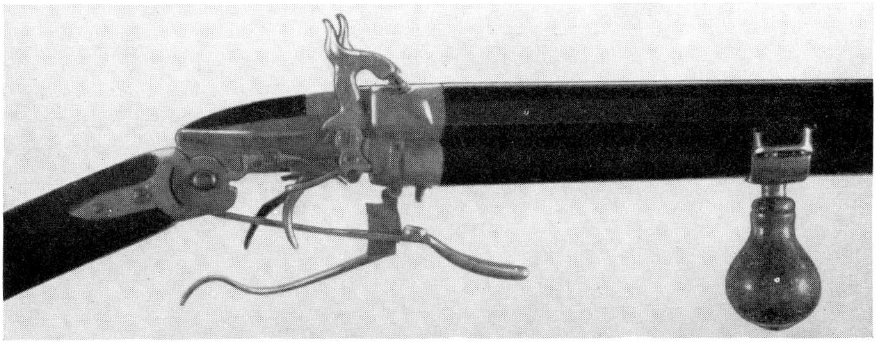

83 Three-barrel gun (*Collection: Paul Westergard*)

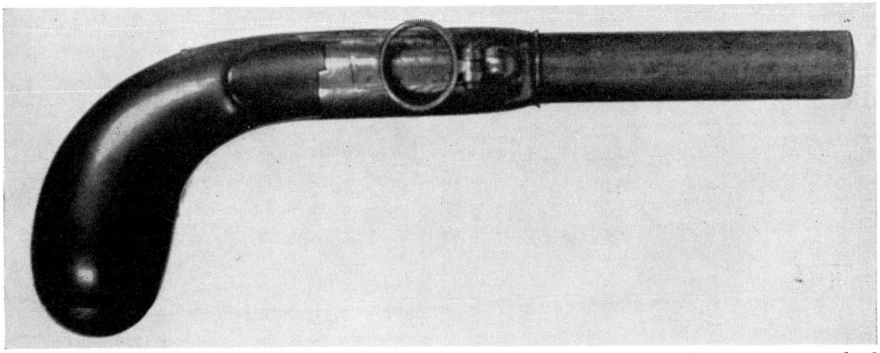

84 Side-hammer pistol, with hammer, nipple and trigger concealed (*Collection: Lewis Winant*)

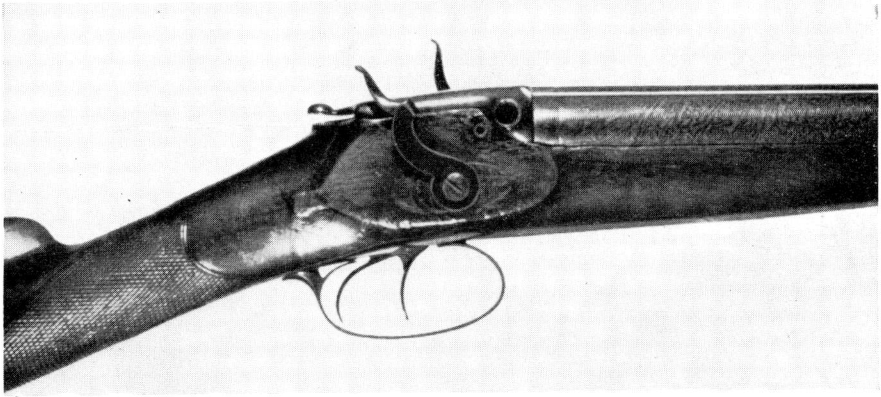

85 Charles Jones "centre-fire" gun (*Collection: Robert Marron*)

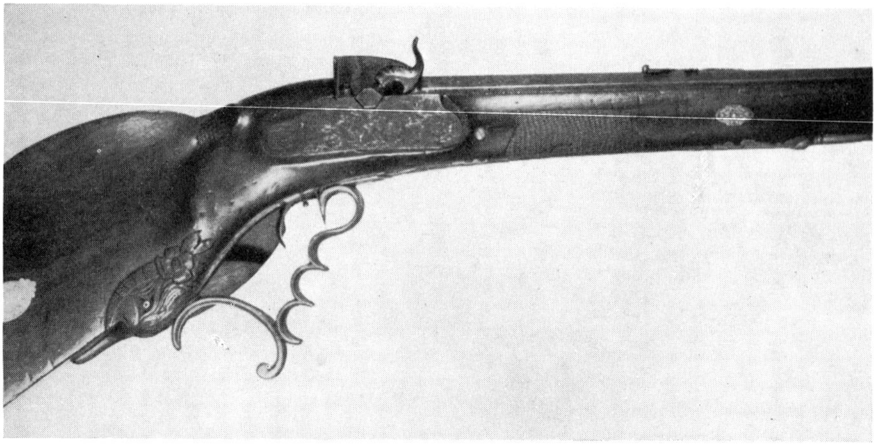

86 Tyrolese Schuetzen rifle (*Collection: Lewis Winant*)

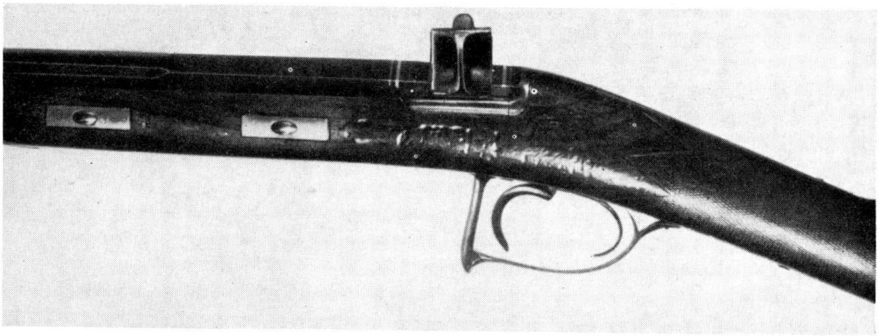

87 Stocker & Bentley hammerless "centre-fire" cap gun, with cover raised for capping nipple (*Collection: Robert Marron*)

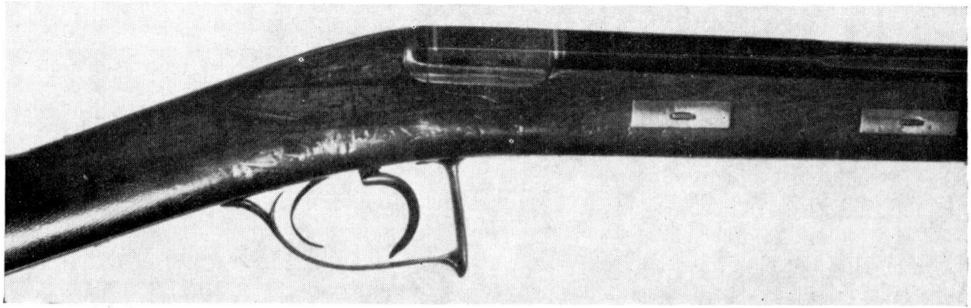

88 Stocker & Bentley hammerless "centre-fire" cap gun, ready to fire (*Collection: Robert Marron*)

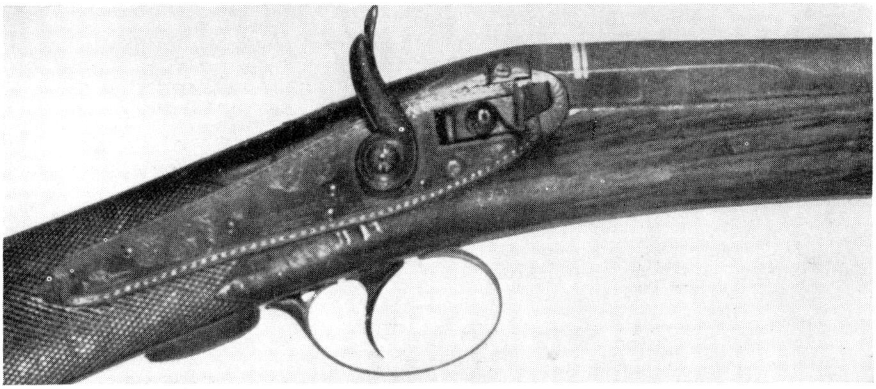

89 Crundwell gun showing gate open for capping (*Collection: Robert Marron*)

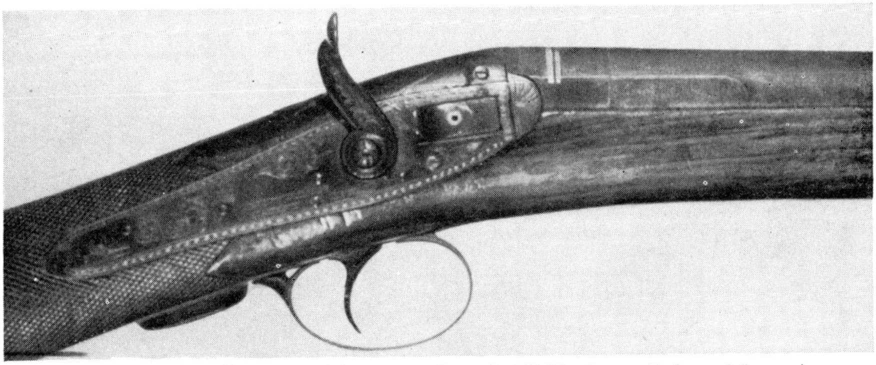

90 Crundwell gun with gate closed (*Collection: Robert Marron*)

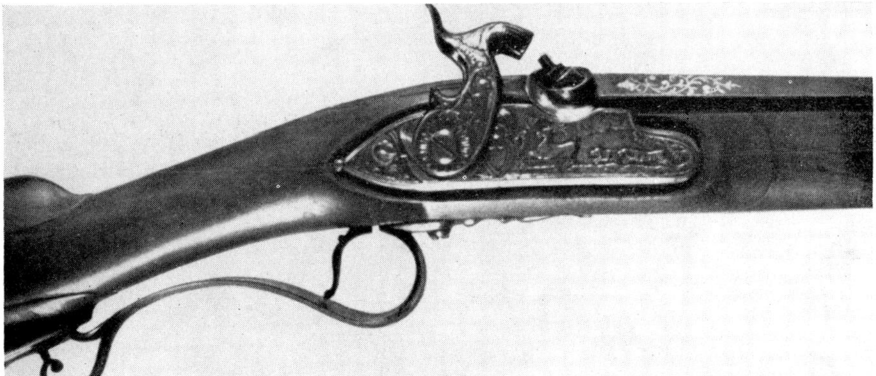

91 Madrid lock gun (*Collection: Lewis Winant*)

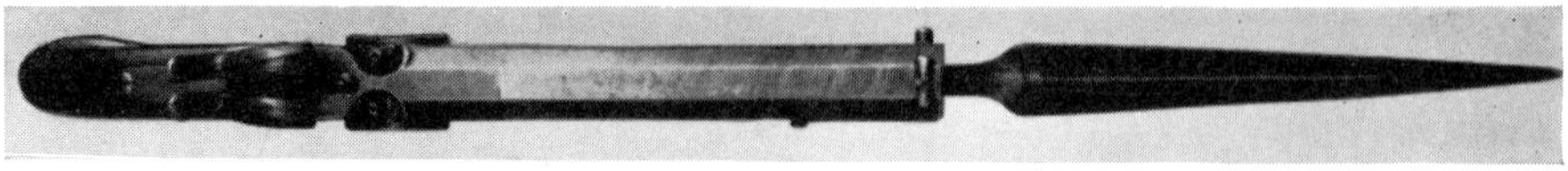

92 Correvon pistol with two nipples and dagger (*Collection: Frank Bivens*)

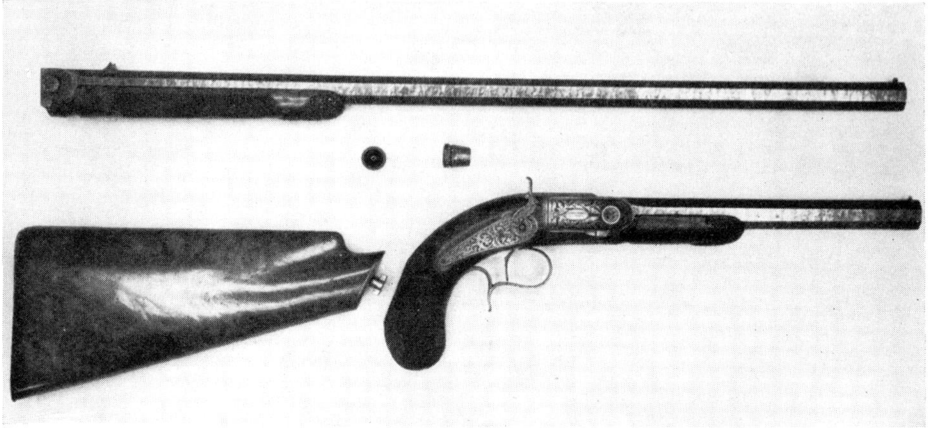

93 Pottet pistol with shoulder stock, extra barrel, and cartridge cases (*Collection: Henry M. Stewart*)

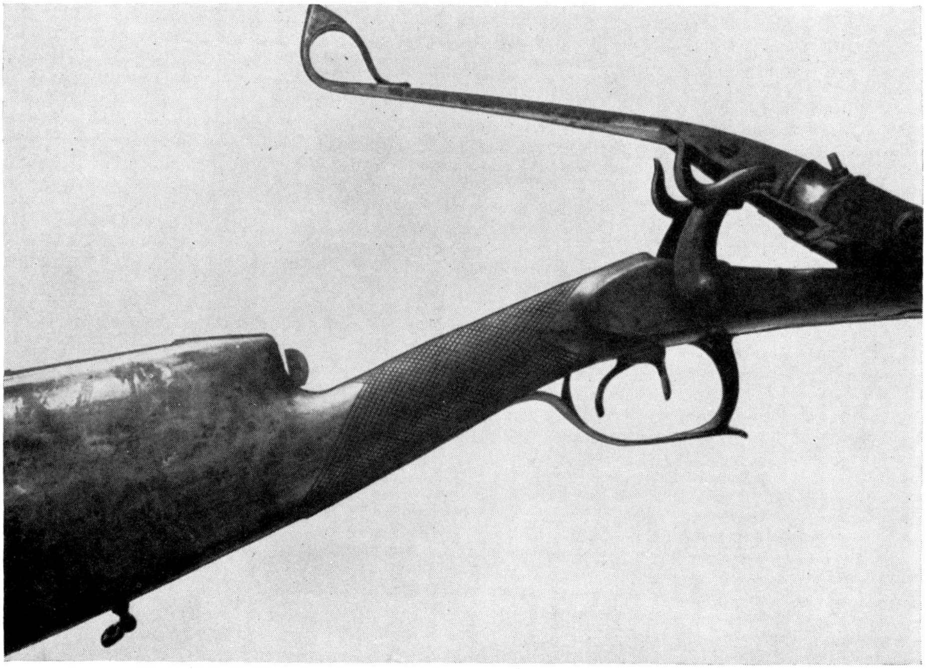

94 Pauly shotgun, showing lock section (*Collection: Lewis Winant*)

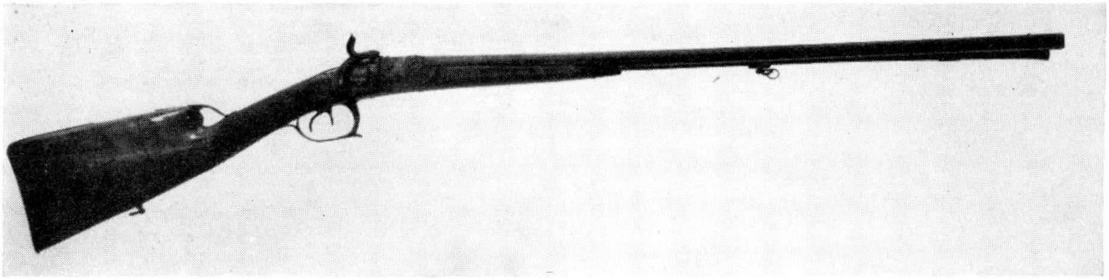

95 Pauly shotgun, full length (*Collection: Lewis Winant*)

96 Renette & Gastinne tilting-barrel shotgun (*Collection: George Cummings*)

97 Lobnitz capping breechloader ready to fire (*Collection: Paul Westergard*)

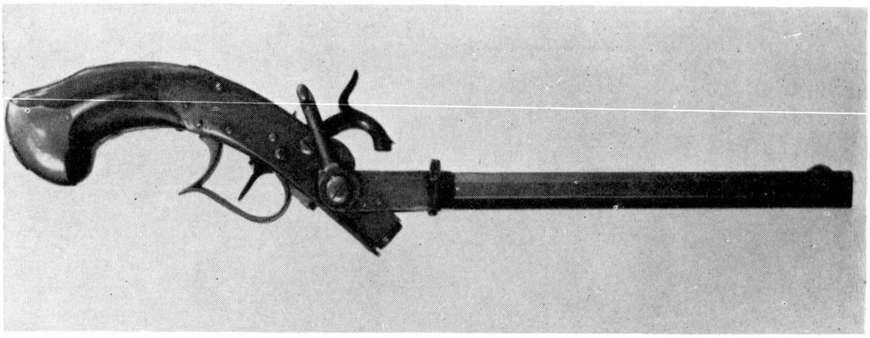

98 Lobnitz capping breechloader in charging position
(*Collection: Paul Westergard*)

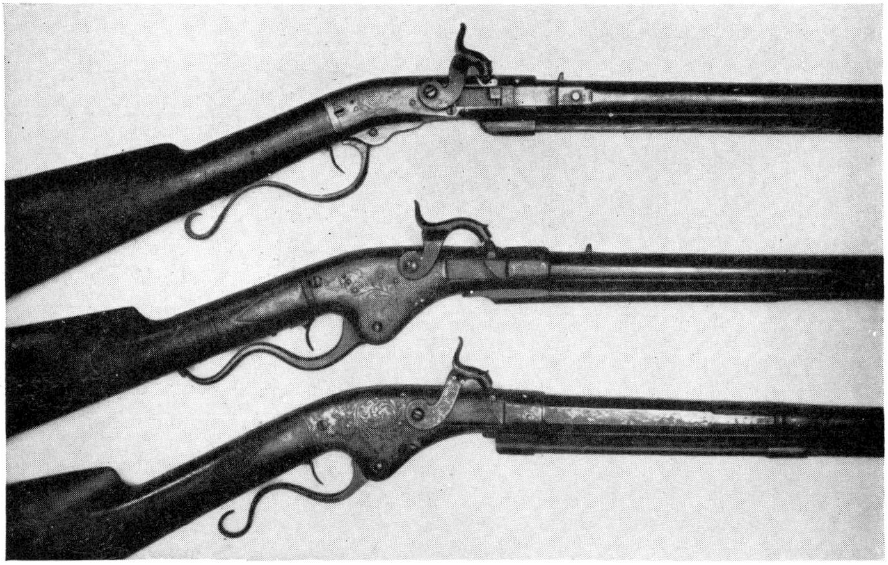

99 Two Marston rifles (*top*), and a Marston shotgun (*bottom*)
(*Collection: Henry M. Stewart*)

100 Marston pistol with cartridges (*Collection: Henry M. Stewart*)

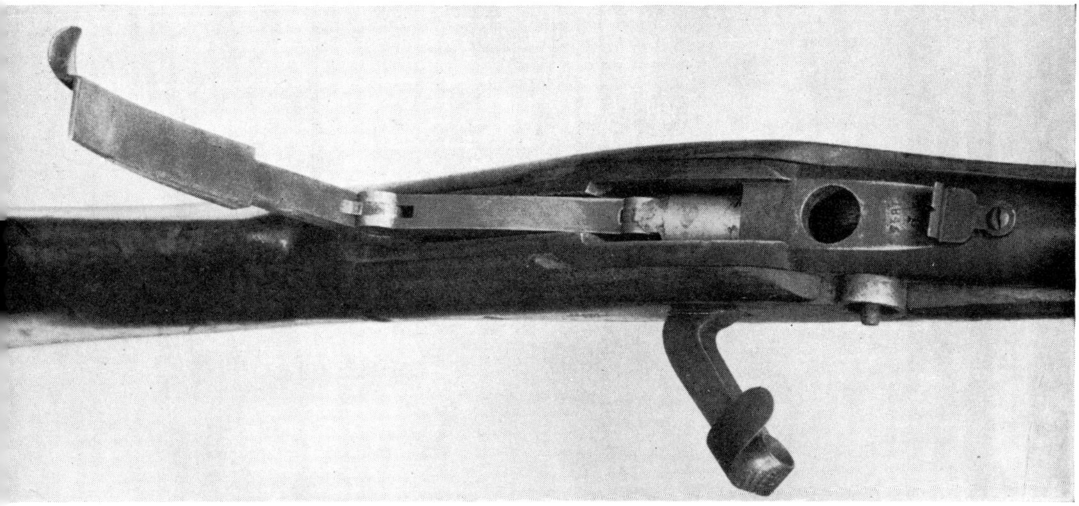

101 Jenks sliding-breech carbine (*Collection: Smithsonian Institution*)

102 Calisher & Terry sliding-breech-bolt rifle (*Formerly in the Harrod Collection*)

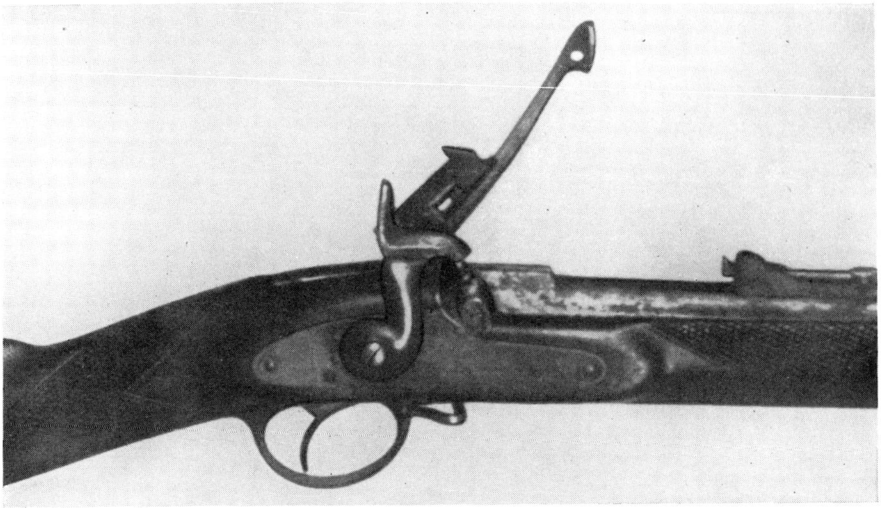

103 Westley Richards sliding-breech-bolt carbine
(*Formerly in the Harrod Collection*)

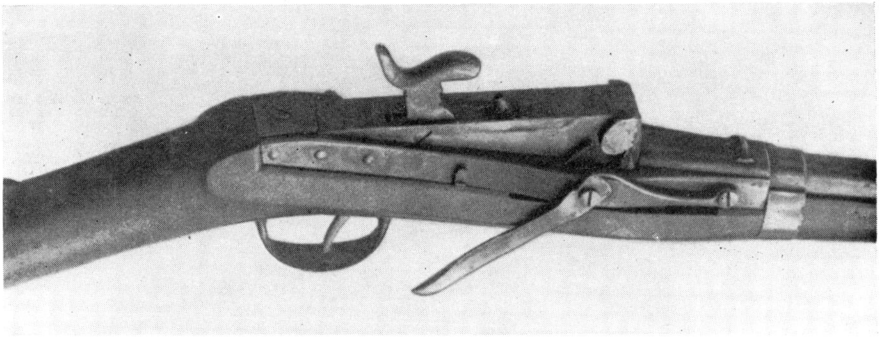

104 Hall chamber-loading rifle (*Formerly in the Harrod Collection*)

105 Lindner chamber-loader ready for loading
(*Formerly in the Harrod Collection*)

106 Larsen chamber-loading underhammer (*Formerly in the Harrod Collection*)

107 Mont Storm rifle with chamber open (*Formerly in the Harrod Collection*)

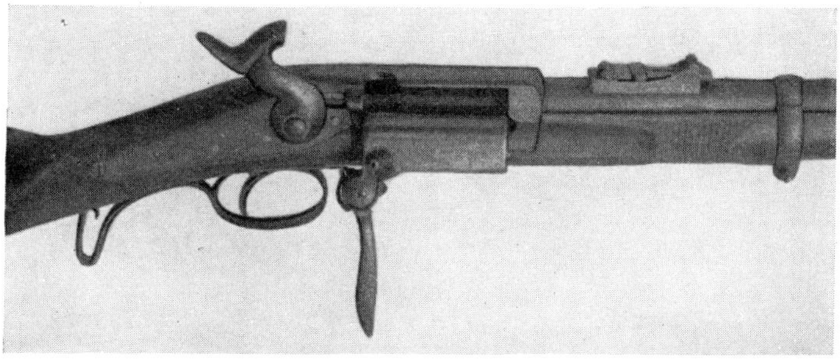

108 Leetch chamber-loader (*Formerly in the Harrod Collection*)

109 Spanish sporting gun (*Formerly in the Harrod Collection*)

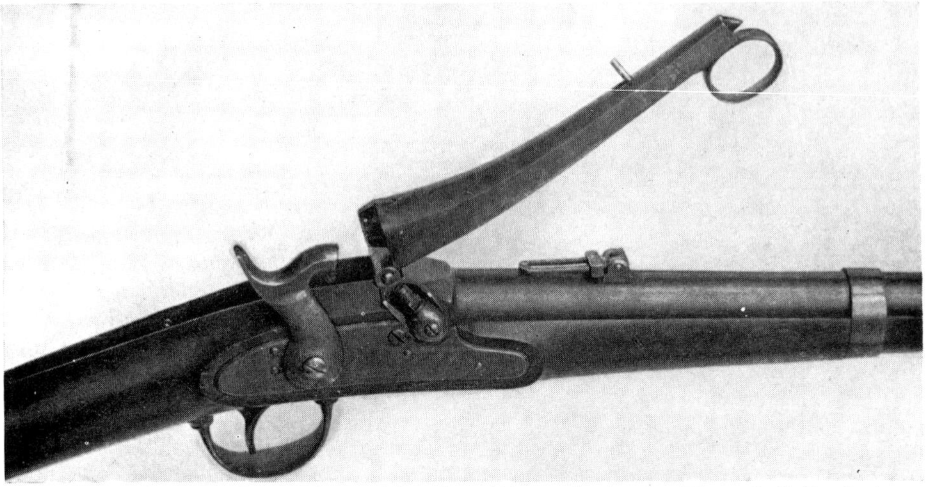

110 Joslyn top-lever breechloader (*Formerly in the Harrod Collection*)

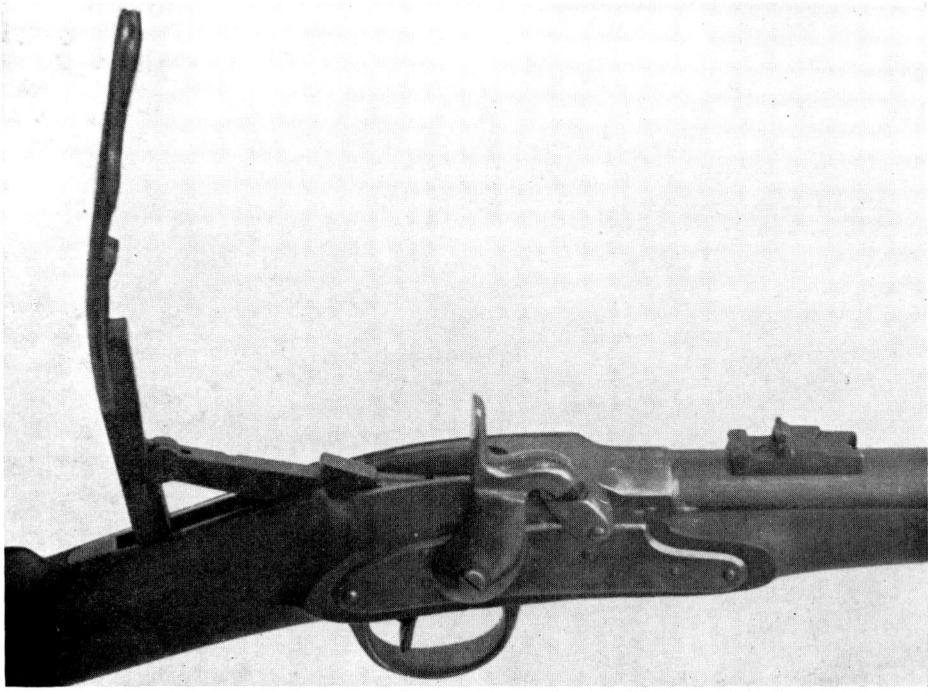

111 Merrill top-lever carbine (*Formerly in the Harrod Collection*)

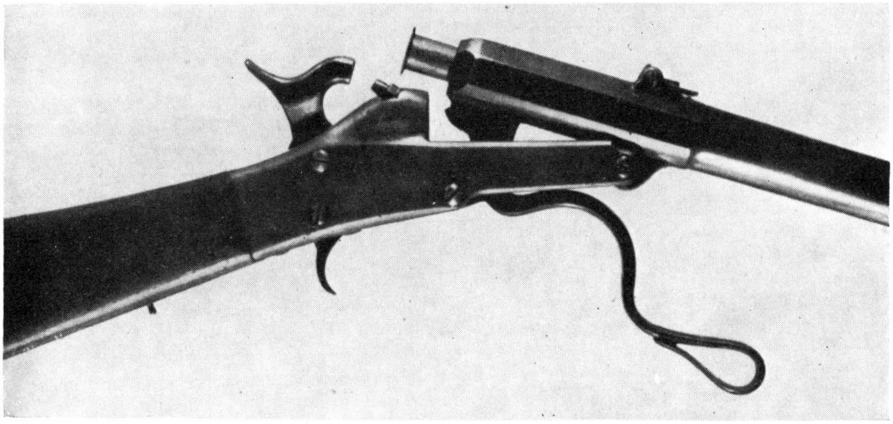

112 Maynard carbine (*Collection: Lewis Winant*)

113 Smith tilting-barrel carbine (*Collection: Smithsonian Institution*)

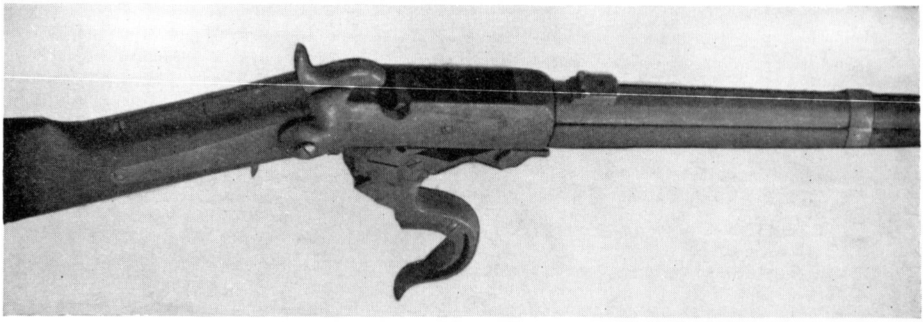

114 Burnside rifle with rotating breechblock (*Formerly in the Harrod Collection*)

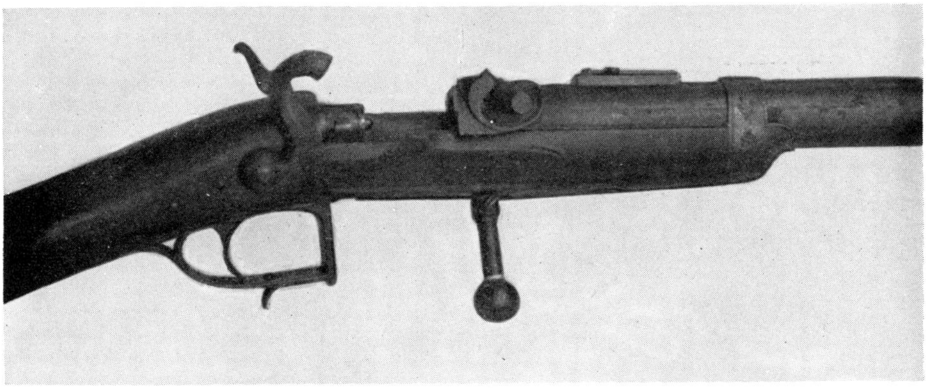

115 Prince sliding-barrel carbine (*Formerly in the Harrod Collection*)

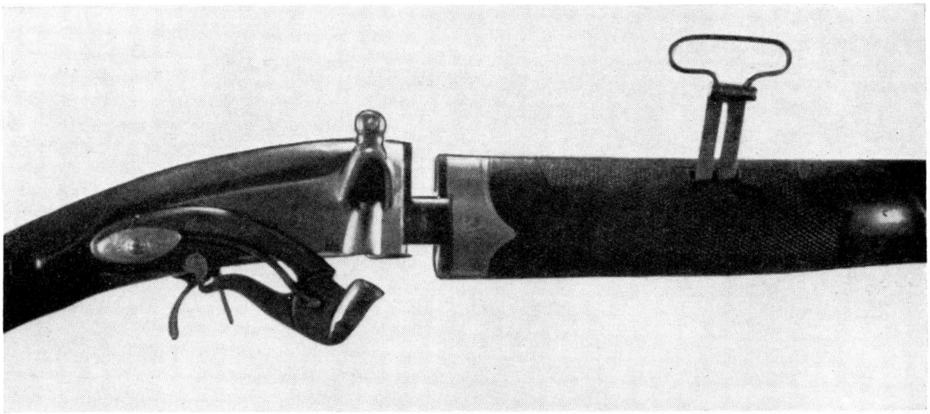

116 Double-barrel shotgun, probably French, sliding barrel extended (*Collection: Paul Westergard*)

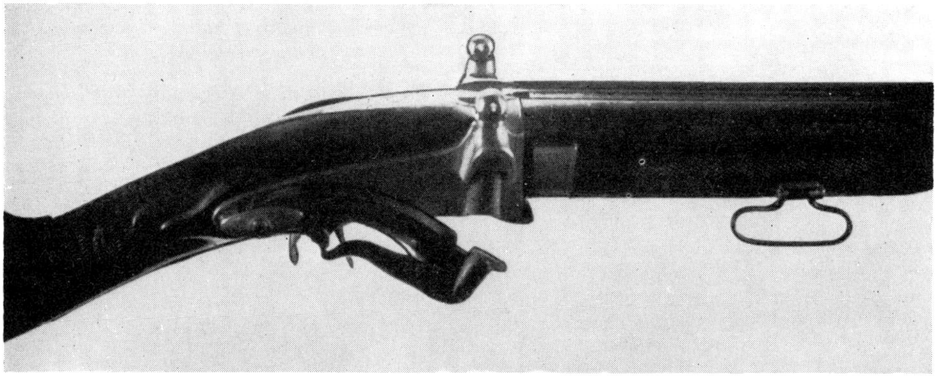

117 Double-barrel shotgun, probably French, sliding barrel closed
(*Collection: Paul Westergard*)

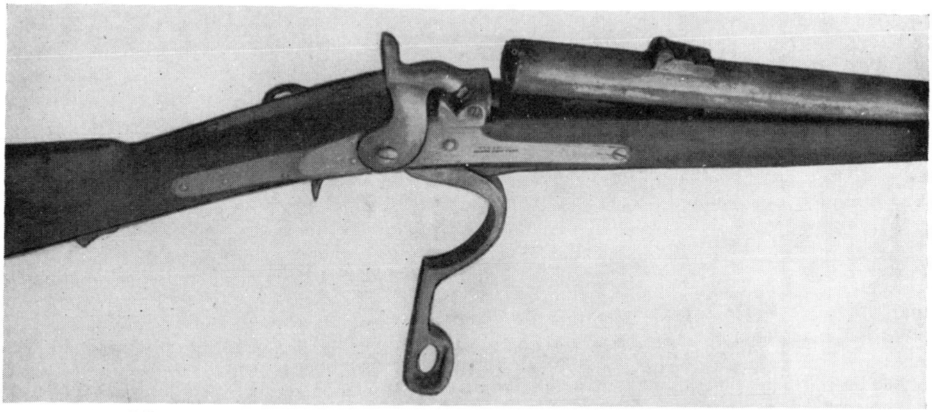

118 Gibbs sliding-barrel carbine (*Formerly in the Harrod Collection*)

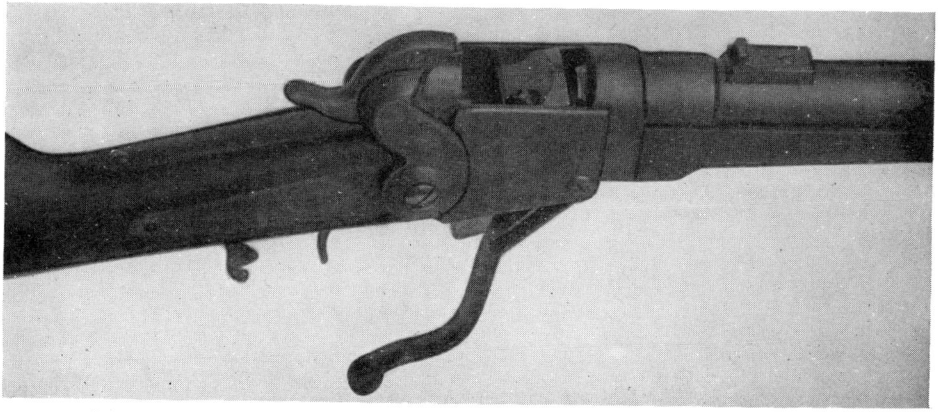

119 Starr carbine with breechblock started on its downward journey
(*Formerly in the Harrod Collection*)

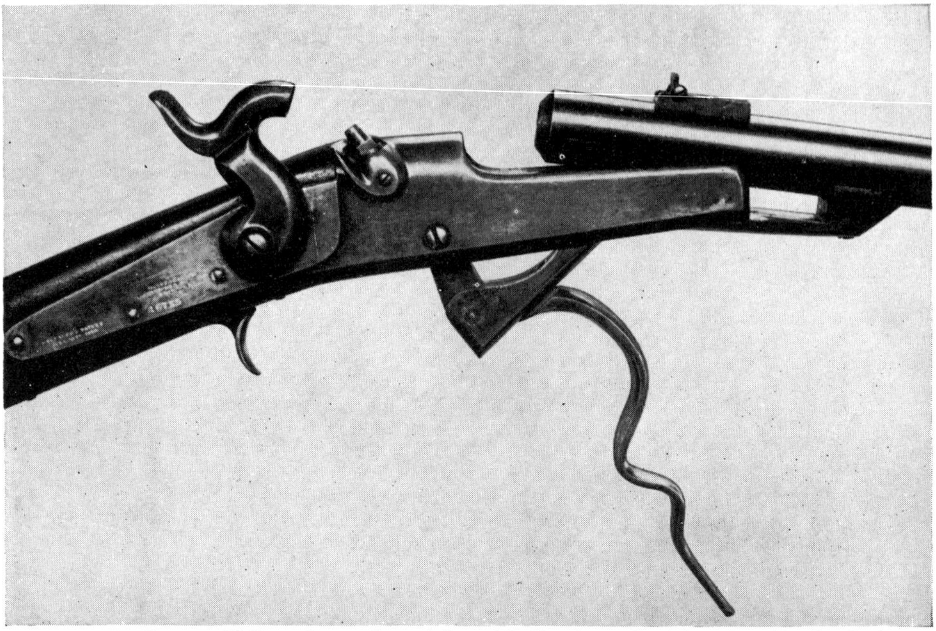

120 Gallager sliding-barrel carbine (*Collection: Smithsonian Institution*)

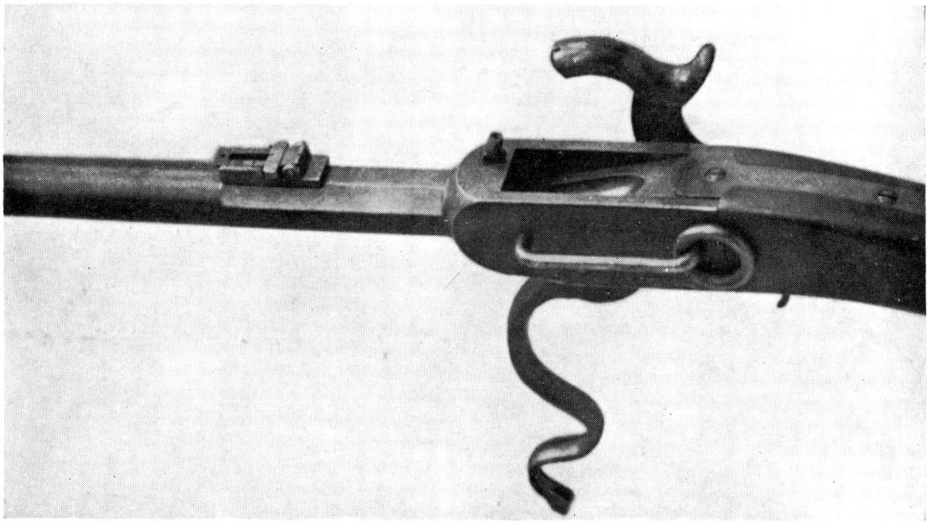

121 Gwyn & Campbell tilting-breechblock carbine
(*Formerly in the Harrod Collection*)

122 Greene bolt-action rifle, in bullet-seating position
(*Collection: Lewis Winant*)

123 Greene bolt-action rifle, cocked, ready to fire (*Collection: Lewis Winant*)

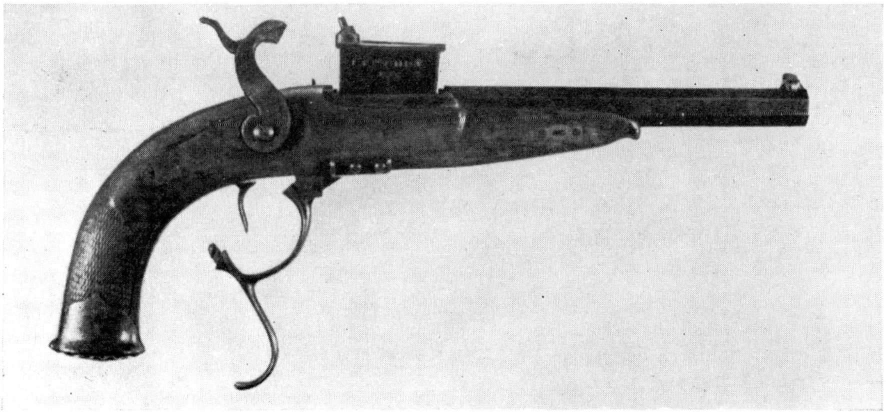

124 Knocke pistol with vertically rising chamber
(*Collection: Dr. W. R. Funderburg*)

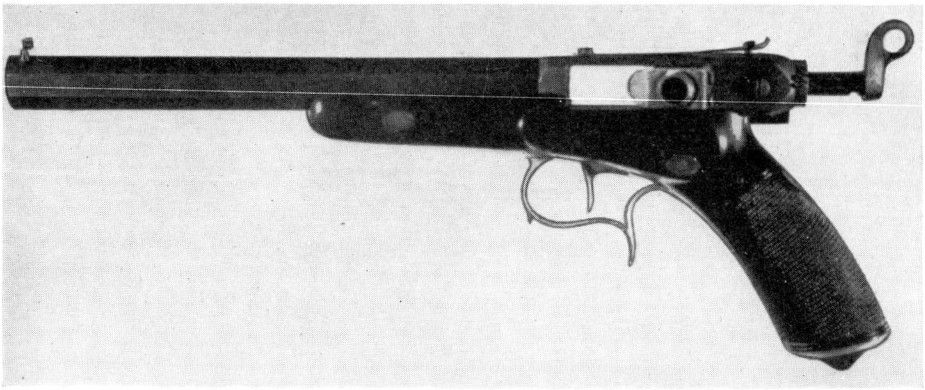

125 Chamber-loading pistol, in loading position (*Collection: Dr. Jack Strassman*)

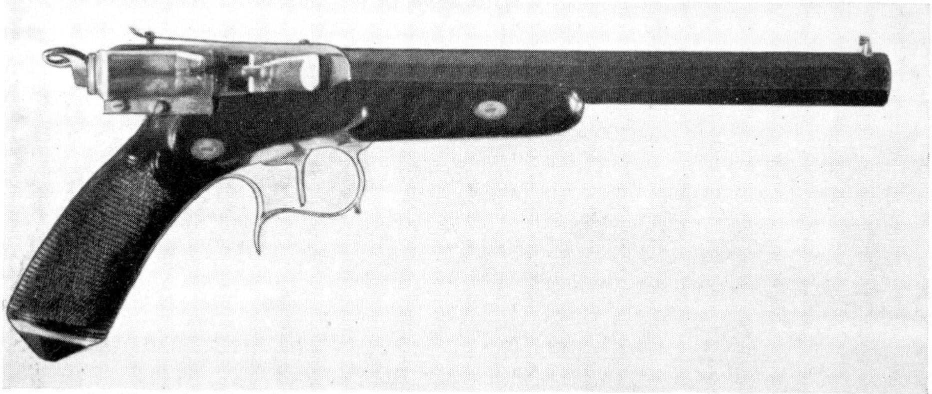

126 Chamber-loading pistol, ready to fire (*Collection: Dr. Jack Strassman*)

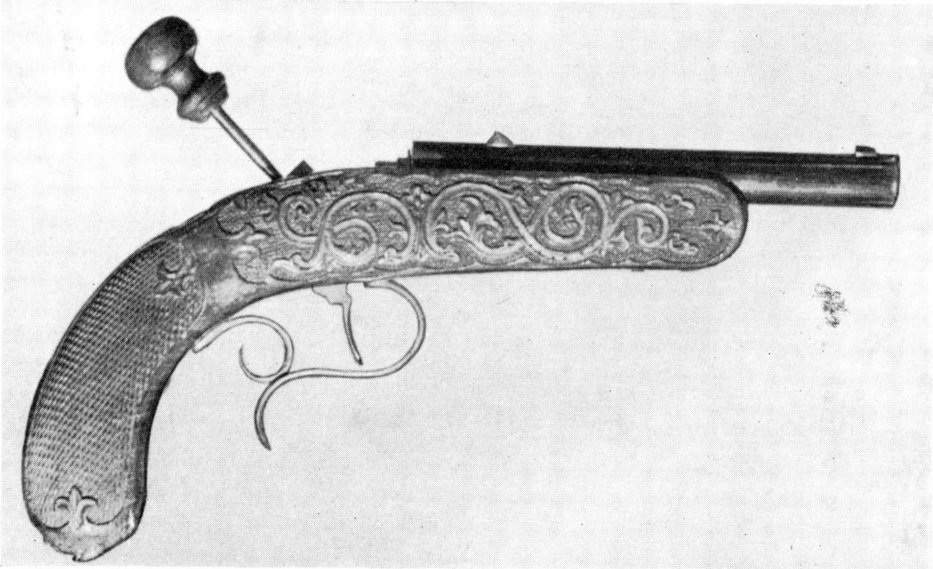

127 German muzzle-loading saloon pistol (*Collection: Paul Westergard*)

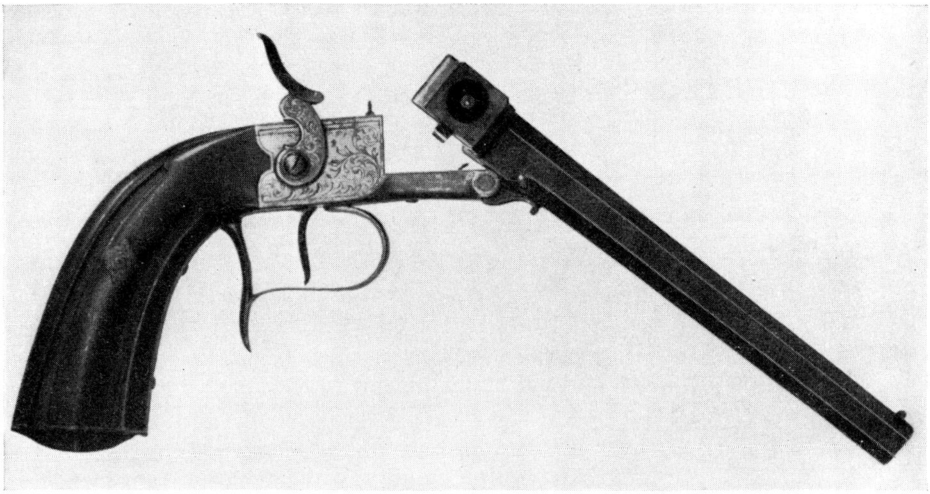

128 French saloon pistol open for loading (*Collection: Louis Hart*)

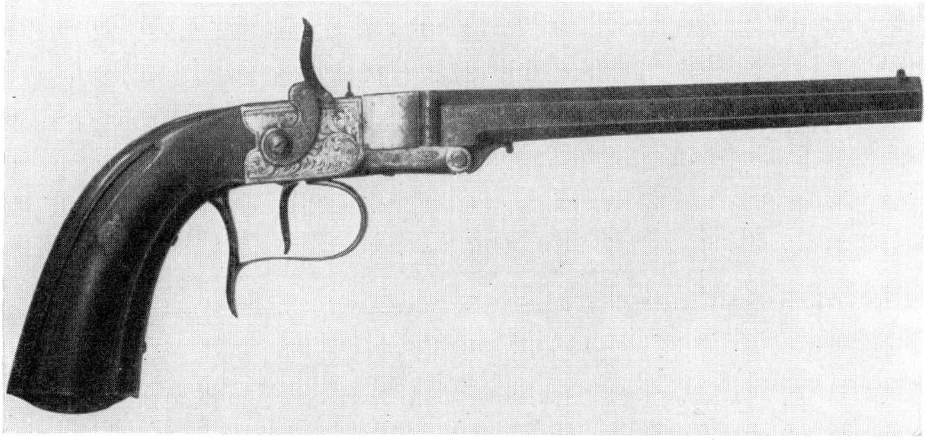

129 French saloon pistol in fired position (*Collection: Louis Hart*)

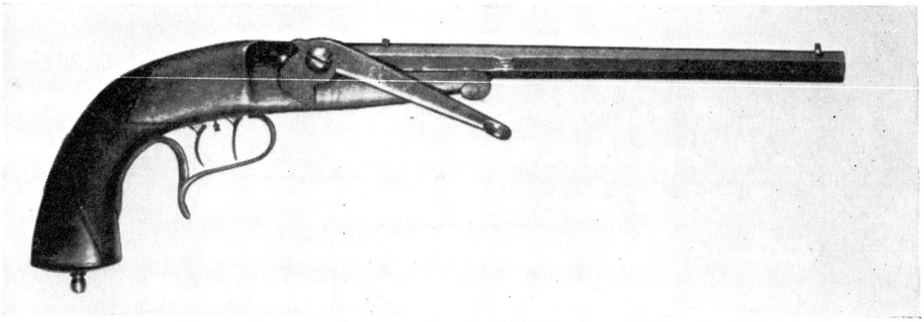

130 Contriner saloon pistol (*Collection: Lewis Winant*)

131 European saloon pistol (*Collection: Dr. W. R. Funderburg*)

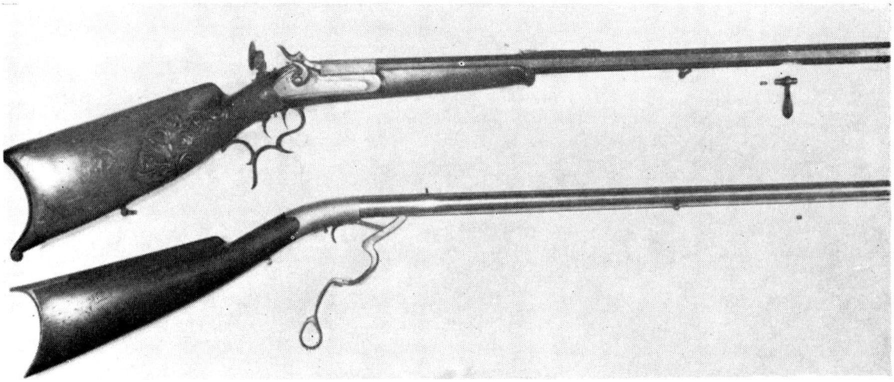

132 German *Zimmerstutzen* (*top*), Forker American indoor rifle (*bottom*). (*Collection: Lewis Winant*)

133 Remington ·17 calibre pistol (*Collection: Henry M. Stewart*)

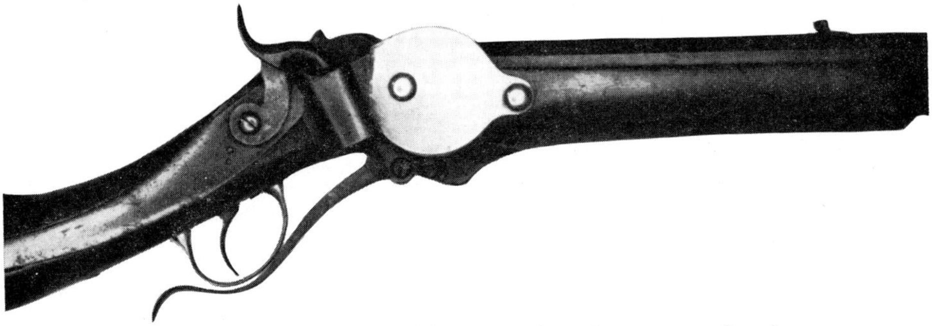

134 First model Sharps with magazine for conventional caps (*Collection: Henry M. Stewart*)

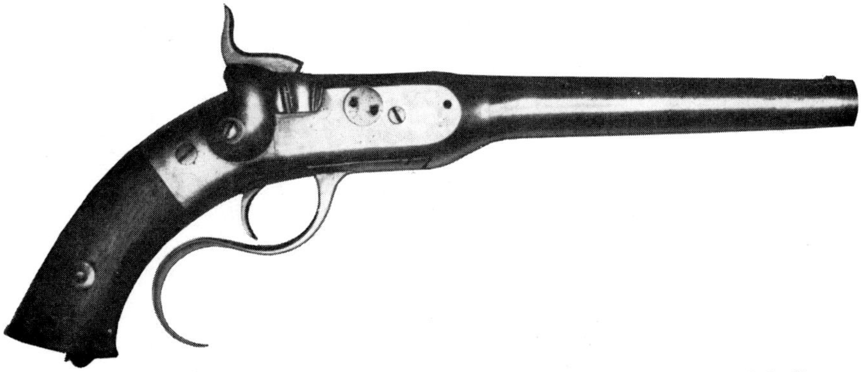

135 Perry pistol with automatic cap magazine (*Collection: Henry M. Stewart*)

136 Brown Bess with tubular cap magazine (*Collection: Lewis Winant*)

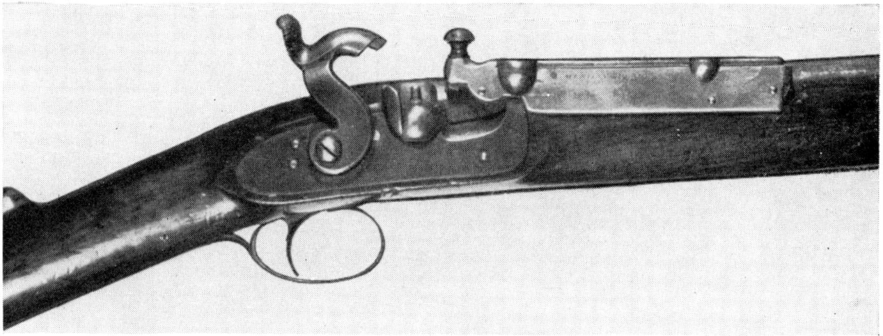

137 Westley Richards carbine with capping magazine (*Collection: Lewis Winant*)

138 Blanch gun with a purported Ritchie self-capper
(*Formerly in the Harrod Collection*)

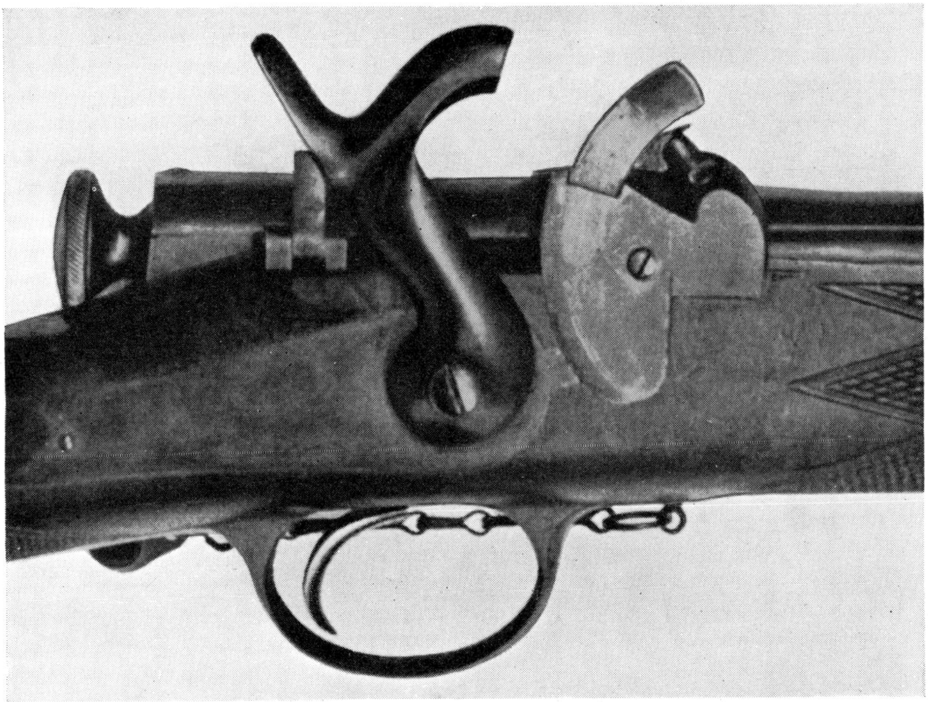

139 Lock with Della Noce automatic capper (*Formerly in the Harrod Collection*)

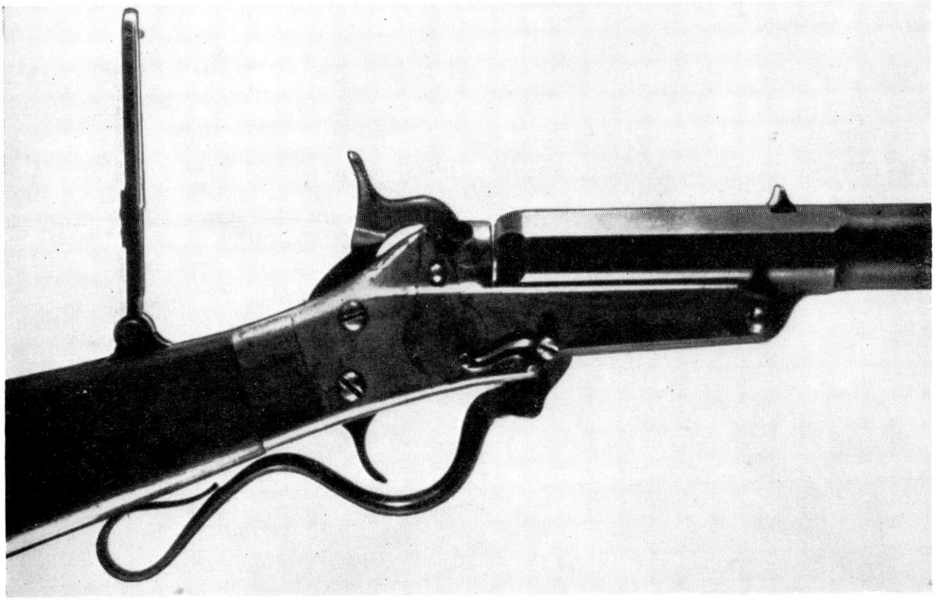

140 Maynard rifle designed to fire either of two early outside-primed cartridges
(*Collection: Lewis Winant*)

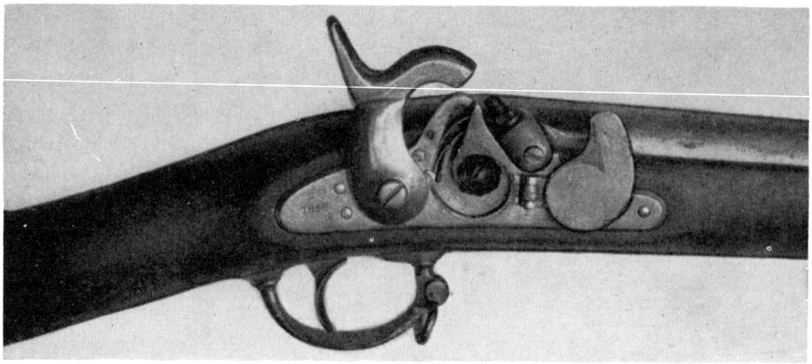

141 U.S. rifle-musket Model 1855 with Maynard tape-feeder
(*Formerly in the Harrod Collection*)

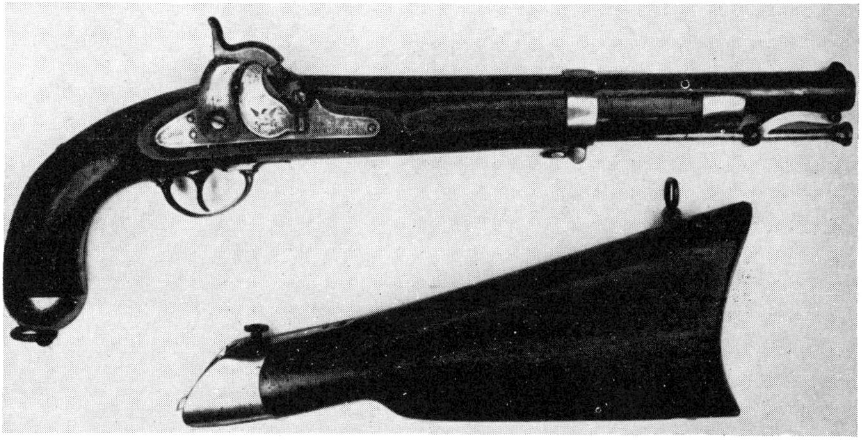

142 U.S. pistol-carbine Model 1855 design with shoulder stock
(*Collection: Henry M. Stewart*)

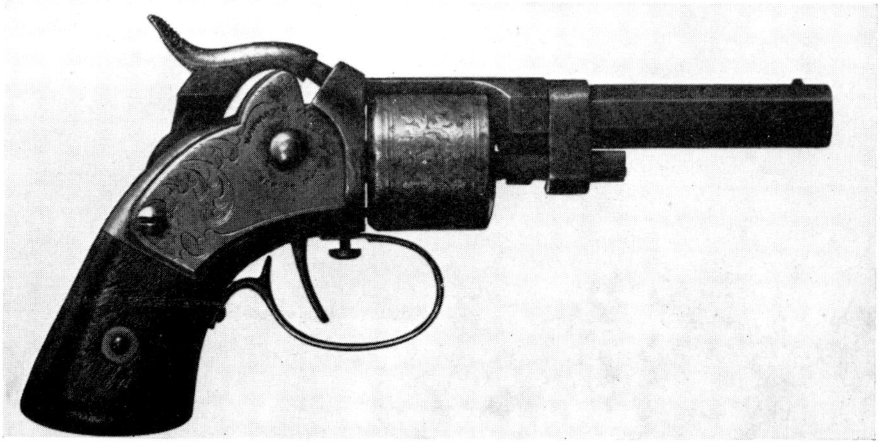

143 Massachusetts Arms Co. revolver, closed in fired position
(*Collection: Lewis Winant*)

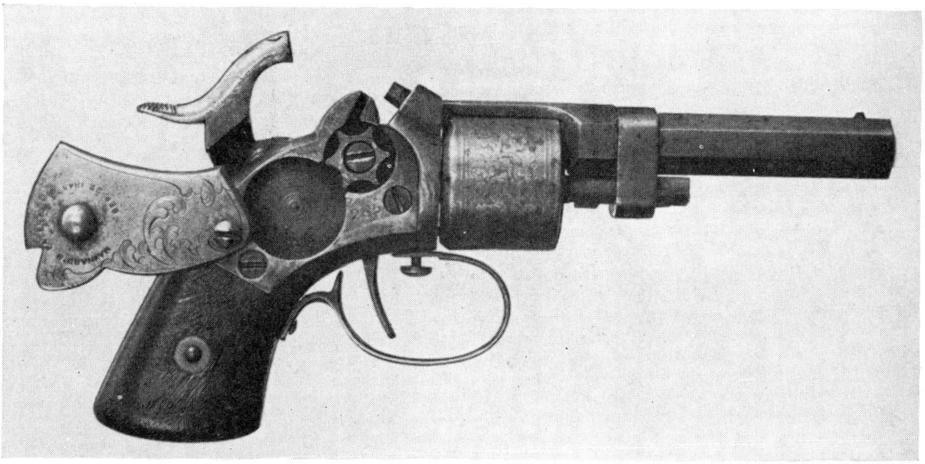

144 Massachusetts Arms Co. revolver, open to show the tape-priming mechanism (*Collection: Lewis Winant*)

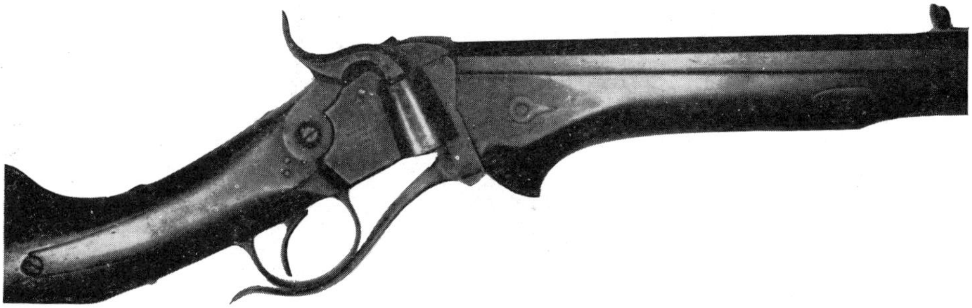

145 Maynard primer on Sharps second model (*Collection: Henry M. Stewart*)

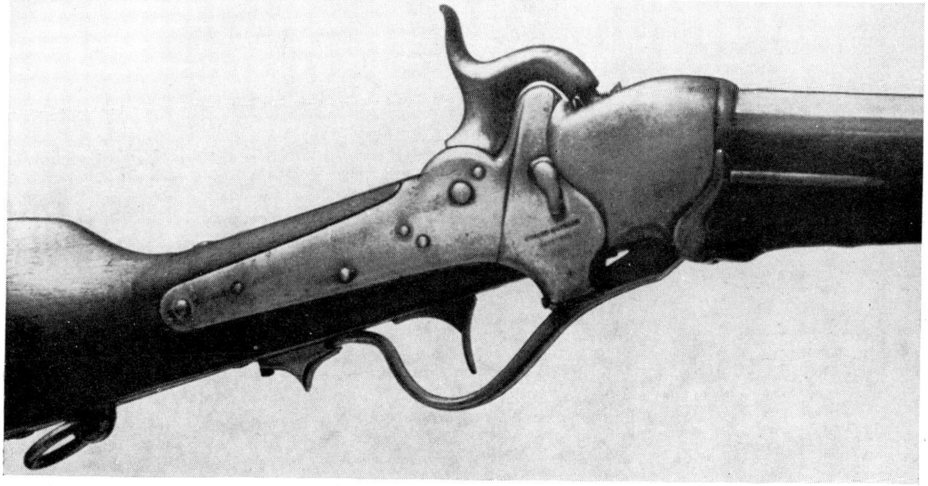

146 1851 model Sharps rifle with Maynard primer (*Collection: Lewis Winant*)

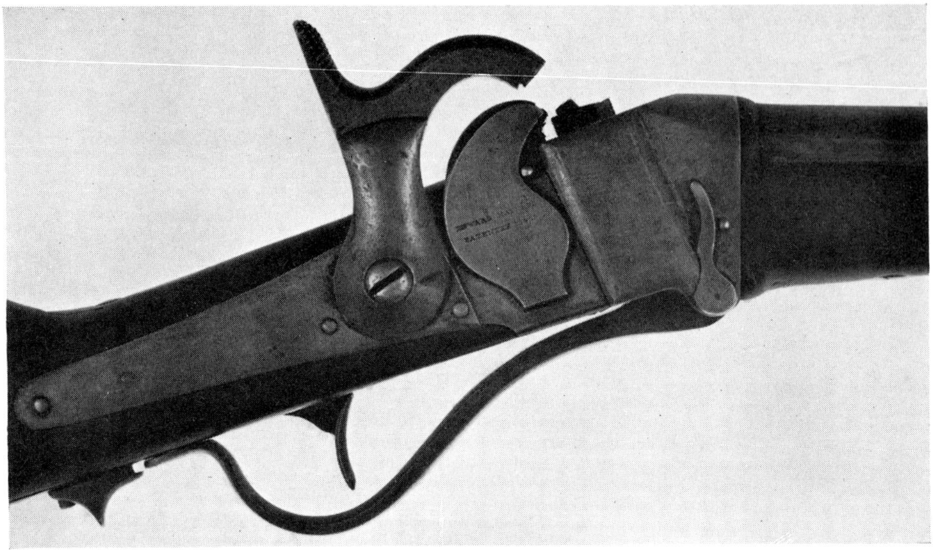

147 1855 model Sharps with Maynard primer (*Winchester Collection*)

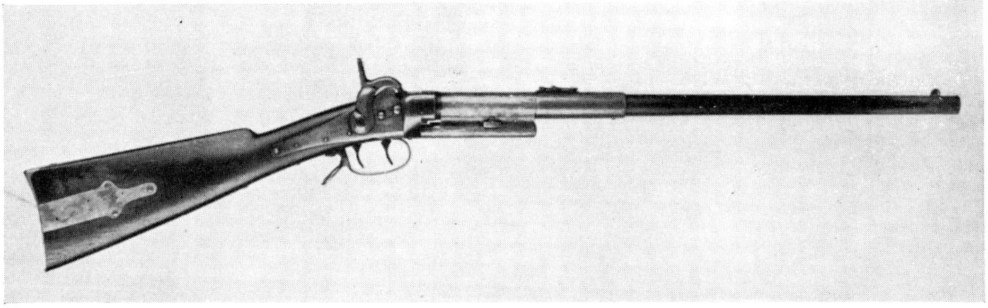

148 Greene carbine with Maynard primer (*West Point Museum Collection*)

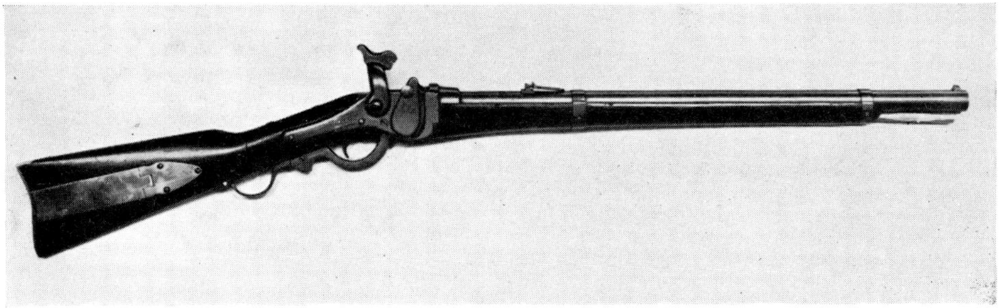

149 Symmes carbine with Maynard primer (*Collection: Smithsonian Institution*)

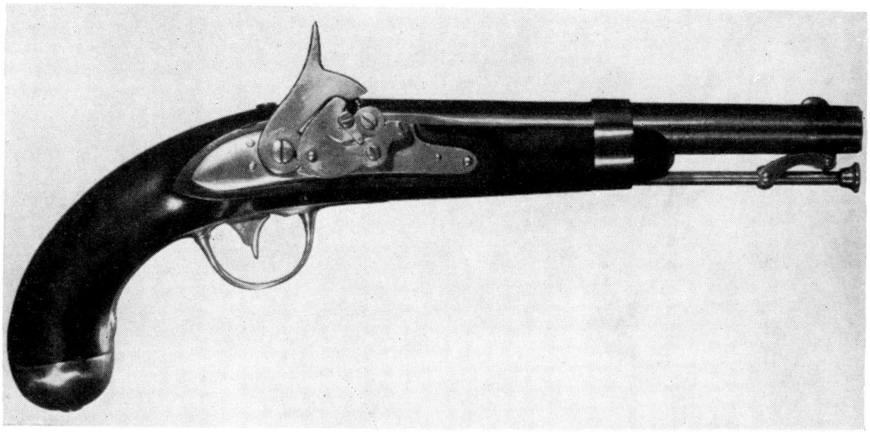

150 1842 model U.S. martial pistol with Maynard primer
(*Collection: William M. Locke*)

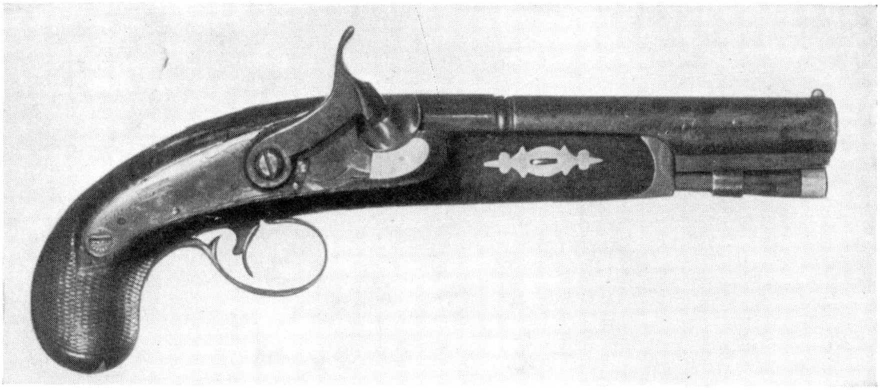

151 Deringer pistol with tape primer (*Collection: William M. Locke*)

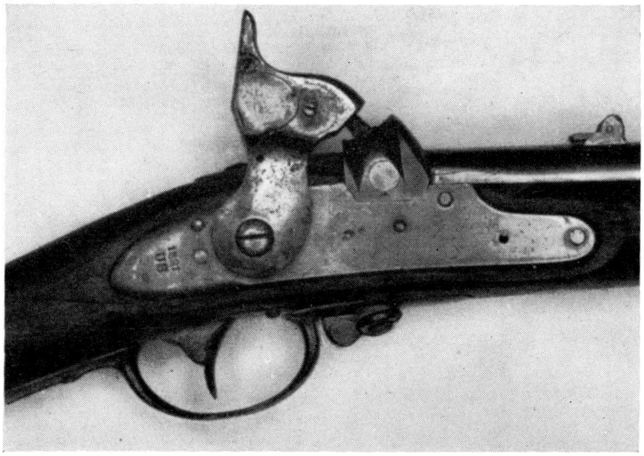

152 U.S. Musket using Ward invention
(*Collection: Henry M. Stewart*)

153 Heurteloup lock just after firing (*Collection: Lewis Winant*)

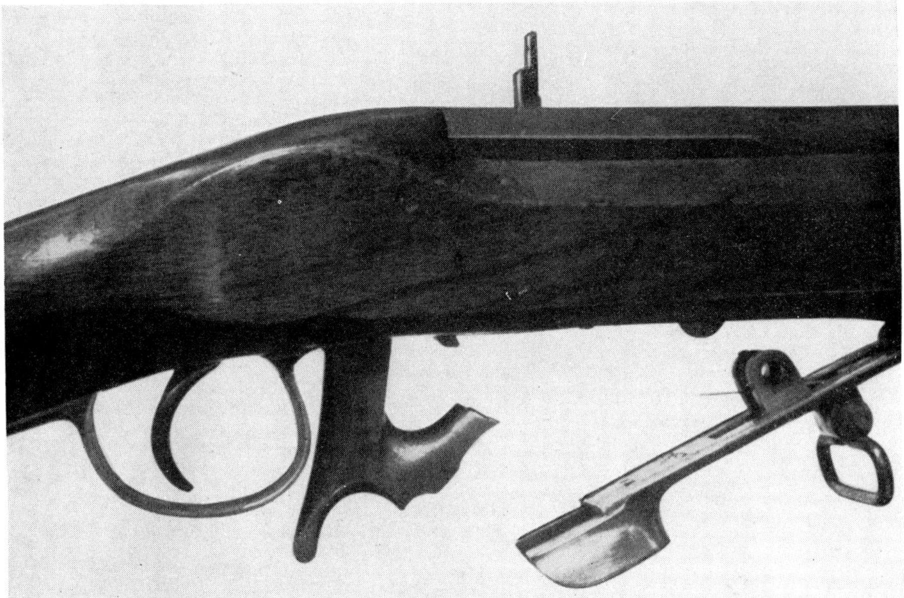

154 Heurteloup lock open (*Collection: Lewis Winant*)

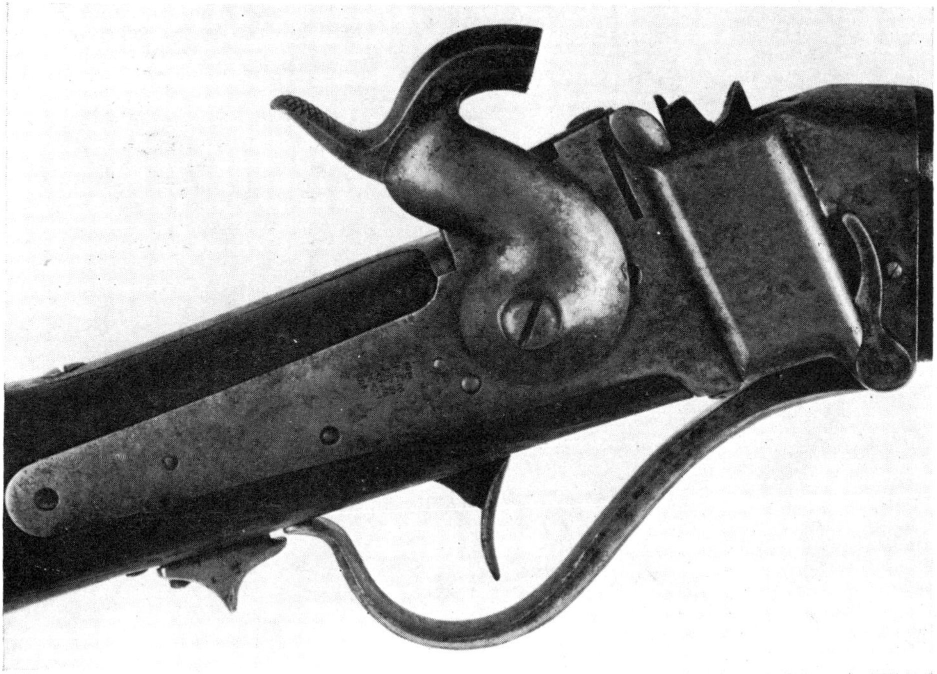

155 1853 model Sharps with disk primer (*Winchester Collection*)

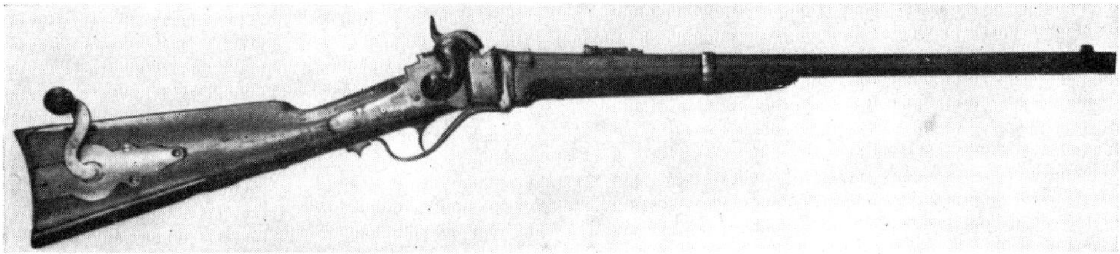

156 "Coffee-mill" Sharps (*Collection: John K. Watson*)

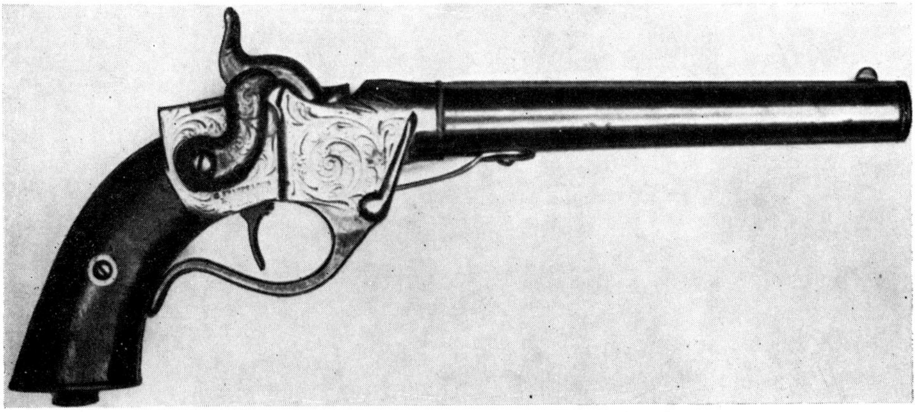

157 Sharps pistol with disk-primer lock, and Lawrence cutoff (*Collection: Henry M. Stewart*)

158 Two Sharps disk-primer "pistol-rifles" (*Collection: Henry M. Stewart*)

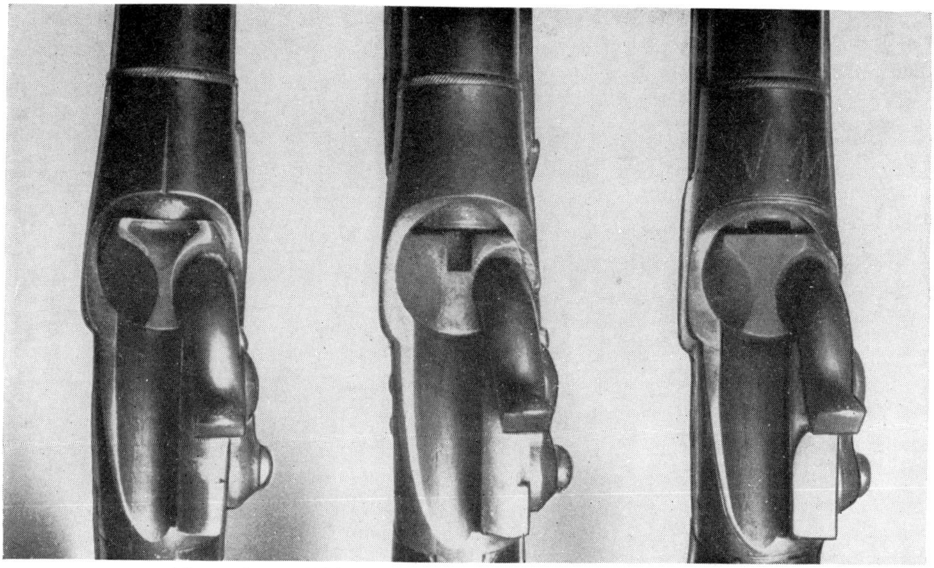

159 Breeches of Sharps guns (*Collection: Henry M. Stewart*)

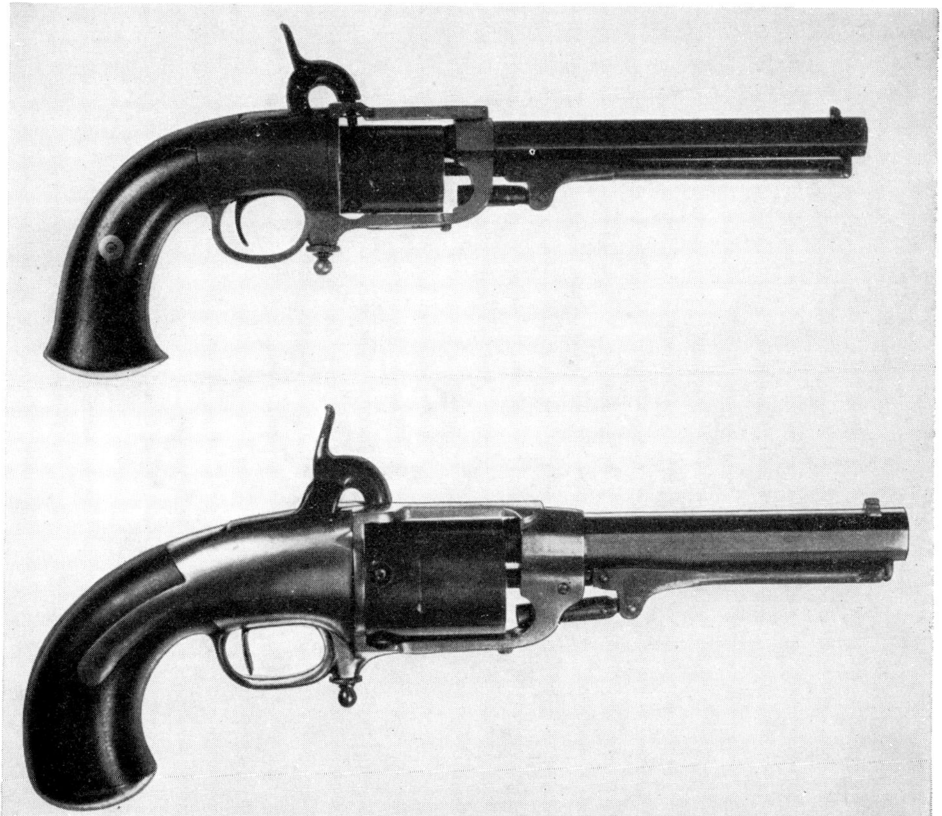

160 Two Butterfield revolvers (*Collection: William M. Locke*)

161 Butterfield derringers (*Collection: George Hyatt*)

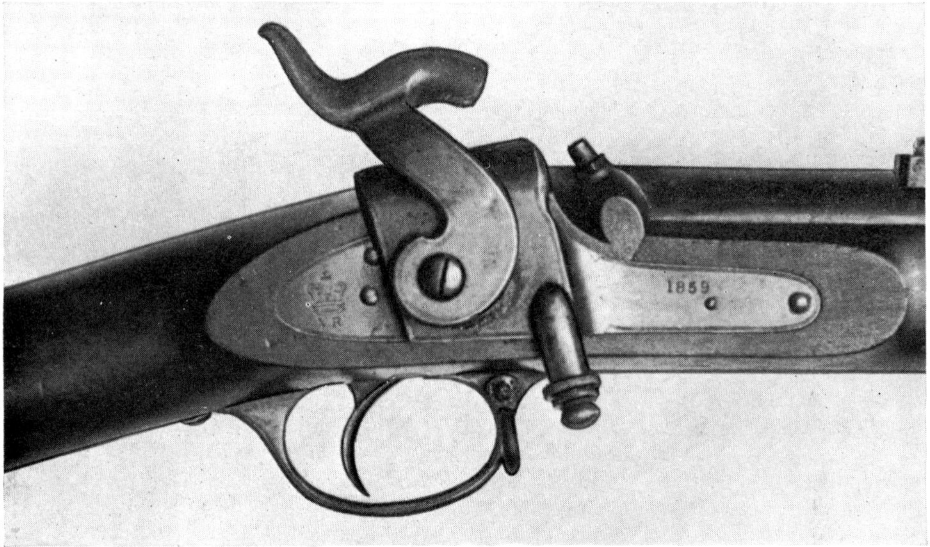

162 Enfield rifle with Chester lock (*Formerly in the Harrod Collection*)

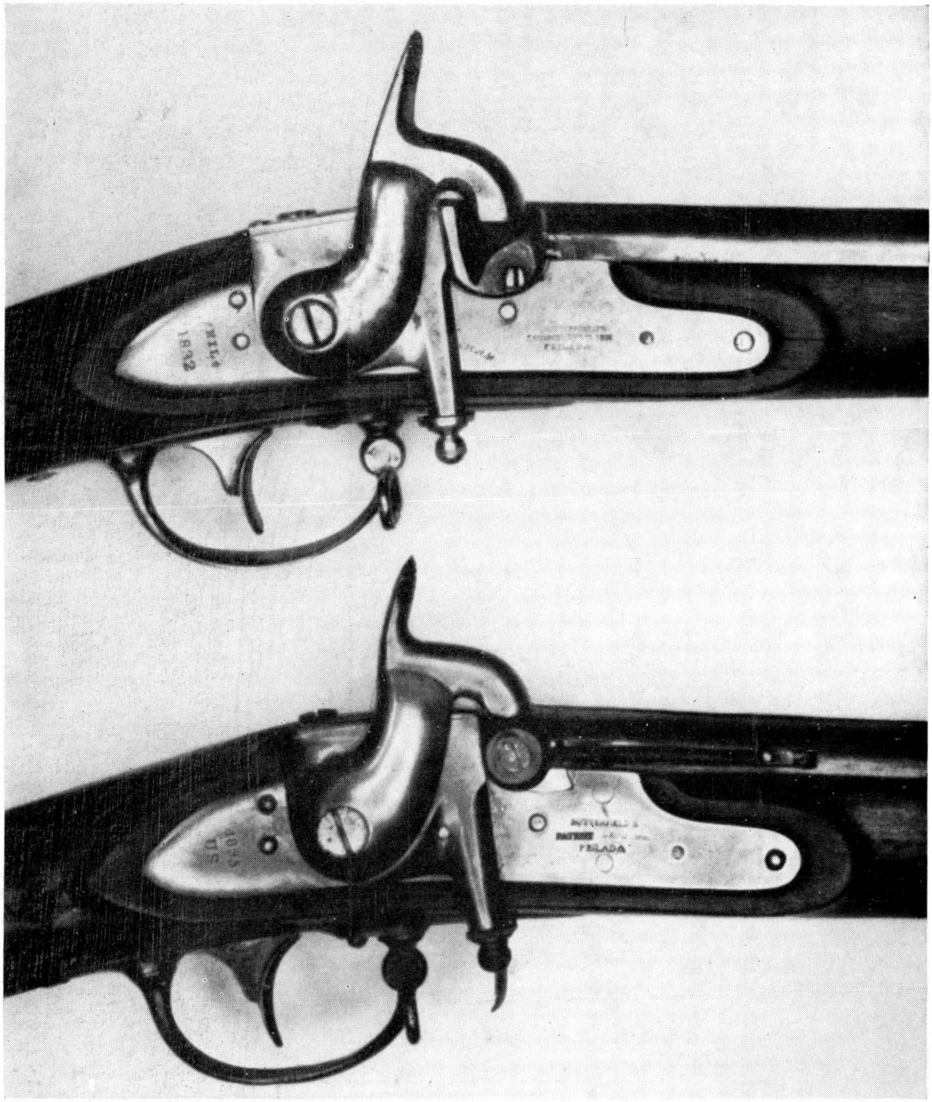

163 U.S. muskets using Butterfield primers (*Collection: Henry M. Stewart*)

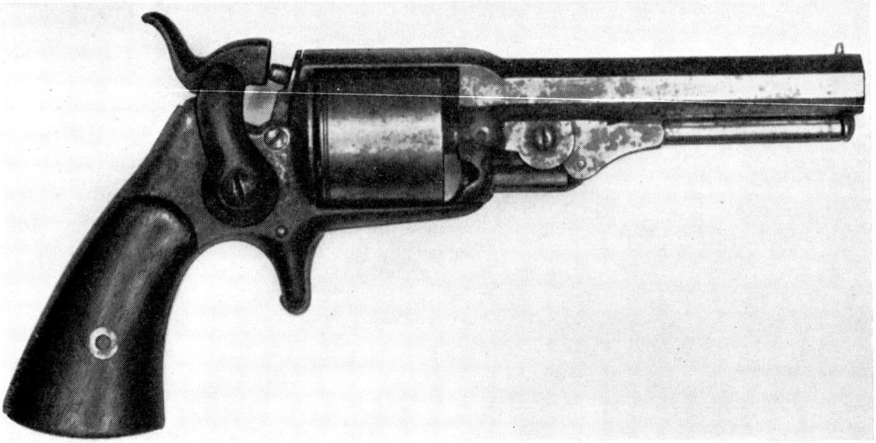

164 Jacob Rupertus revolver with April 19, 1859, primer
(*Collection: Henry M. Stewart*)

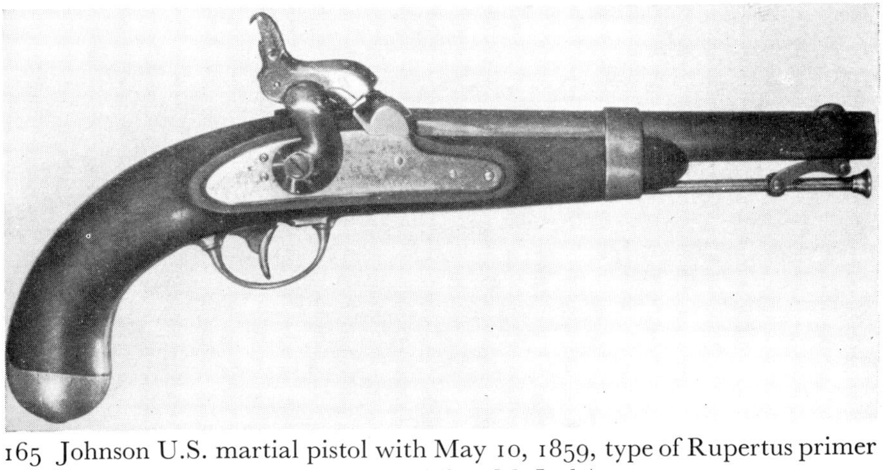

165 Johnson U.S. martial pistol with May 10, 1859, type of Rupertus primer
(*Collection: William M. Locke*)

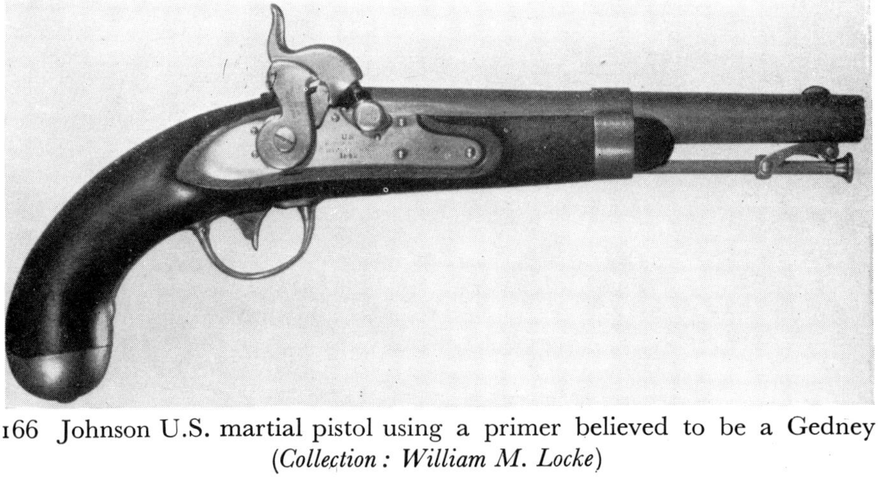

166 Johnson U.S. martial pistol using a primer believed to be a Gedney
(*Collection: William M. Locke*)

167 Bell 1860 patent model (*Collection: Henry M. Stewart*)

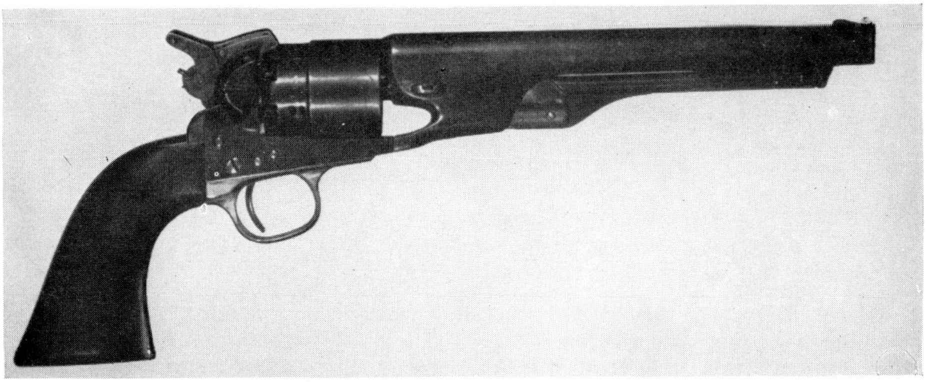

168 Colt 1860 Army revolver with a disk primer of uncertain origin (*Collection: William M. Locke*)

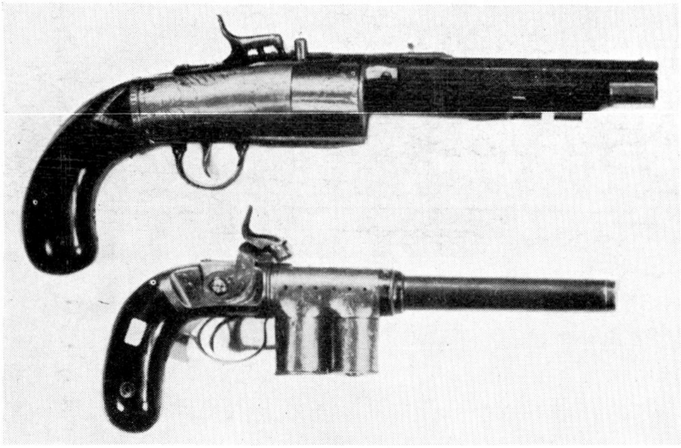

169 Edwards revolver and Percival & Smith revolver
(*Collection: Smithsonian Institution*)

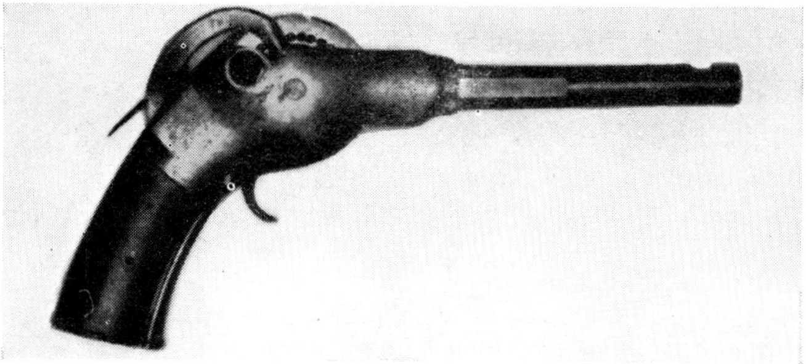

170 Wright vertical-turret revolver (*Collection: William M. Locke*)

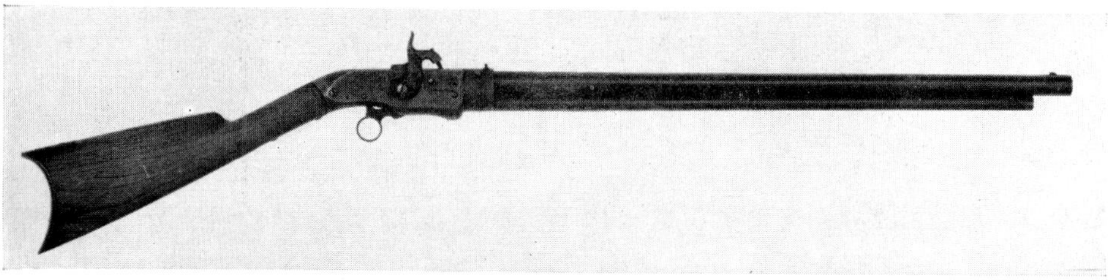

171 Jennings repeating rifle (*Winchester Collection*)

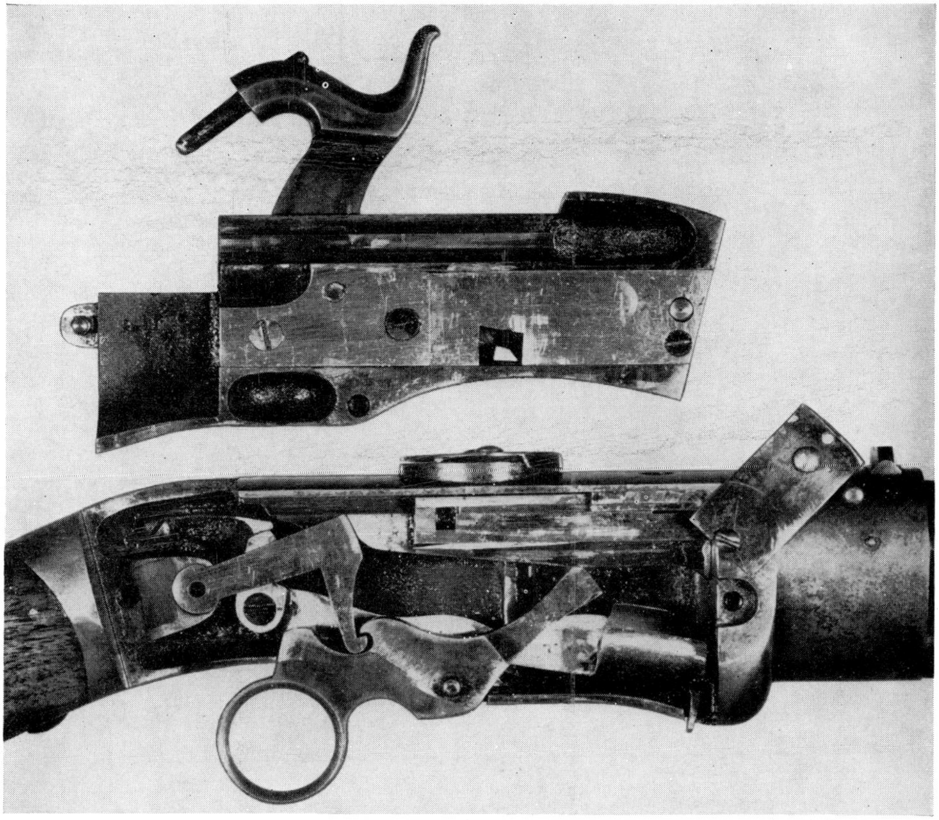

172 Jennings action mechanism exposed in closed position
(*Windsor Collection*)

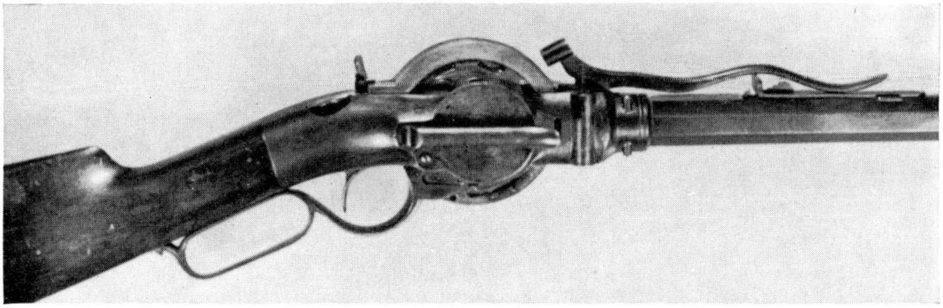

173 Porter rifle with vertical turret (*Collection: James E. Serven*)

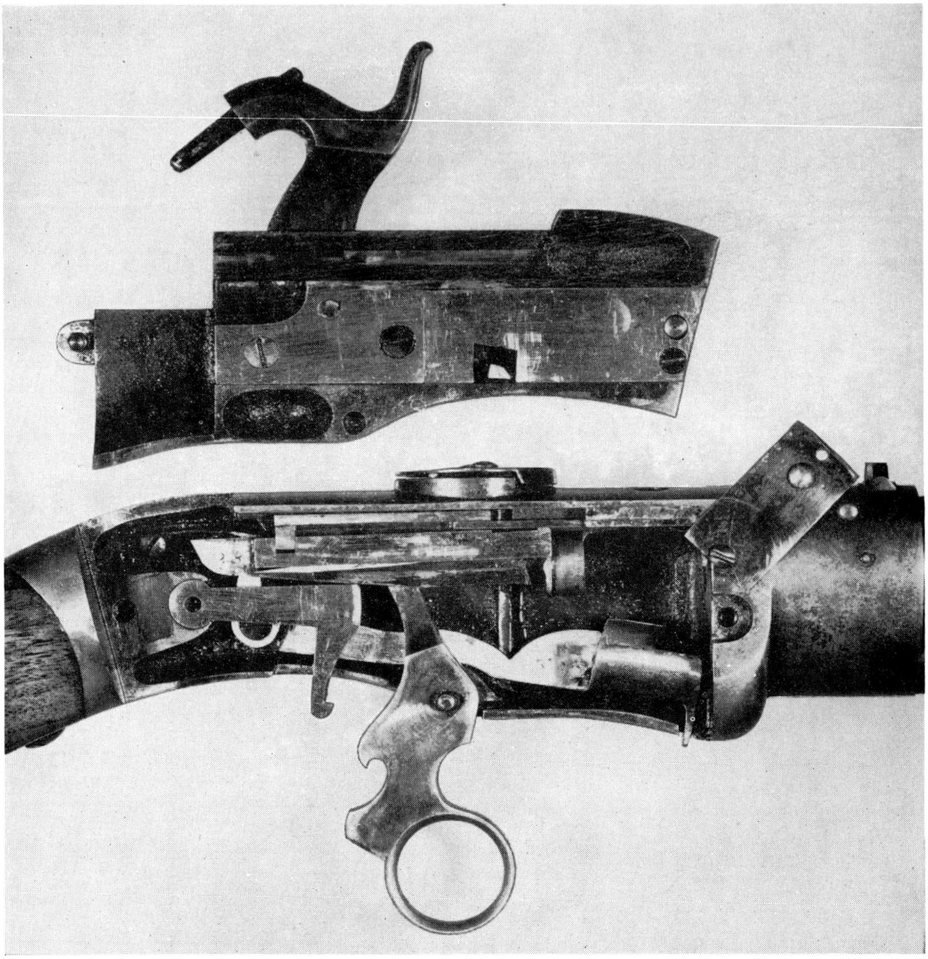

174 Jennings action mechanism exposed in open position
(*Windsor Collection*)

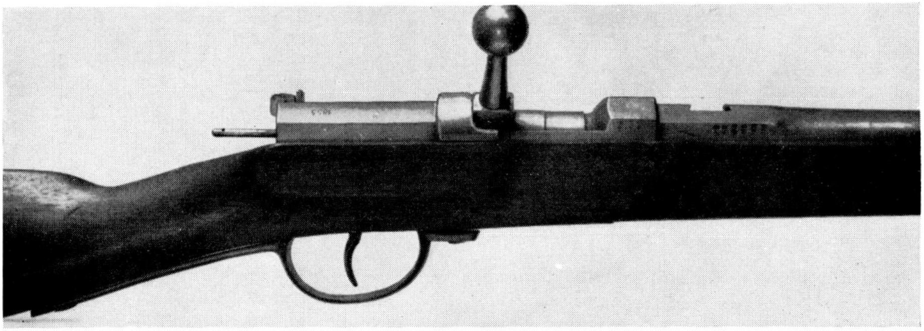

175 Dreyse bolt-action needle-fire rifle (*Collection: Lewis Winant*)

176 Dreyse needle-fire double shotgun (*Formerly in the Harrod Collection*)

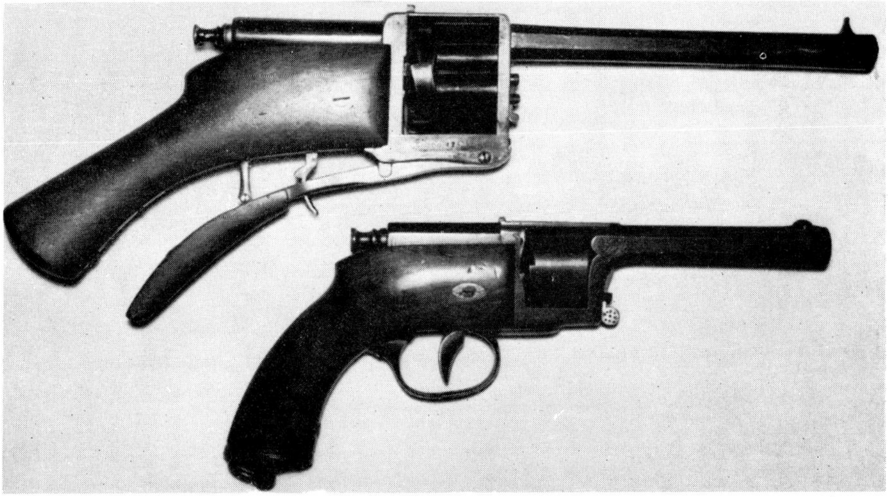

177 Dreyse needle-fire revolvers
(*Collections: Frank R. Horner and Lewis Winant*)

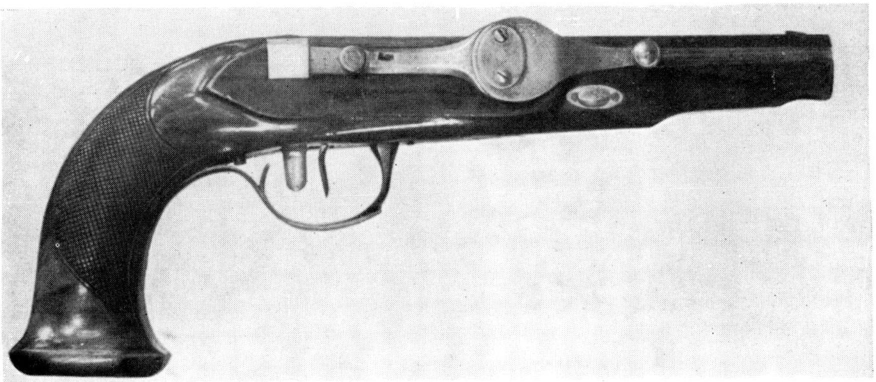

178 Dreyse & Collenbusch muzzle-loading needle-fire pistol
(*Collection: R. H. McLeod*)

179 Schroeder needle-fire breechloader (*West Point Museum Collections*)

180 Needham needle-fire gun (*Formerly in the Harrod Collection*)

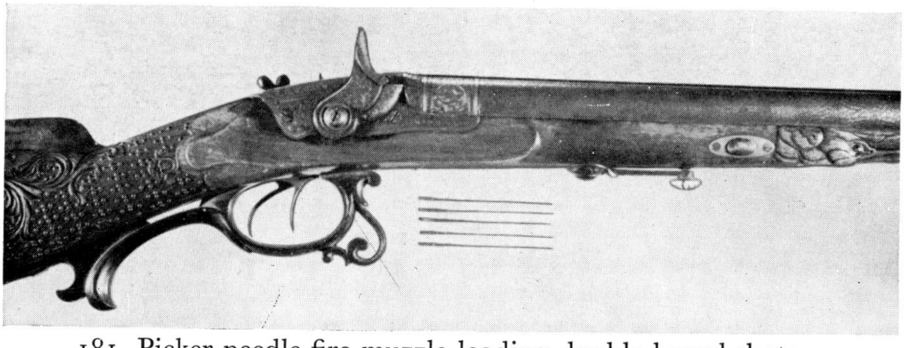

181 Picker needle-fire muzzle-loading double-barrel shotgun (*Collection: Lewis Winant*)

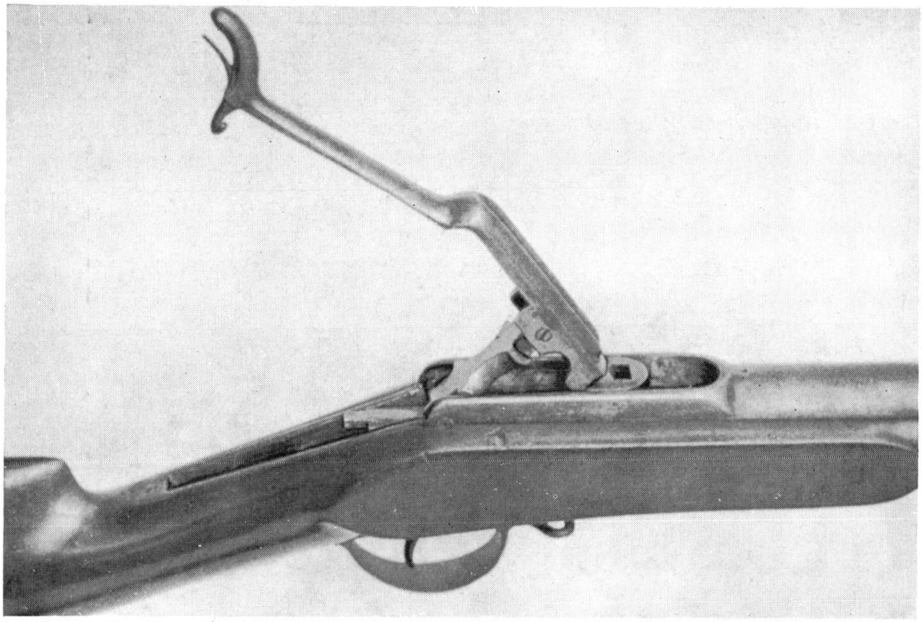

182 Chatauvillard needle-fire gun (*Formerly in the Harrod Collection*)

183 *Mousqueton des Cent Gardes* (*Formerly in the Harrod Collection*)

184 Allen & Wheelock lip-fire revolver (*Collection: Lewis Winant*)

185 Perrin revolver using inside-primed centre-fire cartridges
(*Collection: Lewis Winant*)

186 Robert pistol with breechblock raised
(*Collection: Dr. W. R. Funderburg*)

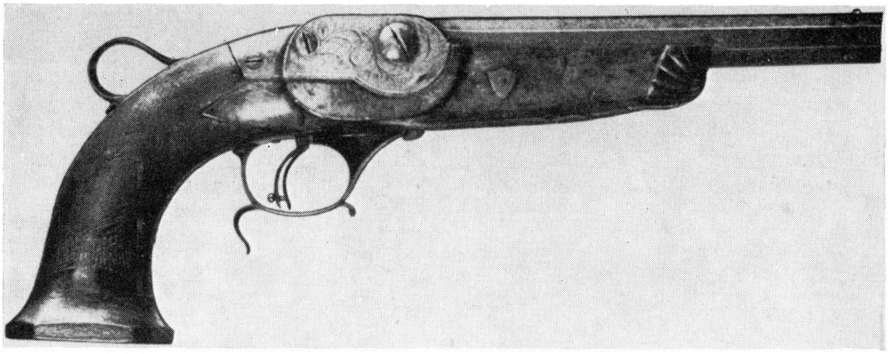

187 Robert pistol with breechblock closed (*Collection: Dr. W. R. Funderburg*)

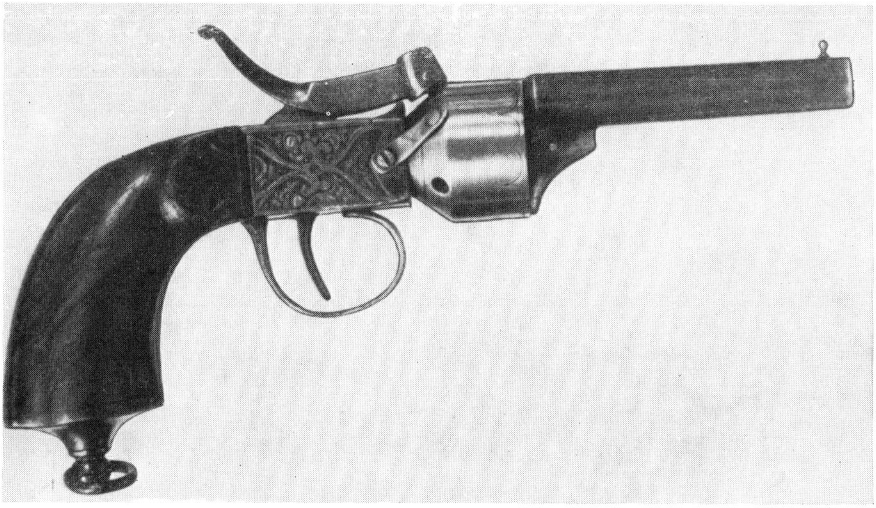

188 Michallon revolver (*Collection: Lewis Winant*)

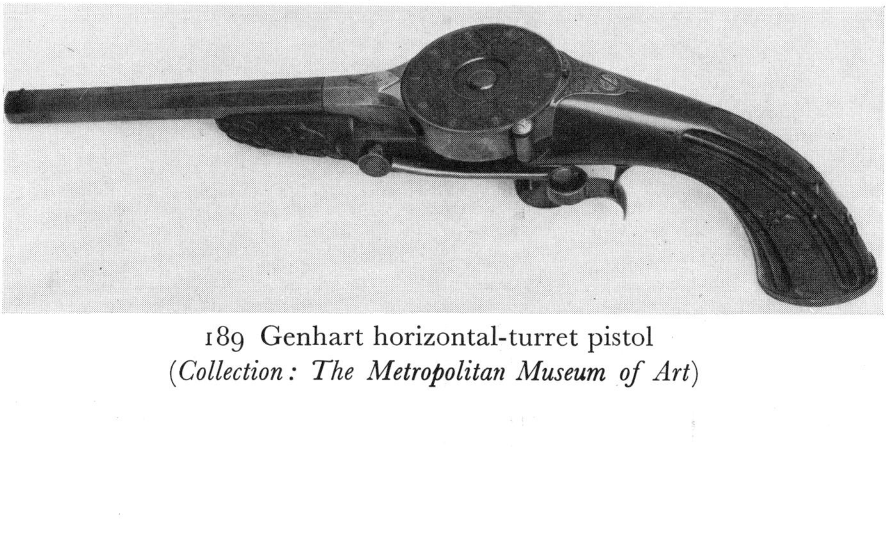

189 Genhart horizontal-turret pistol
(*Collection: The Metropolitan Museum of Art*)

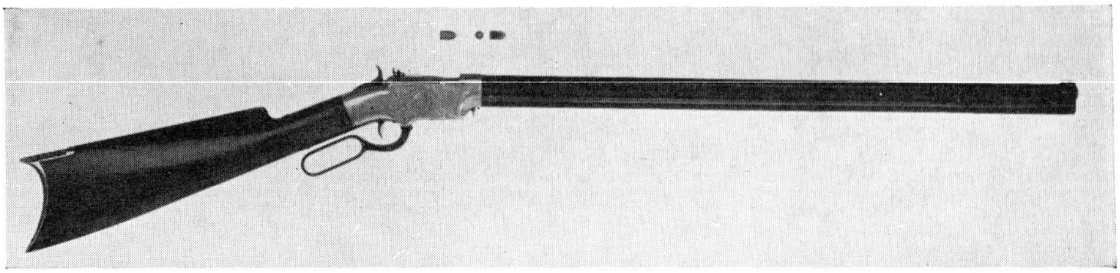

190 Volcanic rifle (*Winchester Collection*)

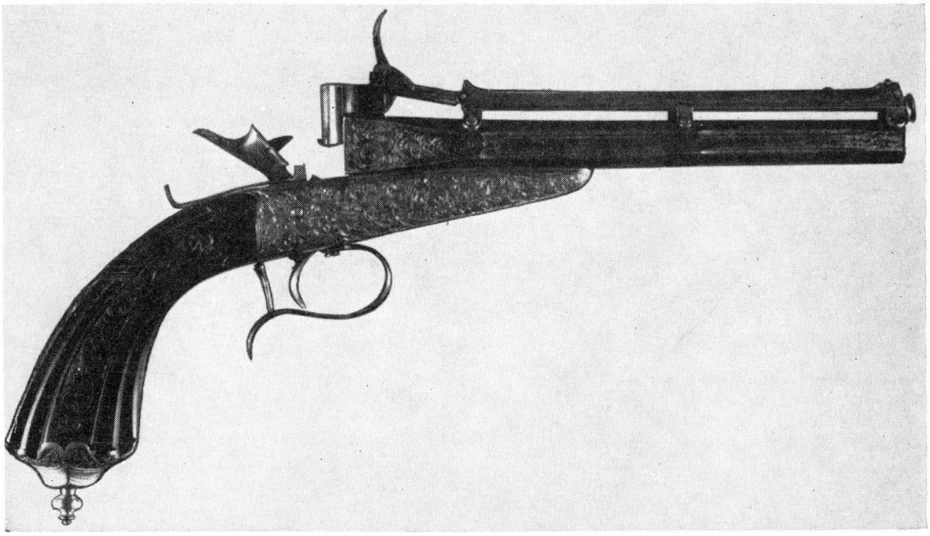

191 Gravity-feed pistol, probably Belgian (*Collection: Lewis Winant*)

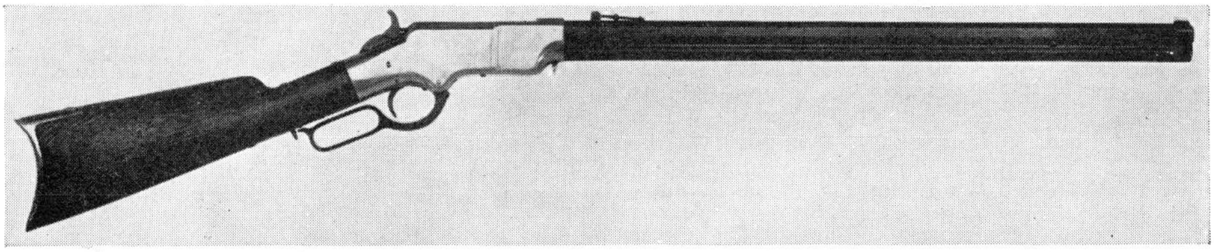

192 Henry rifle (*Winchester Collection*)

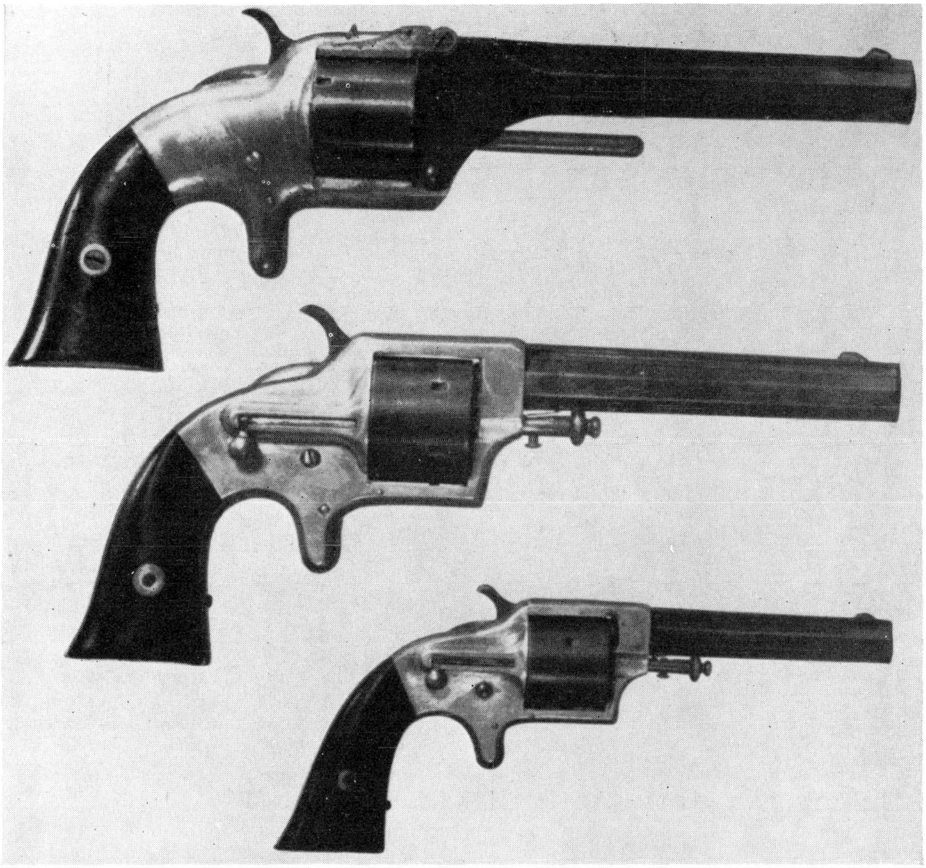

193 Cup-primer revolvers. Two Plant revolvers (*top*); Eagle Arms Company (*bottom*). (*Top and Bottom from collection: Lewis Winant; centre from collection of Henry C. McMullen*)

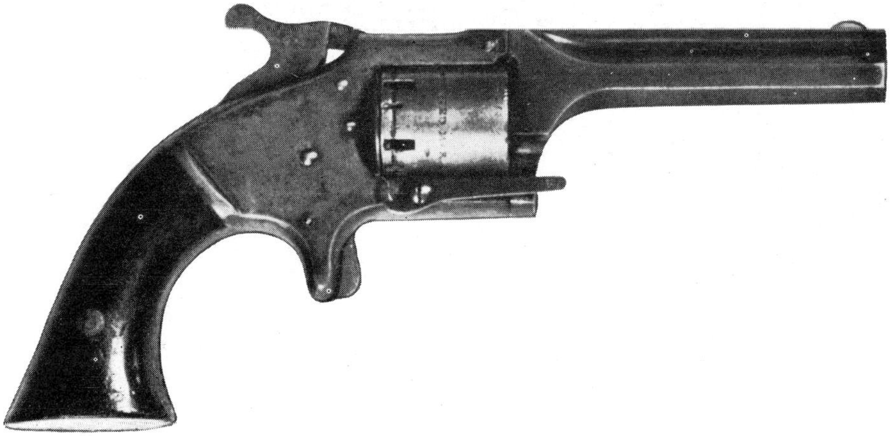

194 Connecticut Arms Company revolver (*Collection: Herbert Green*)

195 National ·45 calibre revolver (*Colt Collection*)

196 Moore ·32 calibre revolver (*Collection: Lewis Winant*)

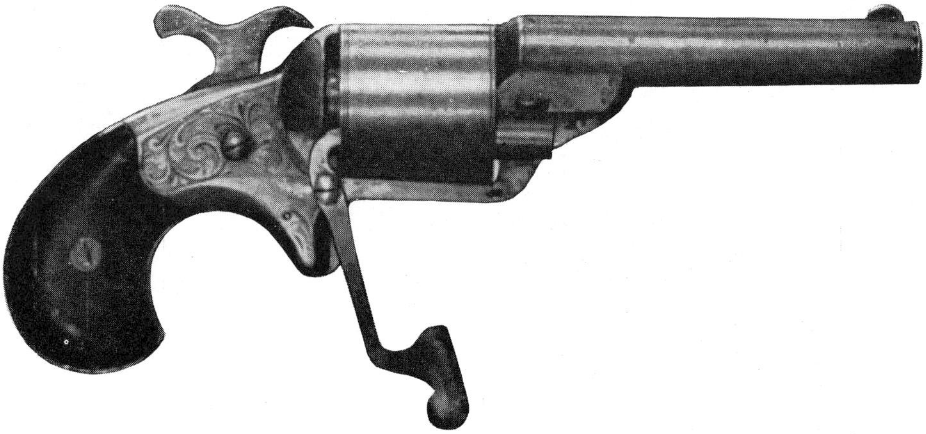

197 National ·32 calibre revolver (*Collection: Arnott Millett*)

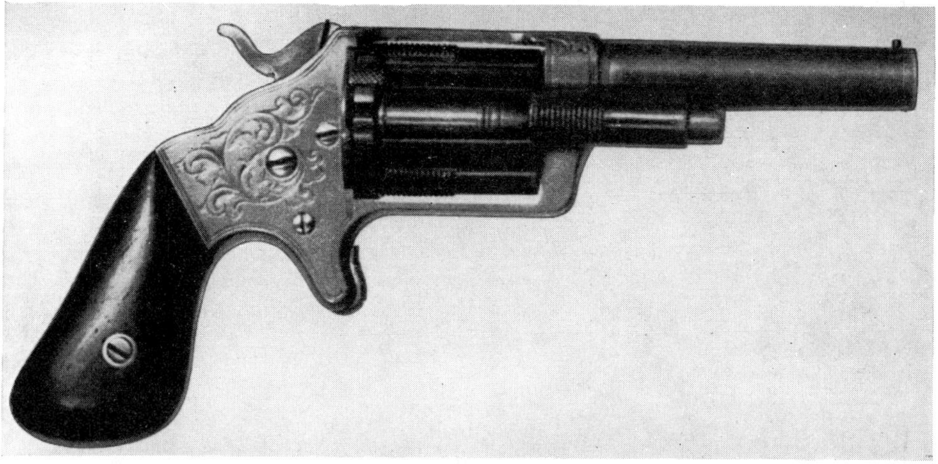

198 Slocum Patent Side-Loading Revolver (*Collection: Lewis Winant*)

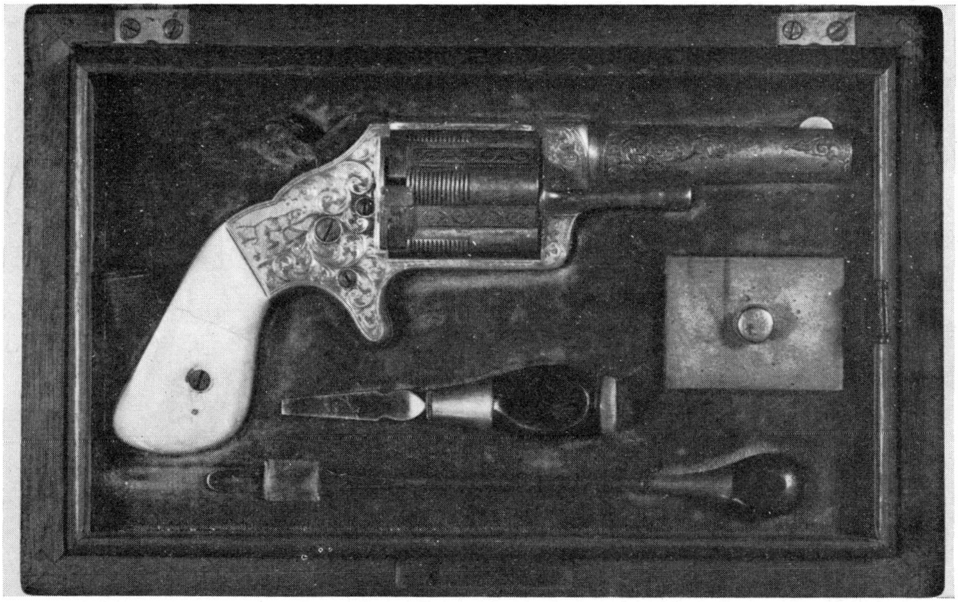

199 Gold-mounted, engraved, presentation Slocum revolver (*Collection: Smithsonian Institution*)

200 Pond Separate-Chambers Revolver (*Collection: Lewis Winant*)

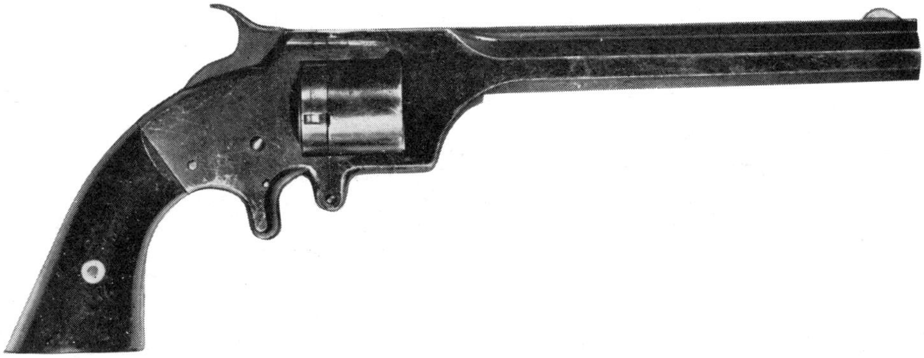

201 Crispin revolver (*Collection: Smithsonian Institution*)

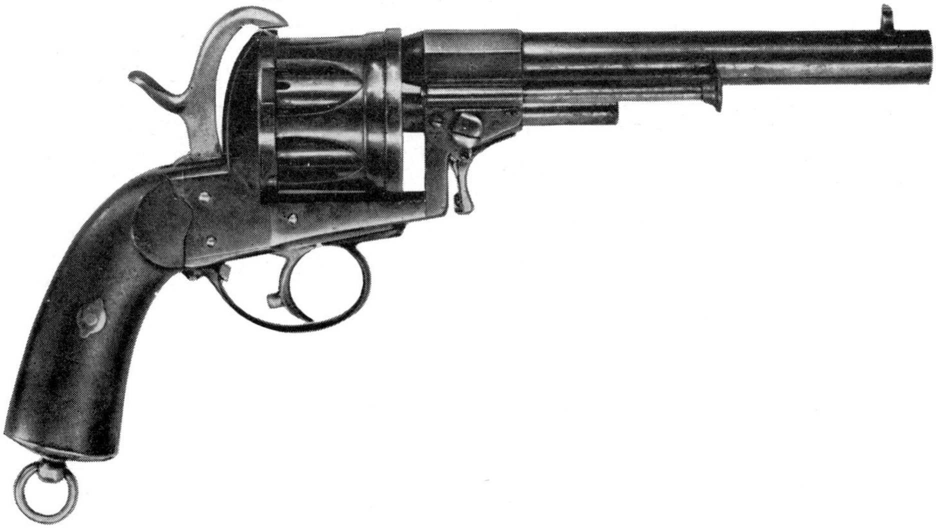

202 Polain revolver (*Colt Collection*)

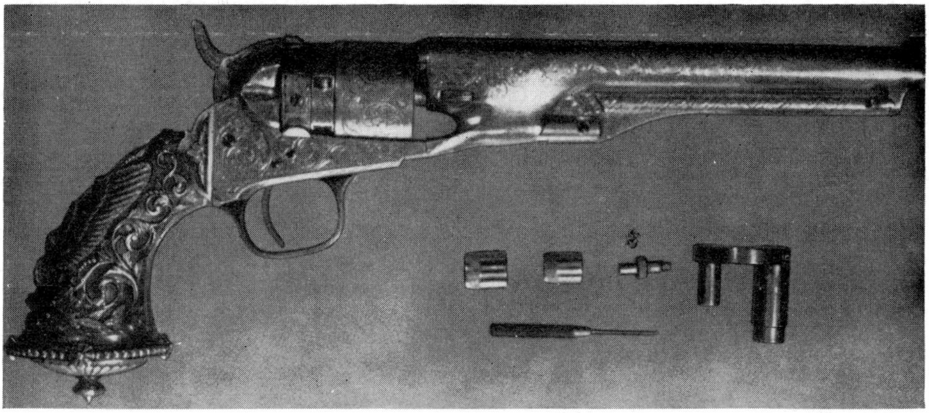

203 1862 model Colt with Thuer cylinder (*Collection: Henry M. Stewart*)

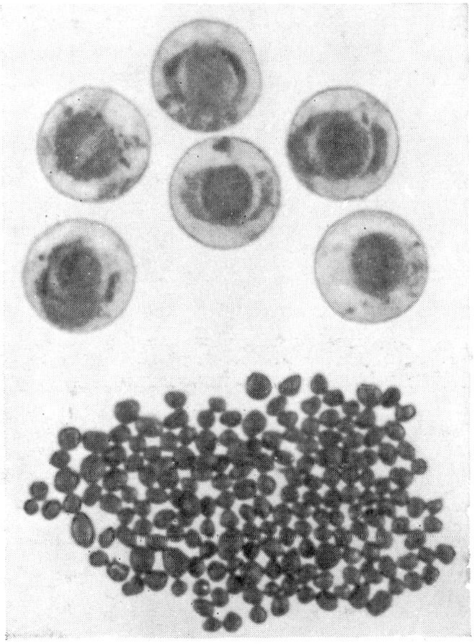

204 Priming patches and pills
(*Collection: Lewis Winant*)

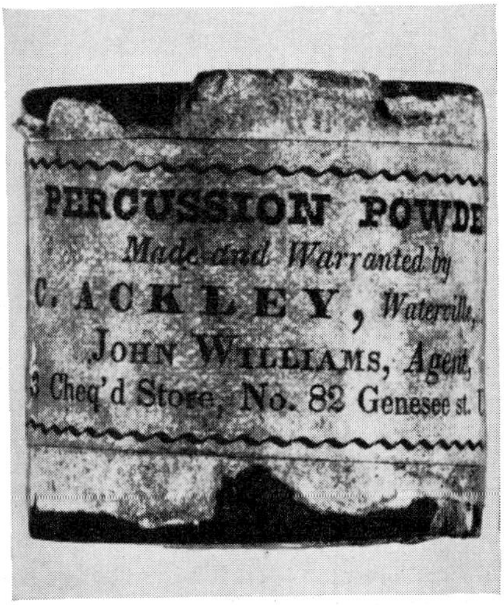

205 Percussion powder box
(*New Haven Historical Society Collection: Photograph courtesy of Winchester*)

206 Pills and chargers
(*Collection: W. Keith Neal*)

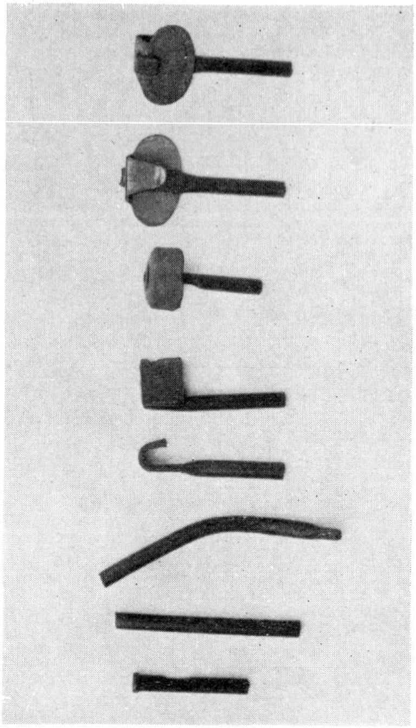

207 Tube primers
(*Collection: W.Keith Neal*)

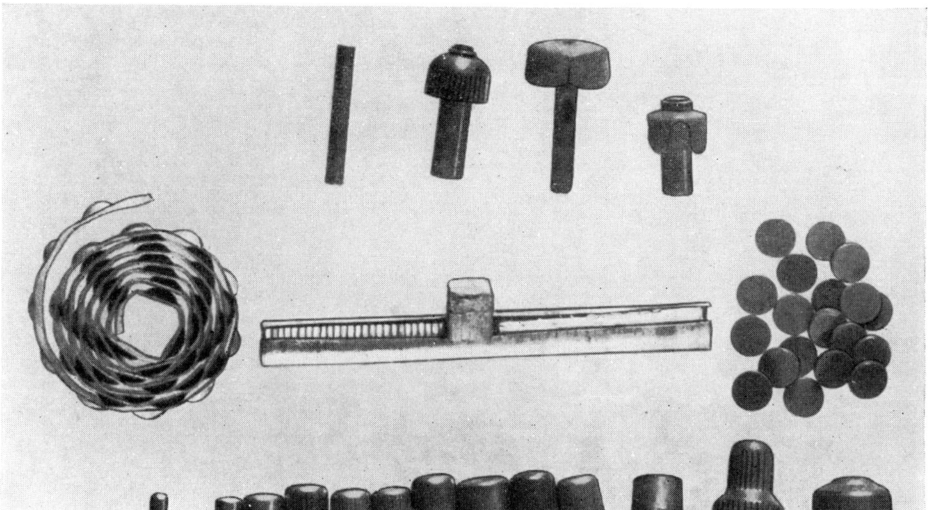

208 Various priming agents (*Collection: Lewis Winant*)

209 Primers and caps (*Collection: Paul Westergard*)

210 Various cappers (*Collection: Paul Westergard*)

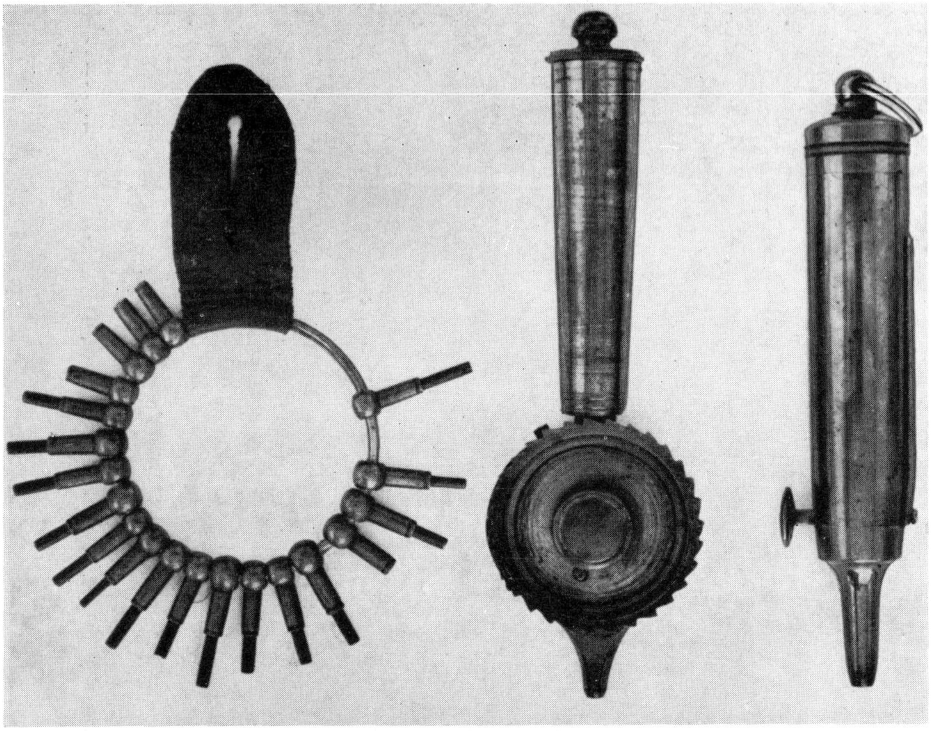

211 Cap and tube dispensers (*Collection: W. Keith Neal*)

212 Various cartridges. (*Left to right*) British Enfield; 1855 model Springfield; Colt ·36 calibre; Colt ·44 calibre (*Collection: Lewis Winant*)

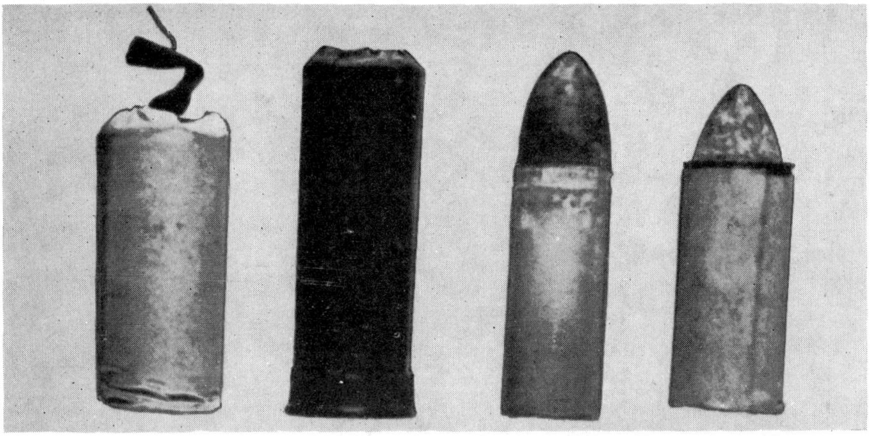

213 Various cartridges. (*Left to right*) Eley shot cartridge; Renette & Gastinne shot cartridge; Sharps linen cartridge; brass-foil-and-paper cartridge (*Collection: Lewis Winant*)

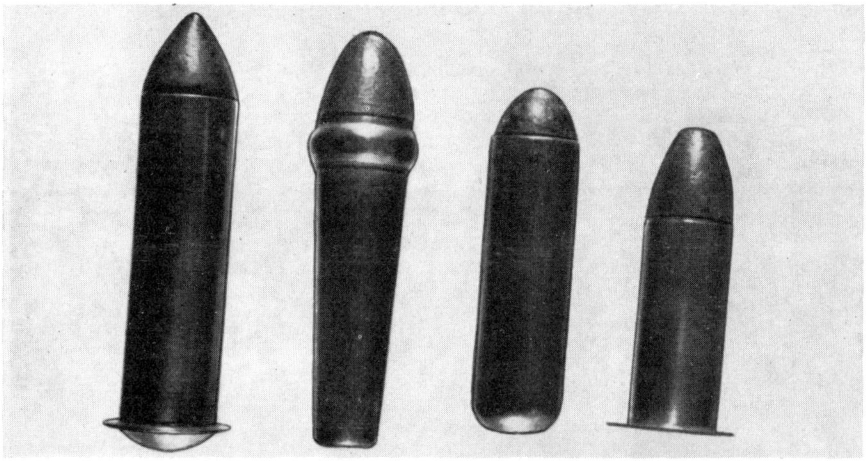

214 Various cartridges. (*Left to right*) Requa-Billinghurst; Burnside; Gallager; Maynard (*Collection: Lewis Winant*)

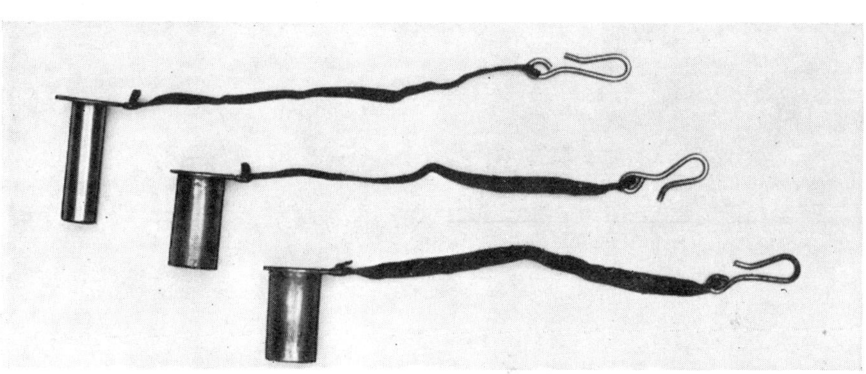

215 Maynard cartridges (*Collection: Henry M. Stewart*)

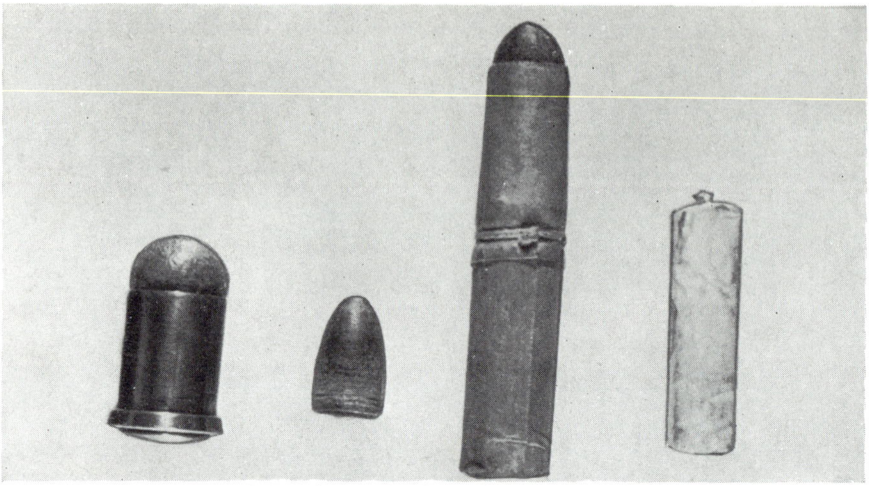

216 Early types of fixed ammunition
(*Collections : Dr. W. R. Funderburg and Lewis Winant*)

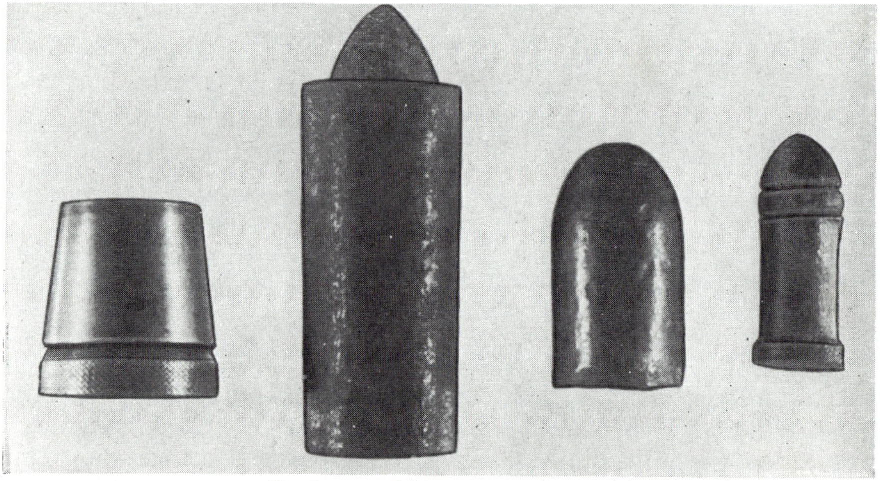

217 Early cartridge case and cartridges
(*Collections : Eugene Miller and Henry M. Stewart*)

218 Various cartridges. (*Left to right*) French pin-fire; Crispin used in Smith carbine; Plant front-loader; Moore front-loader (*Collections : Paul Westergard and Lewis Winant*)

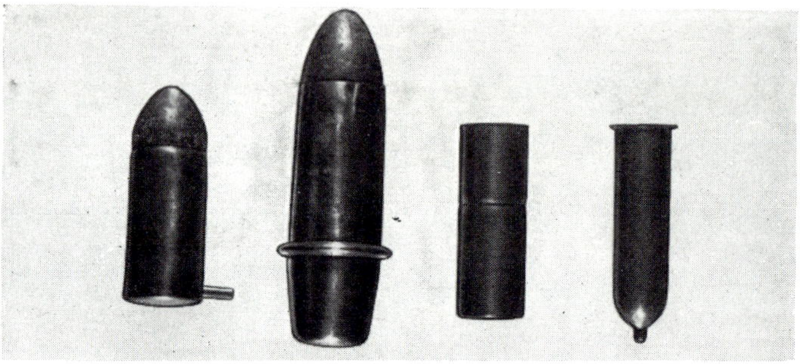

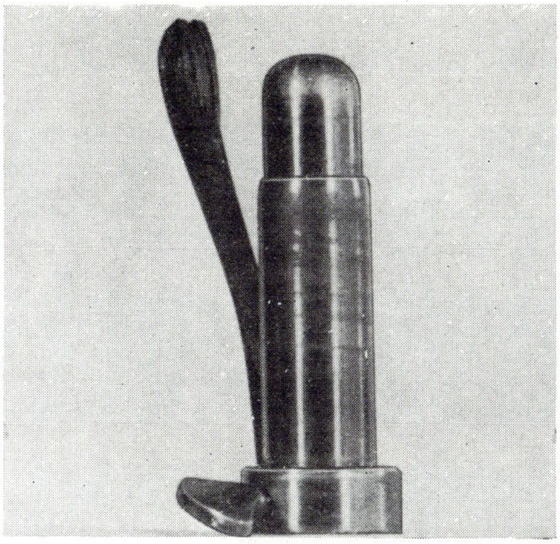

219 Pin-fire reloading tool, side view (*Collection: Paul Westergard*)

220 Pin-fire reloading tool, top view (*Collection: Paul Westergard*)

221 Centre-fire cartridges (*Collection: Lewis Winant*)

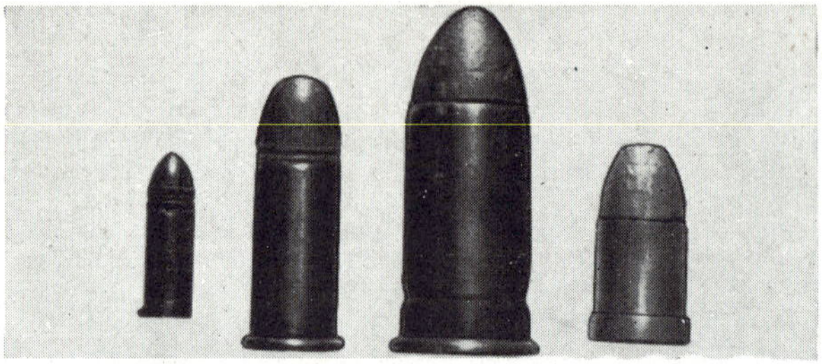

222 Various cartridges. (*Left to right*) Allen & Wheelock lip-fire; ·44 Henry Flat rim-fire; inside-primed musket cartridge; inside-primed cartridge for Perrin revolver (*Collection: Lewis Winant*)

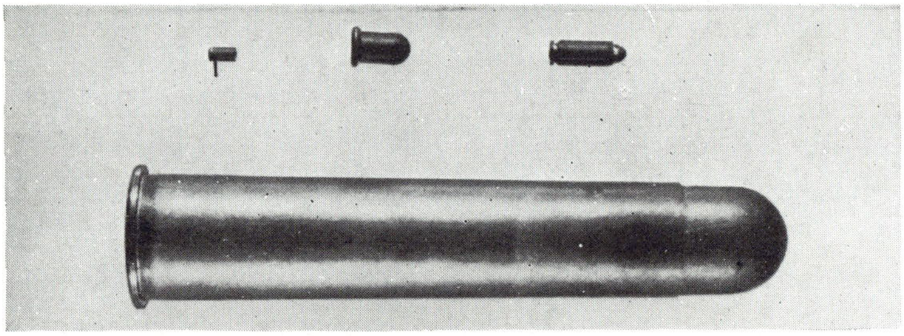

223 Various cartridges showing extreme variation in size (*Collection: Lewis Winant*)

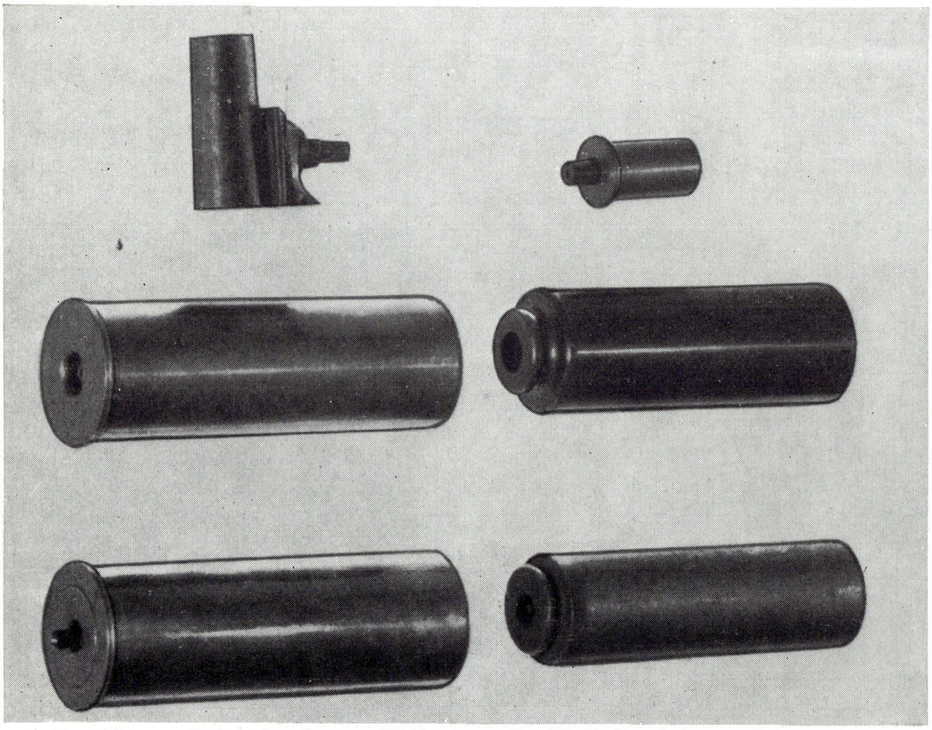

224 Cartridges and chamber inserts (*Collections: Dr. W. R. Funderburg and Paul Westergard*)

CHAPTER VI

PERCUSSION-CAP MUZZLE-LOADERS

IN the 1820's great numbers of percussion-cap guns were made, but many of the older sportsmen clung to the flintlock, because the flint guns were stronger shooting than the early percussion guns.

Though the flint guns shot stronger the cap guns shot quicker. A young man with a percussion gun could become proficient in shooting flying with brief practice. The skill needed to shoot flying with a flint gun took long to acquire.

For those who wanted to espouse the new percussion ignition but were reluctant to cast off the friction ignition of the flintlocks, guns were made combining both systems.

The idea of fitting a second lock to a single-shot firearm, so there would be a reserve lock in case of a misfire, was not new. Usually the two locks were alike. Guns loaded with a single charge had been made with two matchlocks, others with two wheel locks—and others would be made with two percussion-cap locks to fire one charge.

When the wheel lock was invented men who did not place full confidence in friction ignition had a wheel lock and a matchlock fitted to the same gun. It is not surprising that after three hundred years of friction ignition, men would ask for guns having flintlocks along with the newfangled cap locks.

It is probable that some of the men who bought the combination flint and cap guns they had demanded did so only because they feared they might run out of caps when more could not be had quickly.

Guns with these combination locks are hard to come by. It seems that many gunmakers experimented with the dual ignitions, but that only two makers, both English, produced more than a few examples. Sampson (or possibly Samson) Davis was one; Ezekiel Baker was the other. The Davis lock was patented in 1822; the Baker lock, though apparently about a year earlier, was not patented as far as I can learn.

Brief reference to the Davis lock was made in Chapter III, when it was mentioned as the first percussion-cap lock pictured in an English patent. What was called the Devolving Pan lock, patented by Sampson Davis, British patent of 1822 numbered 4648, is shown in Plate 70. A flash pan and a nipple are both contained in a piece pivoted on the lock plate. This piece may be turned so either the pan will be in line with the chamber vent for flint ignition, or the nipple will be in line for percussion ignition. The lower jaw of the flint cock was made large and acted as the hammer which detonated the cap when the "movable touch-hole piece" was turned so the nipple was in proper alignment for percussion ignition. Certainly the Davis and the Baker combination locks, and probably all the other similar locks, were designed to use copper caps. However, it is true that the Davis lock in particular could in an emergency have been made to function with one of the paper caps stuck to the wide concave lower jaw of the hammer. It is perhaps interesting to notice that the name "copper cap" did not come into use quite as early as the product. The cap was "detonating priming" in the Abridgement of Specifications for the Davis patent: "The charge may be fired by detonating priming placed on the nipple . . ."

The early patented caps were of copper—Deboubert's *chapeau de cuivre*—but not all metal caps were copper. A few sportsmen used iron caps. The elder Greener made a strong plea for iron caps in his *Science of Gunnery*, published in 1841. In his next, his last, book, which came seventeen years later, *Gunnery in 1858*, Mr. Greener omitted any reference to iron caps, but he did say, "Copper caps are now a misnomer: very few are to be met with. Brass caps boiled to the colour of copper are the rule".

Which is the ignition the shooter primarily relied on in these guns with combination locks? I had thought it likely that as long as the caps held out the percussion system was first choice, and the flint system would be the one in reserve. However, when I studied the features of the Baker lock, I concluded it was Mr. Baker's idea the flintlock would be the one commonly used, and that caps would be resorted to only if the flintlock was not functioning satisfactorily. There is a little lever, pivoted on the lock plate, which could well be dispensed with if the man firing the gun intended to keep the flint as the ignition in reserve, but which seems to be at least strongly desirable if the intention was to have the cap ignition held in reserve in primed readiness.

Two views are shown of this Baker lock. Plate 71 shows the pistol with the steel—or what we now call the frizzen—covering the pan, and with the cock raised, ready for firing by flint. Plate 72 shows the steel raised and out of the way, and with the hammer having descended on the nipple to explode the cap. It can be noticed in the second illustration the nipple has moved forward—less than a half-inch, but enough to get it at a point exactly in the curve made by the small striking nose under the lower jaw of the flint holder. It can perhaps be noticed in the photograph that the small pivoted lever has also changed its position in relation to the nipple. The bar of steel containing the nipple and the flint pan was moved forward by pushing ahead the knob that protrudes below the block on which the bar slides. In the Davis lock the hammer that strikes the cap is simply a much thickened lower jaw of the cock. In the Baker lock it is a separate piece of metal secured under a normal lower jaw.

Alongside the nipple on the Baker lock there is a small depression with a tiny hole in the bottom. This leads to the space between the nipple and the touch hole. The little lever previously mentioned has a small cover on its end which ensures the tiny hole is stoppered when the sliding bar is in position for flint use, Plate 71, but that the hole is not plugged when the bar is in position for cap use, Plate 72. Men who shoot the muzzle-loaders frequently put a little 4F priming powder through the nipple when they want to make doubly sure there will be no misfire. It is surmised this tiny vent alongside the nipple was there to give the shooter added percussion priming. The small cover would be desirable if the shooter were to prime his gun for both flint and cap ignition and then use the flint ignition first, because without the cover the sparks from the flint would probably set off the priming powder under the nipple. It seems the little cover was constructed so it could not close the tiny hole when caps were used because with the hole unplugged a safety feature was provided: the open hole would let excess gas escape if too much of the fine priming powder had been used. If the surmises are all true, it reasonably follows that the shooter generally tried the flint ignition first, and held the percussion ignition in reserve.

The markings on the Baker pistol should be mentioned, "Baker London" on the barrel, and "E. Baker 1821" on the lock plate. The date is the year before the Sampson Davis patent, the first patent in England that showed a percussion-cap nipple.

An undated pair of pistols with combination flint and cap locks is shown in Plate 73. These are English screw-barrel pocket pistols,

Birmingham proved, marked "Mabson, Labron & Mabson". A thickened lower jaw of the cock, like that on the Davis pistol, serves as a striker for the cap. This is the only pair I know of constructed so the pistols could be fired as flintlocks only, as cap locks only, or as flint and cap locks together. The upper of the pair is ready for firing with cap ignition; the lower, for firing with flint ignition. The upper pistol has a cap on the nipple; the lower does not have. If a cap were placed on the nipple of the lower gun, that gun would fire with both flint and cap ignition with the pulling of the trigger.

In addition to guns that permitted a choice of either flint or percussion ignition without any change of lock, there were guns that permitted interchanging of locks, so the sportsman could quickly substitute a cap lock for a flint, or vice versa. Such a lock for percussion ignition is shown in Plate 74. This lock does not permanently convert a gun from flint to percussion. It is one of a set of two locks that give dual ignition. The other of the pair is, of course, a flintlock that may be put in place of the cap lock in a moment's time with the aid of a screw-driver.

In the 1820's in England some guns were also made that could be fired either with a metallic percussion cap or with loose powder. The idea was to provide an alternative if caps could not be obtained, as it was with the makers of locks using either caps or flints. A drawing of such a gun appeared on the front page of the London *Mechanics' Magazine* for February 5, 1825, and is reproduced in Illustration I. I should like to call attention to the fact that though many drawings in early nineteenth-century periodicals were of uncompleted and sometimes manifestly unworkable inventions, this drawing is of an actual gun that had already been well tested. The editor of *Mechanics' Magazine* stated, "We have prefixed . . . a side-view and sections of the Lock of the Gun, with the inspection of which we have been kindly favoured . . . and which may be seen by any of our readers at 55, Paternoster-row, during the ensuing week". The gun was supplied with a nipple for caps, and also a cup for percussion powder, as well as with "screws", or firing pins, of two lengths. The man, unidentified except as "S. R.", who sent the gun for examination, stated it "was made by Mr. Beckwith two years back". To explain the operation of the lock, S. R. said: "If the sportsman is inclined to use a copper cap, the nipple is put into the breech, and a short screw is put into the hammer. If, however, no caps are to be got, and the sportsman has some percussion powder, or wishes to use it instead of a cap (which powder is most convenient for use when made into a small pellet or ball, the size of a large pin's head),

Mechanics' Magazine,

MUSEUM, REGISTER, JOURNAL, AND GAZETTE.

No. 76.] SATURDAY, FEBRUARY 5, 1825. [Price 3*d*.

" Ingenious Art, with her expressive face,
Steps forth to fashion and refine the race.
Not only fills Necessity's demand,
But overcharges her capacious hand.
Capricious Taste itself can crave no more
Than she supplies from her abounding store;
She strikes out all that Luxury can ask,
And gains new vigour from her endless task." *Cowper.*

BECKWITH'S PERCUSSION GUN.

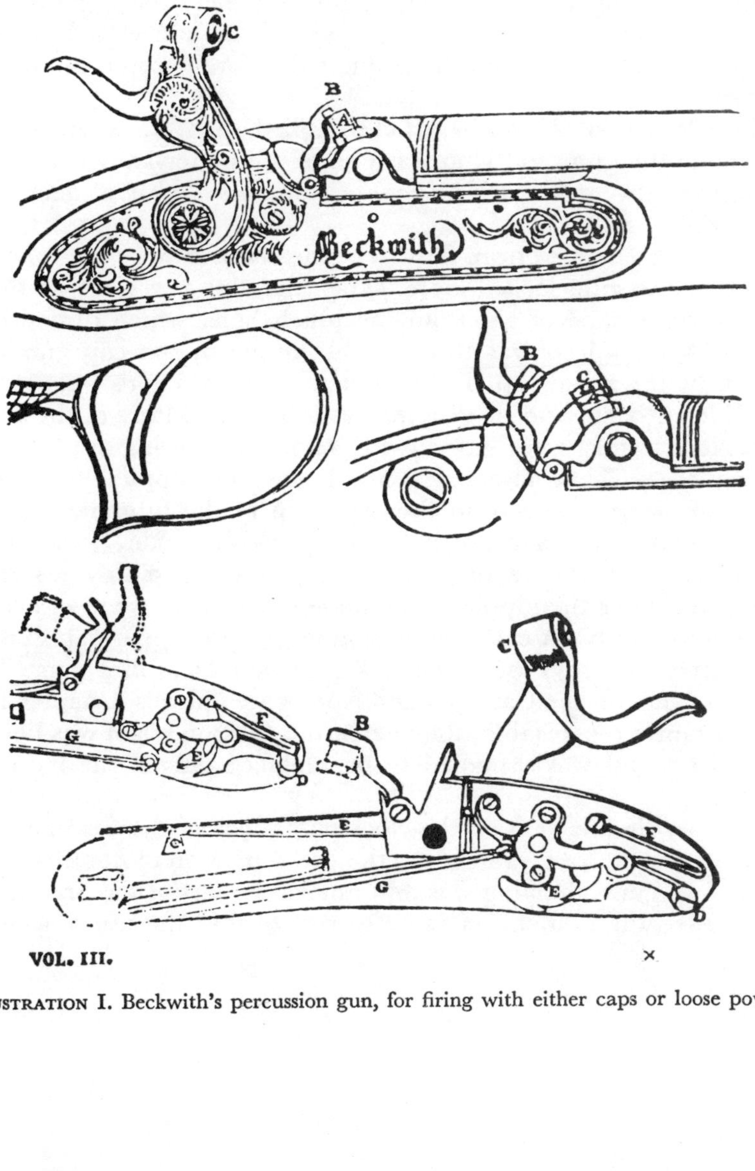

ILLUSTRATION I. Beckwith's percussion gun, for firing with either caps or loose powder

then the nipple is taken out and the cup screwed into the breech in its place, and a longer screw put into the hammer to reach the pellet in the cup; and to prevent the pellet falling out of the cup, or the copper cap from coming off the nipple, as the hammer is drawn up from the cup or nipple after loading, a small cap falls down and covers the cup, so that no wet can touch the priming, which cap rises up and makes way for the hammer when the trigger is pulled". The "small cap" that "falls down and covers the cup" is like the cover that was later used in the Shrapnel gun, described in the previous chapter.

A popular demonstration of this gun "to prove the rapidity with which the hammer falls upon the cup" involved priming with loose powder, covering the cup, cocking the hammer, turning the gun over, and pulling the trigger. The cover of the cup would get out of the way and the priming be detonated before it could fall out of the cup.

The *Mechanics' Magazine* article implied that W. A. Beckwith, who made the gun, and who was one of the better-known London gunsmiths, also made self-priming detonators "with a magazine sliding on a bar".

Men who changed from flint to percussion cap were apt to complain that cap guns kicked more. When the flint gun went off there was a large escape of gas from the touch hole, which diminished recoil. The escape of gas through the nipple in the cap gun was shut off by the metal cap. The hammers of the cap guns were sometimes blown back, and in extreme cases broken. Many of the early percussion pistols were fitted with hammers having replaceable striking noses. They also had vents below the nipples, to permit escape of gas resulting from the explosion of the fulminate in the cap. In Plate 75 is a pistol by a good British maker, Jackson, of Nottingham. This has a platinum plug pierced by a tiny gas vent, to be seen under the nipple in the photograph. This vent was commonly found only on early percussion guns. On copper-cap guns it was a carryover from the patch-lock guns, and from flint guns. The hammer noses on the Cartmell and Nock patch pistols, Chapter III, were instantly replaceable; the one on the Jackson pistol was tightly screwed on and was supposed to be replaced only if the hammer broke.

The needle-fine vent on the Nock patch-lock pistol was in a plug made removable for cleaning. On the Jackson, as on most other early copper-cap guns, the plug was an immovable part of the breeching. About 1830 the gunmakers came to realize that the use of a vent, while it reduced the kick, also reduced the power of the charge. Stronger mainsprings, and uniformity in strength of caps, removed the trouble of blown-back and broken hammers, and so the vents for gas escape were discontinued, and so were the detachable noses, at about the same time.

The Samuel & Charles Smith gun in Plate 76 has a hammer with a demountable nose, but the gun achieved a measure of fame not because of the hammer but because of the special cap and nipple. The cap, called "Smith's Patent Imperial Cap", and so marked, was patented in 1830, British patent 5978. The cap was made much wider and flatter than an ordinary cap, and the patent claim was simply for the placing of the priming in a small indentation in the centre of the inside surface of the top of the wide cap. This idea of concentrating the priming in a small area and sending its flash through a shorter channel was well received by British sportsmen.

One of the earliest types of British pistols to use copper caps is the one made by Fisher, of Bristol, shown in Plates 77 and 78. This pistol is not a conversion from flintlock though it looks like similar pistols that were conversions. It was made when caps were first produced and when there was little uniformity in nipples and caps. When a nipple was to be capped the hinged guard, which resembles the frizzen on a centre-hammer flint pistol, was pushed up, as in the first illustration. When pressed down and in firing position, as in the second illustration, the guard held the cap securely. For this type of lock the "top-hat" cap, one which had a "brim" like that on an opera hat, was preferred.

The use of guards to retain caps on nipples while carrying hunting guns in the field was not unusual. Such guards are less frequently found on pistols. A fancy German pistol, equipped with both a shoulder stock and a nipple guard, is shown in Plate 79.

Some of the early locks were of singular appearance. In Plate 80 is the invention, British patent 6046 of 1830, of John George Lacy and Samson Davis. I suspect this Samson Davis is the same as Sampson Davis who invented the Devolving Pan lock eight years earlier. The patent covers the application of a bent lever to gun locks, to take the place of the conventional tumbler. As may be seen, the bent-back lever has notches in it for retaining the hammer either at half or full cock.

Makers never did come to agreement as to whether the nipple should be set in the breech from the top, from the side, from underneath, or from directly in the rear. As a result we find that though most hammers struck downward some struck up, some struck sideways, some struck straight ahead, and some even struck backwards.

The type of lock most frequently found on cap-lock muzzle-loaders has the hammer striking downward with the nipple either vertical or tilted back about halfway between horizontal and vertical. Plate 81 shows the type. The pistol is one of a pair made in Liège in 1867 by Julian and engraved by Potgisser for Emperor Leopold II and shows the extraordinarily fine workmanship of which the best Belgian makers were capable.

The underhammer guns which had the nipples below the barrel were moderately popular both in Europe and America. Three American underhammer bootleg pistols are shown in Plate 82. An advantage of the underhammer construction is the decreased danger of being hit in the face by fragments of metal if a cap flies in pieces. A disadvantage is that a badly fitting cap is more likely to drop off.

An altogether unusual firearm which has both top-hammer and underhammer locks is pictured in Plate 83. This unmarked, apparently European gun has two side-by-side octagon barrels over one round barrel. The trigger guard for the triggers for the two top hammers is itself the trigger for the underneath hammer. It is hardly the safest of guns, but it is an interesting oddity.

Hammers and nipples are visible on underhammer guns here illustrated. The hammer and the nipple are usually in sight on a side-hammer lock, but on the unmarked side-hammer pistol in Plate 84 the hammer and the nipple are concealed, and the trigger is also concealed. When the ring on the side is pulled the folding hammer comes out and locks in the cocked position, as does the folding trigger. The breech is recessed, slightly to hold the bar hammer, and deeply to hold the nipple out of sight.

In most percussion guns the nipples were at an angle to the barrel bore. Some guns were made with the nipples set in the centre of the barrel breech in line with the axis of the bore, so the flash from the cap went straight to the middle of the powder charge. Those guns, made forty years before modern centre-fire cartridges were known, were called centre-fire guns. An early centre-fire gun that was well thought of in England was the Charles Jones. An example is shown in Plate 85. The strikers, which drive straight ahead to hit the anvils set in the centre of the barrel breech, are concealed and are actuated by the external cocking levers, one of which is seen cocked in the photograph. There is a sliding cover which must be drawn back when the gun is capped. This cover is what made the gun so popular. When pushed forward it prevented flying pieces of a broken cap getting in the shooter's eyes. The gun had one most unusual and probably unique feature. The caps had the fulminate on the outside of their closed ends, not on the inside, and they were installed on the hammer noses, not on the nipples.

Guns with hammers that strike backward were frequently produced in the Tyrol both in flint and in percussion cap, but rarely were they made in any other part of the world. A Schuetzen rifle from the Tyrol, full stocked and of outstanding quality, with the hammer reversing the usual motion in firing, is pictured in Plate 86. The lock has a very intricate hair-trigger assembly which may be set to go off at a touch much more delicate than an ordinary man can control. With the trigger set the gun may be fired either by touching the forward trigger or by pressing a button set in the stock just ahead of the lock plate. There is a large protective fence above and in back of the nipple.

It may seem that early gunmakers took unneeded precautions against flying bits of copper, but it should be remembered that early caps were apt to shatter and that many a man who took chances had an eye blinded.

Another gun designed to confine the particles of a shattered cap to a small enclosed space is shown in two Plates, 87 and 88. This was made and patented by George Stocker and Joseph Bentley in England, patent 8024 of the year 1839. It might be called a hammerless centre-fire cap gun. There is no external hammer or cocking lever. There is a long firing pin within the stock which is retracted when the large reversed trigger is pressed forward. When this large trigger is in its forward position a pivoted cover may be raised and the nipple may be capped, as shown in the left-hand view of the gun, Plate 87. Extending down from the middle of this cover is a baffle plate with a small hole in its centre. This baffle provides an added safety feature. It prevents the firing pin getting through to the cap except when the cover is closed and the hole in the baffle comes in line with the pin.

One more example of guns which required no external cock and which were designed to ensure the shooter would not be hit by flying fragments is shown in Plates 89 and 90. This gun, patented in England in 1829, British 5845, by David Lawrence and John Crundwell was made in London by Crundwell & Co. and provided an extra feature, a safety in back of the trigger guard which must be pressed when the trigger is pulled in order to release the cocking lever for firing. Just ahead of this cocking lever is a small rectangular metal plate, or gate. In Plate 89, which shows the gate open for capping, you may be able to see the end of an uncapped nipple. Opening the gate cocked the gun. In Plate 90, which shows the gate closed, the nipple has disappeared and you see only a vent for gas escape. This hiding of the nipple gives protection to the shooter. When the gate was closed the nipple was turned through 90 degrees, and lined up between the small striker and the touch hole in the centre of the barrel breech.

Most collectors know that for many years, especially in the days of flint guns, Spanish barrels were considered superior to barrels made in any other country. Wealthy sportsmen of the different European countries ordered new guns made up around fine old barrels of any famous Spanish maker. The entire gun would be new, except the barrel and possibly metal furniture of exceptional merit. Such a gun, equipped with a rare Madrid lock in percussion, is shown in Plate 91. Most Madrid locks are in flint. The peculiarity of the Madrid lock is that it has two sears coming through the lock plate, one acting on the breast of the cock and one on the tail. It has some resemblance to a miquelet lock, but it has its mainspring inside the lock plate. The new gun with its new lock was made by Esteban and is marked with the date 1838; the barrel is signed by Bustindui and dates about 1780; the trigger guard is signed by Zegarra and also dates about 1780.

A single-shot pistol with double percussion-cap ignition is pictured in Plate 92. The piece is French, marked "Correvon à Yverdon". There are two nipples, both leading to the single powder chamber. The hammer is bifurcated and has two noses. When the trigger is pulled two caps will be detonated at the same time and the slight possibility of a misfire will be substantially lessened.

An added point of interest in the pistol is its long dagger, shown locked in position for attack. The blade may be folded and fastened out of the way under the barrel.

CHAPTER VII

BREECH-LOADING CAP GUNS

BREECHLOADERS firing self-contained metallic cartridges and breechloaders firing separate-primed cartridges both had their first great tryout in the American Civil War. No more than passing mention will be made in this volume to the guns in that struggle that fired fixed ammunition—such famous rifles as the Spencer and the Henry—but in this chapter or in Chapter IX will be found examples of all makes of capping breechloaders approved and put in service by the Union forces in the Civil War. I have chosen to place all capping breechloaders in two main categories, those that use only caps which are placed on nipples one at a time by hand, and those that have auxiliary primer magazines. The guns in this latter category will be found in Chapter IX, which will be devoted to many forms of cap, tape, and disk magazine primers employed both with muzzle-loading and with breech-loading firearms.

The capping breechloaders which use only hand-applied caps, and which are pictured in this chapter, I have placed, for convenience, in the minor categories listed below. After each category designation, I will list the names of the apposite firearms identified in this chapter, with the names in *italic* type of those guns actually used in military service by the North in the Civil War.

Top Lever: Pauly, *Joslyn*, *Merrill*
Tilting Barrel: Renette & Gastinne, *Maynard*, *Smith*
Rotating Breechblock: *Burnside*
Chamber Loading: Lobnitz, Larsen, Leetch, Mont Storm, *Hall*, *Lindner*
Sliding Breech Bolt: Marston, Terry, Westley Richards, *Jenks*
Sliding Barrel: Prince, *Gibbs*, *Gallager*
Dropping Breechblock: *Starr*

Tilting Breechblock: *Gwyn & Campbell*
Bolt Action Underhammer: *Greene Rifle*

Just what is a capping breechloader? It is a gun loaded at the breech and fired by means of a percussion cap set on an external nipple. In this country the best known of all capping breechloaders is probably the Sharps.

A gun which has its percussion cap placed on a breech-loading cartridge, as the Pottet has, rather than on an external nipple, is a percussion-cap breechloader, but I shall not class it as a capping breechloader.

Because it seems proper and because it is customary to include what W. W. Greener called "chamber loaders" among capping breechloaders, I too shall do it. Chamber loaders have the barrels cut into two sections, one long and one short. The short section is at the breech and is loaded from its front end. Such guns, of which a notable example is the *Hall*, are sometimes called muzzle-loading breechloaders.

Percussion-cap revolvers, short or long, are chamber loaders and are in a sense capping breechloaders, but no revolvers will be discussed in this chapter.

When guns were first made it was realized there were advantages in loading at the breech rather than at the muzzle. Many of the earliest guns, those using match ignition, were breechloaders. Around 1750 the majority of flint hunting rifles made in England were probably breechloaders, being of the screw type exemplified by the Ferguson rifle.

A truly successful breechloader, one that would not cause endless trouble by reason of gas escape at the breech, was out of the question until percussion ignition arrived. All during the percussion era there was sporadic use of breechloaders. The first detonator breechloader to use a self-contained cartridge was the Pauly, described in Chapter II. The first capping breechloader may also have been a Pauly.

Let's give attention to the early percussion-cap breechloaders that are prized by collectors because of their history, unusual construction, or dependability, before getting to the military capping breechloaders, those of the Civil War especially.

One gun which is a breechloader using a percussion cap, but not what a collector calls a capping breechloader, is the Pottet. The Pottet, of which a superb example complete with two interchangeable barrels and supplied with a shoulder stock is shown in Plate

93, is the earliest instance of the use of a copper cap as part of the cartridge. The two small objects in the centre of the illustration are cartridge cases. Another picture of a Pottet cartridge will be found in the final chapter of this volume.

Two misstatements have often been made regarding the Pottet invention. One is that the patent was obtained in 1857, the other that the Pottet was the first firearm to employ a metallic centre-fire reloadable cartridge. The Pottet patent for both the gun and the cartridge was actually taken out in France by Clément Pottet on March 3, 1829, and was patent 3930. (French Patents—Series 1, volume 39, page 165, plate 17.) Pottet was not the first to make a gun to use a metallic centre-fire reloadable cartridge. Pauly was the first, in 1812, with his gun with fulminating powder tamped in the centre of a cartridge head. Pottet was first, however, to patent a gun that successfully fired a metallic centre-fire cartridge with a copper cap attached to it. It should be stressed that the Pottet cap was simply an adjunct, pressed by the fingers on a nipple built into the cartridge head: the cap was not a fixed part of the cartridge.

Pottet had been a workman for Pauly, and his gun shows the Pauly influence. It is a breechloader with an external cocking lever and an internal striker much like Pauly's. In his patent specification Pottet illustrated two kinds of cartridges and said either could be used. One kind had an anvil for a cap in the form of a nipple; the other had a depression in the head into which fulminate could be pressed (*pressée dans le petit bassinet*) as was done in the Pauly cartridges.

Now let's look at a top-lever capping breechloader bearing the Pauly name. Pauly was surely the first maker of guns firing self-contained cartridges, and guns bearing his name were probably the first breechloaders using metal caps. This Pauly double-barrelled percussion-cap shotgun, probably produced very soon after 1820, is pictured in two views, the lock section in Plate 94, and full length in Plate 95. (According to Deane, in *Deane's Manual of the History and Science of Fire-arms*, it would appear that the first use of an external nipple and cap in Pauly guns was by Picherau, a successor to Pauly who was himself succeeded by Lefaucheux in 1826.) Guns of this type bearing both the name of Pauly and the name of one or another of Pauly's successors are in existence, but the piece pictured here bears no name other than that of Pauly. Deane says the nipple and the cap were the invention of Deboubert. Deboubert's invention was patented in 1820. This capping breech-loader has the same breech action as Pauly's earlier fixed-cartridge gun, but this gun is supplied with a rod carried under the barrels, whereas the earlier cartridge gun made no provision for carrying a cleaning rod. The earlier Pauly had rabbeted chambers to take rimmed self-contained cartridges; this gun does not have rabbeted chambers and takes cartridges that are neither rimmed nor self-contained. The operation of the gun requires little comment. When the pivoted arm is raised the barrel chambers are accessible; when it is pressed down the nipples are in line with the chambers.

Another double-barrelled French shotgun, produced by Renette & Gastinne, is shown in Plate 96. This is a tilting-barrel type, later than the Pauly, and uses an improved and much favoured method of locking the barrels to the frame. The cartridge has a cardboard case with a metal head having a flame hole of about $\frac{3}{16}$ inch diameter in the centre. The metal head is covered with thin paper which prevents loss of powder through the flame hole. There is a projecting metal knob about $\frac{1}{8}$ inch high in the centre of the inside face of the standing breech, and there is a vent leading from the nipple through the middle of this projection. When the loaded gun is closed by means of the lever under the trigger guard the projection breaks the paper on the cartridge head and the passage for flame to the charge is uninterrupted.

An interesting capping breechloader, certainly among the very early ones, is shown in Plates 97 and 98. It is marked as having been made in Kiobenhavn (Copenhagen) by N. Lobnitz. The French Pauly has the nipples on an arm which pivots on a stationary barrel, the Danish Lobnitz has a movable barrel with the nipple set in a rigid breech. This rare gun is one of a pair.

Most breechloading guns are opened either by sidewise turning of the barrel or by depressing the muzzle. The Lobnitz is opened by raising the muzzle after a release lever is pressed upward. A most important feature of the Lobnitz construction is that when the gun is opened the barrel moves not only up but also a short distance forward and away from the chamber. When the gun is closed, by turning the lever back to its position alongside the barrel, the protruding mouth of the chamber enters the barrel. The construction results in a joint almost completely leakproof.

The Lobnitz was a chamber loader form of capping breechloader, but it was unlike most chamber loaders in that the chamber was not itself turned for loading. The powder chamber is in the standing breech, in back of the barrel breech, so that the powder was not loaded in the barrel itself.

A capping breechloader that is highly rated by collectors, whether it be in rifle, shotgun, or pistol form, is the sliding-breech-bolt Marston. Two models of the Marston rifle and one model of a Marston shotgun are shown in Plate 99. A Marston pistol is pictured in Plate 100. The vertical lever, with its curved end extending to the butt of the pistol, would, when drawn or pressed forward, pull back a sliding breech bolt and give space at the side for insertion of a cartridge in the chamber. The cartridge is interesting and was probably the first American one having a greased base which was driven through the barrel as a swab by the next discharge. The cartridge, for the pistol shown, is of paper and has at its base a well-greased leather disk with a small hole in its centre to permit the flash from the cap to reach the powder charge. Each loading pushes the leather disk of the antecedent cartridge to the chamber mouth and discharge then causes the disk to clean the fouling from the barrel. The disk is slightly greater in diameter than the barrel bore and requires the mechanical force of the lever to force it into the barrel. At the front end of the lever there is a bushing which surrounds the rear of the cartridge and prevents gas leakage. The breech bolt is held firmly against the cartridge at the time of its discharge. Mr. Marston effectively employed the principle of the arch to resolve a vertical pressure of a lever to a horizontal thrust of a sliding bolt.

The January 8, 1853, issue of the *Scientific American*—an issue still on the shelves of many large libraries—has an interesting and well-illustrated article on the Marston guns and cartridges. The following month, in the February 19th issue, there is a supplemental report telling of the success of a trial of a Marston rifle in England. It would seem the idea of a greased leather disk to clean the barrel was sound, for one sentence of the notice reads: "On the first trial, persons unaccustomed to the use of this rifle fired 100 shots in 15 minutes, and after firing a thousand shots the bore was perfectly clean".

Up to this time no description has been given of a Civil War capping breechloader. It may be well to precede the introduction of the first one by setting forth the manifest superiority of the breechloader in warfare.

The many considerations, of which speed and ease of reloading and cleaning were foremost, that made the sportsman prefer the breechloader in hunting, also made the soldier prefer it in war. In addition, the soldier might have some one shooting back and he might become more agitated than any hunter with buck fever. If someone were shooting back he did not want to present a standing target or expose himself more than necessary. He could reload a breechloader while in motion or when prone. He had a difficult task if he tried to load a muzzle-loader without coming to a halt or while lying on the ground. If he had to stand to load a muzzle-loader his realization that he presented a better target might hurry him and might make him heedless to a point where his unreliability strained credulity. Proof of the mental block and disorientation in men under fire was given by their actions at Gettysburg. On that battlefield it is said 150,000 men were engaged, and from that battlefield after the engagement 27,000 muzzle-loaders were collected. Of those it was reported 24,000 were loaded. The further report, the one that proved the case for breechloaders, was that, of those 24,000 muzzle-loaders, 12,000 were double-loaded. Of the abandoned breechloaders none was double-loaded, because none could be double-loaded.

Actually, of the final 12,000 muzzle-loaders a large proportion were charged with from three to ten loads, and many had the bullet rammed in the barrel ahead of the powder.

The breechloaders did away with the nuisance and hazard of a ramrod. The ramrod being dispensed with, there was no shooting it away because the soldier in his excitement had forgotten to withdraw it from the barrel.

Muzzle-loaders were quite unsuitable for cavalry. Most of the breechloaders could be rapidly reloaded by a cavalryman even while sitting on a restive horse.

I will attempt to include, as part of the remainder of this chapter, descriptions of one each of all the principal makes of capping breechloaders of American manufacture used by Northern forces during the Civil War, except those using priming magazines. Some of these rifles and carbines were rugged, accurate, and very efficient in operation, and received acclaim. Some fine guns failed to get proper recognition and support, and some had nothing to recommend them. Many makes were produced in both rifle and carbine types. Some were made only in rifle form, and some only as carbines. As mentioned earlier, the American guns which saw service in our Civil War will have their names in *italic* type.

Of capping breechloaders in the sliding-breech-bolt category, like the Marston already described, the only example among the Civil War guns is the *Jenks*. It is strange that no other American martial firearm was made in that construction. Two British military rifles of the sliding-breechblock type, the Terry and the Westley Richards, attained fame.

Some of the *Jenks* percussion guns were equipped with Maynard primers. The carbine in Plate 101 was not supplied with any priming magazine. *Jenks* carbines used in the Civil War by the Navy and probably by some units of cavalry had the action patented by William Jenks, May 25, 1838, United States patent 747. A few of the first ones, in flintlock, went in military service in 1839. In addition to being the only sliding-breech United States carbine, the *Jenks* was the only "mule-ear" gun put in service by our forces. Raising a lever caused a sliding breech bolt to move back, permitting loading the chamber with loose powder and ball.

I prefer to class the *Jenks* as a sliding-breech-bolt type, but it could as well be classed as a top-lever type.

A later *Jenks* conversion is called the *Jenks-Merrill.* This has an improvement which permits loading with a paper cartridge and also replaces the "mule-ear" hammer with a conventional side hammer. What the conversion looked like will be shown in the picture of the top-lever *Merrill* (Plate 111).

Plate 102 shows a Terry rifle, made by Calisher & Terry, London. This has a sliding breech-bolt and is sometimes referred to as a bolt-action rifle. The Southern forces in the Civil War brought many of these carbines and called them the "door bolt guns". A lever, when turned, raised, and pulled back, exposed a cavity in which a cartridge was dropped. When the lever was closed it plunged the cartridge into the chamber to a point where the centre of the side of the cartridge was under the flame hole in the nipple. The base of the paper cartridge was made of tallow-saturated felt. Mr. Terry's object in having the powder ignited in the centre, instead of at the end, was to detain the wad in the barrel while the bullet was being ejected. The ball from the next cartridge would force the wad out of—and at the same time lubricate and clean—the barrel. The system worked well. Jewitt reported in *Rifles and Volunteer Rifle Corps* that a Terry carbine tested on H.M.S. *Excellent* in 1858 fired 1800 rounds without cleaning.

A Westley Richards sliding-breech-bolt carbine is shown in Plate 103. This is often called the "monkey tail" gun. There is a hinged arm which when lifted to a vertical position withdraws a plunger and permits manual insertion of a cartridge in the barrel chamber. When the lever is pressed down, the plunger slides forward until its front end fits as a plug in the chamber, and its rear end bears solidly against an extension of the barrel, preventing the action's blowing open. The cartridge for the Westley Richards was similar to that fired by the Terry. It had a grease-soaked wad at the base which acted effectively as an obturator and which was driven out by the bullet in the next charge.

The Westley Richards carbine was the official British cavalry arm before the Snider was adopted. It was the first British official arm in which the cartridge itself was designed to do the work of stopping escape of gas at the breech.

Percussion-cap chamber loaders were produced in many styles. Four varieties from Europe (apart from the already described Lobnitz) as well as two United States martial rifles will now be shown.

The *Hall* chamber loader was the first gun loaded at the breech to be adopted by any nation for its armed forces. The *Hall*, with flint ignition, was patented by John Hall, May 21, 1811. It was issued in small numbers to United States troops in 1826.

According to the inventor's description: "The barrel is in two pieces. That which forms the breech rises at its fore end upon touching a spring, or by any other method which may be found more convenient". The charge was rammed down this short part of the barrel, which was called by Mr. Hall the "receiver".

The particular *Hall* rifle shown, Plate 104, has percussion-cap ignition and is supplied with the fishtail lever improvement for opening and closing the receiver.

The collector with an investigative mind will find several unusual, often overlooked features in a *Hall*. If he rub his finger around the barrel bore at the muzzle he will find it smooth. If he then look through the barrel he will probably find it rifled, but not quite to the muzzle. If he will check the muzzle calibre with the bore of the "receiver" he will find the latter is of greater diameter. A bullet of slightly more than barrel-bore diameter was used, so that gas from the powder explosion would not escape past the bullet and be wasted. A careful check will show the barrel bore to be slightly tapered, funnelling to greater calibre at the breech end. The *Hall* was furnished with a set trigger; one that could be adjusted by means of a screw to whatever weight trigger-pull the soldier liked.

Of much greater importance than these features just mentioned was the fact that *Hall* rifles had interchangeable parts. John Hall was a pioneer in advocating interchangeability of parts, and he vigorously fought any minor changes in design that might cause parts of one gun not to fit another gun of the same model. Deviations in sizes and shapes were not tolerated.

The other American military chamber loader is the *Lindner.* Plate 105 shows one of these guns with its chamber tilted for loading. It was put in the position shown by turning from right to left the flat round knob to be seen just in front and below the muzzle of the chamber. To put the chamber in shooting position, it is pressed down with a thumb and held while the knob is turned from left to right. The knob is fastened to a cylindrical casing which covers the front end of the chamber and holds it in place when the knob is at the right. The mechanism was patented March 29, 1859, by Edward Lindner, United States patent 23,378, and the gun was manufactured in Manchester, New Hampshire, by Amoskeag Manufacturing Company.

A Larsen chamber loader, the underhammer arm adopted in the 1840's by Norway for military service, is pictured in Plate 106. The chamber is tilted by means of a lever having an eccentric action that forces the chamber mouth hard against the barrel breech to prevent gas escape.

Another chamber loader of Belgian provenience which attracted favourable attention both in Europe and in the United States was the Mont Storm. One of these rifles, with the chamber open, is shown in Plate 107. It will be noticed that the Mont Storm, unlike the other uptilting chamber loaders, has the chamber hinged at the front so that when in loading position it lies flat on its back. As a result of this unfortunate design a cartridge could be, and sometimes was, inserted wrong end first. The chamber when in firing position was held by a stout bolt actuated by the hammer. Mr. Mont Storm was granted United States patent 15,307 on July 8, 1856. There has been some misunderstanding about this patent. It should be noticed that the patent dealt with the conversion of percussion-cap muzzle-loaders to percussion-cap breechloaders, and not with conversion to rim-fire breechloaders.

Plate 108 pictures an English chamber loader which does not have the chamber tilt upward, as do the chambers on the four chamber loaders just described. In this gun, the Leetch, brought out in 1859, the chamber turns at the side, much as the cylinder swings out in a modern solid frame revolver. Contemporary authorities praised the gun but, though it was designed for the service cartridge, it was not accepted for military service. (The inventor's name is sometimes found spelled "Leech".)

Still another type of chamber loader is the Spanish sporting gun, Plate 109. As the photograph shows, the chamber turns sideways.

Two top-lever Civil War capping breechloaders are the *Joslyn* and the *Merrill*. An 1855 model *Joslyn* is shown in Plate 110 with the lever raised to permit insertion of a paper cartridge. The lever on the *Joslyn* is much like the lever on the earlier Pauly guns. It normally rests, latched, in a mortise cut in the stock. It is raised after the hammer is put at half-cock, by sliding the oval ring forward to release the latch and then pulling the ring up. This gun was patented by B. F. Joslyn, August 28, 1855, United States patent 13,507.

The percussion-cap *Joslyn* carbine was used in less numbers in the Civil War than the later model *Joslyn* which used rim-fire cartridges. The rim-fire arms of the Civil War do not come within the scope of this volume. An exception will be made later in the case of the (American) Henry rifle.

The other top-lever Civil War carbine, the *Merrill*, is pictured in Plate 111. As the photograph shows, the lever is pulled up and back to open the breech. Its front end latches under the base of the rear sight. The breech bolt, which seats a combustible paper cartridge in the chamber when the lever is lowered, has a copper face which acts as an efficient gas check. Mr. James H. Merrill, the inventor of this breech-loading system was granted several United States patents. The system was applied to new guns and was also widely used to convert many guns from muzzle-loading to breech-loading.

Perhaps the best Civil War capping breechloader was the tilting-barrel *Maynard*. A *Maynard* carbine, one without a tape primer, is shown with one of the distinctive wide-rimmed brass cartridges partly inserted in the chamber in Plate 112. For further description of Maynard arms and cartridges the reader is referred to Chapters IX and XII.

The second of the tilting-barrel Civil War carbines was the *Smith*, Plate 113. This gun, patented by Gilbert Smith, August 5, 1856, United States patent 15,496, was designed to fire either a cartridge with a rubber case or one with a paper-wrapped foil case. This gun opens for loading across the middle of the chamber. The cartridge is pressed back into the standing-breech part of the chamber, with the bullet protruding. When the gun is closed the bullet end slips into the barrel part of the chamber. The barrel is held closed by a long spring catch lying over the barrel and hooked to a lug in the standing breech. The catch is released by pushing up a lifter located just in front of the trigger. It should be mentioned that the *Smith* carbine which fired the oddly shaped Crispin cartridges, the ones with the fulminate-filled belt, was a model different from that illustrated here.

A capping breechloader with a rotating breechblock that used an all-metal cartridge—and some say it was better than the *Maynard*—was the *Burnside*. Of the single-shot Civil War carbines only the *Sharps* was purchased by the North in greater numbers. A late model *Burnside* is pictured in Plate 114. At the time Ambrose Burnside, the inventor, designed his first breech-loading rifle, he was a lieutenant in the United States Army. In 1852 he resigned his commission to devote his time to his invention. In 1856 he obtained United States patent 14,491, and in 1857 he saw his carbine rated best in a competitive test at West Point of 18 breech-loading rifles. Burnside formed a company to manufacture his carbine, but apparently he did not make contributions to the right people in Washington. He failed to get more than token Government orders, and his firm went into bankruptcy. When the war broke, orders were plentiful and manufacturing was resumed on a large scale. Burnside returned to Army service and a distinguished career. He became General Burnside, Commander of the Army of the Potomac, and after the war he was elected Governor of Rhode Island.

When the trigger guard is lowered, as shown in Plate 114, a cartridge may be dropped in the breechblock. Raising the trigger guard to its closed position will move the breechblock forward and seat the bullet end of the cartridge in the barrel chamber. The merit of the gun lay largely in its peculiarly shaped cartridge. At the moment of firing, the metal case of the cartridge effectively sealed the joint between the breechblock and the barrel, preventing the disconcerting gas escape which was sure to take place with continued firing of breechloaders using paper or linen cartridges. A *Burnside* cartridge is described in Chapter XII.

We now come to the sliding-barrel capping breechloaders. Two American carbines, the *Gibbs* and the *Gallager*, one English carbine, the Prince, and one European shotgun will be shown here.

Plate 115 exhibits a Prince carbine, patented in England in 1855, with the chamber open, ready for loading. When in firing position the lever with the knob on the end rests against the front of the trigger guard, where it is locked in place by a bolt on the bow of the guard. To open the chamber the little bolt catch is released, the knob is pressed to the right and forward. A sturdy plug on the standing breech has lugs which lock into recesses on the inside of the rear end of the barrel when the lever is drawn back.

The Prince may or may not have been the best of all the many fine arms that failed to be adopted for military service, in England and elsewhere, but it almost surely came out better in tests and received more praise from authorities than any other gun that similarly failed to be adopted. The Prince defeated other guns in both official and unofficial tests, in durability, accuracy, and rapidity of fire. A group of the most highly esteemed gunmakers of the time, including John Blanch & Son, John Blissett, George Fuller, John Manton & Son, Samuel Nock & Co., Parker, Field & Son, Henry Tatham, and Henry Wilkinson, signed the following testimonial:

> We, the undersigned, being actuated by no other motive than a desire to see the most effective weapon in the hands of our soldiers, and having beyond that no interest whatever in Mr. Prince's breech-loader, do hereby attach our names for the purpose of attesting our belief that its principle is beyond comparison the best we have seen for a breech-loading gun, and in our opinion quite free from those practical objections existing in all the breech-loaders previously introduced.
>
> From its extreme simplicity, we also deem it well adapted to withstand the exposure to wet and to rough usage incidental to a military weapon, while the cartridge itself being waterproof, adds to its superiority.

A double-barrel shotgun with unexpected and fascinating features is shown in Plates 116 and 117. This sliding-barrel gun bears neither proof mark nor maker's name. I would guess it is French.

The right hammer is shown fully cocked. Until I saw this gun I thought fully cocked always meant in position to be fired by trigger pull. In this gun *fully cocked* means in safety position, where trigger pull will not drop the hammer. To put the hammer in firing position it must be eased up to an intermediate notch, an operation requiring careful attention. The nipples are another startling feature, and in common with the hammers have little to recommend them. Instead of being drilled through, the nipples have their tops closed. The fire from the cap, instead of travelling straight through, has to turn through a small hole in the side of the nipple and pass through a hole in the breech, to reach the powder charge. If the nipple is tightened too much, the two holes will not coincide and the gun will probably misfire.

In Plate 116 the gun is shown opened, with the fastening wedge having been drawn out of the keyway by a pull on the large loop.

Removal of the wedge permits sliding the barrels a short distance on a centre pin and turning them for loading. The barrels must be turned completely over when loading.

The *Gibbs* carbine shown in Plate 118 may be called, and is by some, a tilting-barrel capping breechloader. I choose to call it a sliding-barrel type because, though its barrel does tilt for loading, it also slides forward. I prefer to reserve the tilting-barrel classification for those arms whose barrels tilt but do not move forward. Depressing the trigger guard to the position shown in the illustration causes the barrel to rise and move forward. United States patent 14,057 was granted L. H. Gibbs for his invention on January 8, 1856.

The *Gallager* carbine, the other sliding-barrel Civil War capping breechloader, was patented by Mahlon J. Gallager, July 17, 1860, United States patent 29,157. It is like the *Gibbs* in that the barrel moves forward and tilts when the trigger guard is depressed, as Plate 120 shows. The tilting occurs after the forward movement ends. The cartridge chamber is made one half in the standing breech and the other half in the barrel. The cartridges used were cylindrical and made of all brass, or, more commonly, of paper-wrapped brass foil. After a shot was fired and the gun opened, a fired case would protrude from the part of the chamber to which it had adhered, and could be withdrawn.

The *Gibbs* used combustible cartridges, with envelopes of either linen or paper, but the *Gallager* used metal, or paper and metal, cartridges that required extraction after firing. Like the Maynard and Burnside Civil War cartridges, the Gallager cartridge had a flash hole in the centre of the base to permit flame from an external cap to reach the powder. None of the guns that used these metal cartridges had suitable extractors. The Maynard cartridge had a wide rim that was easily grasped; the Burnside fired case would usually fall out if the gun was turned over; the Gallager cartridge usually required prying out.

The records indicate the troops did not have the high regard for the *Gallager* that they had for the *Burnside* and the *Maynard*. The *Burnside* and the *Maynard* were excellent guns of their type, but they were inferior to the Civil War guns that fired self-contained cartridges, such as the Ballard, the Henry, and the Spencer rifles.

The carbine most heavily bought by the United States in the Civil War was the dropping breechblock *Sharps*. As all *Sharps* percussion-cap arms were equipped with either pellet or tape magazines, the descriptions of *Sharps* arms will be given in Chapter IX, along with descriptions of other magazine primer guns.

A total of 89,653 *Sharps* shoulder arms was bought by the United States from January 1, 1861, to June 30, 1866, according to the U.S. Ordnance reports. Most of these *Sharps* were carbines, and by far the most were designed for separate-primed cartridges, either paper or linen. A few at the end of the war were using self-contained copper cartridges.

The only Civil War breechloader that was bought in greater numbers was the famous Spencer repeater. From January 1, 1861, to June 30, 1866, 106,667 Spencer shoulder arms were purchased.

The reader may be interested in some figures showing how total purchases and fabrications of shoulder arms were split between muzzle-loaders and breechloaders.

The grand total of all shoulder arms purchased by the North in this country and abroad, in the period from January 1, 1861, to June 30, 1866, was 3,104,184. This figure includes 801,997 Springfields fabricated by the United States, not bought from contractors.

Of this total of 3,104,184, very nearly 2,681,000 were muzzle-loaders, and just over 423,000 were breechloaders.

Of the 423,000 breechloaders approximately 265,000 were capping breechloaders and 158,000 were users of self-contained cartridges. (*Sharps* accounted for one third of the capping breechloaders, and Spencer accounted for two thirds of the self-contained cartridge guns.)

Stated in percentage, 5 per cent plus were modern-type cartridge breechloaders, 8 per cent plus were capping breechloaders, 86 per cent plus were muzzle-loaders.

The other Civil War capping breechloader of the dropping-breechblock type was the *Starr*. Plate 119 shows one with the trigger guard unlatched and pressed down, so that the pivoted breechblock has started to drop back to expose the chamber for loading.

The *Starr* carbine was patented September 14, 1858, by Eben T. Starr, United States patent 21,523.

The Civil War's tilting-breechblock carbine was the *Gwyn & Campbell*, shown in Plate 121. This arm, patented by E. Gwyn and A. C. Campbell, October 21, 1862, United States patent 36,709, bore other names. It is frequently called the Cosmopolitan carbine because it was manufactured by the Cosmopolitan Arms Company of Hamilton, Ohio. Sometimes it is known as the Union Rifle, because it is so marked. Occasionally it is known as the Gross carbine, after Henry Gross who patented improvements. It is also called the Grapevine carbine because of the shape of the trigger guard. Pushing the trigger guard down causes the breechblock to tilt down at the front, as shown in the illustration, so it is easy to push a cartridge along its groove and into the chamber.

The *Greene* rifle in Plates 122 and 123 should not be confused with the Maynard-primer-equipped Greene carbine to be described in Chapter IX. Except that both guns were bought for military use—the rifle by the United States and the carbine by England—and that they were both invented by the same man, they have little in common. The carbine is reasonably conventional; the rifle is astonishingly unconventional, not in appearance but in construction, method of operation, and type of cartridge used.

The rifle, patented November 17, 1857, United States patent 18,634, by J. Durrell Greene, sometime Lieutenant-Colonel in the U.S. Army, surely has more peculiarities and innovations than can be found in any other martial weapon.

Anyone who looks through the barrel of a *Greene* rifle will see a smooth bore with no lands or grooves. So that it may be understood why the gun is called a rifle, I quote from an 1864 U.S. Ordnance report on the *Greene:* "The bore is elliptical in shape, and the rotary motion is imparted to the bullet by giving the longest diameter of the ellipse a turn of three-fourths in the length of the barrel. The oval form is too slight a variation from a perfect cylinder to be perceptible to the eye, and the appearance of the barrel, on looking through, is precisely like that of a smoothbore musket. But by placing one of the bullets (which are cast round, and assume the elliptical shape on entering the barrel) into the muzzle, and looking through from the breech, a slight crescent of light will be perceived on each side of it".

The *Greene* was the only oval-bored rifle adopted by the U.S. Army. The oval-bore system of rifling was developed in England by Lancaster perhaps twenty years before Greene imitated it. At this point it should be mentioned that the *Greene* was also the first bolt-action and also the first underhammer rifle adopted by the U.S. Army.

The cartridge for the *Greene* rifle was unique. It completely reversed accepted practice. Normally, when a cartridge is properly placed in a barrel breech, the bullet is in front of the powder. When a Green combustible paper cartridge was pressed in the chamber of a *Greene* rifle the bullet was in back of the powder. Consequently, when a Greene cartridge was fired, the bullet in that cartridge was not expelled from the barrel.

To ensure that no one will think Colonel Greene was demented, or that the United States was bereft of reason in buying such an invention, it is necessary to explain the firing of a *Greene*, starting with an empty rifle. A button on the breech tang, which locked the bolt and prevented firing unless the bolt were home, was pressed down, permitting the bolt handle to be turned up and the bolt drawn back. With the bolt back, a hollow-base expanding bullet was dropped in the receiver. The bolt was moved forward to its original closed position but the bolt handle was not then turned down. Forward pressure was continued on the bolt handle, and an auxiliary rod, or inner bolt, moved ahead to seat the bullet. This position is shown in Plate 122. Again the bolt was drawn fully back, and, after a cartridge was placed in the receiver, was moved forward sufficiently to push the cartridge into the chamber. The bolt handle was turned down, the ring hammer was cocked by a pull with the index finger, the nipple was capped, and the gun was ready to fire when the trigger was pulled. Plate 123 shows this position. On pulling the trigger the forward bullet left the gun, but the bullet at the base of the just discharged cartridge had not moved, and it had served as an efficient gas check. It was now ready to be pushed forward and fired by the next cartridge.

The *Greene* rifle was supplied only to a few troops and had little influence on the outcome of the Civil War, but its cartridge did create high excitement among some Confederates who wrongly assumed the foremost end was the bullet end, and who thought the big end of the bullet, not the point, was the striking end. Those men went on to reach the wildly false conclusion that the hollowed end of the bullet contained poison and was placed foremost so the poison would be spread around the wound.

The capping breechloaders which bear makers' names, twenty-three of them so far described, are all noteworthy. Undoubtedly there are a few others of genuine importance. Some guns that were tested and peremptorily rejected for military service were later proved to possess solid merit. They should be in the noteworthy class. On the other hand some guns that, in service, fell far short of expectations should also be in the noteworthy class, because they had, after all, been tested, approved, and purchased by the military.

It is difficult to assess the importance, consequence, value, or fame, of such pieces as the two pistols, both chamber loaders, now pictured.

The pistol in Plate 124 is marked "A. Knocke In München" on the barrel and "K. B. Privlegt 1848" on the chamber. The chamber rises vertically for loading as the trigger guard is lowered.

The chamber loader in Plates 125 and 126 is of fine, though

distinctly unusual, construction. To load this piece a heavy striker lying alongside the barrel breech is first drawn back against pressure of two coiled springs. When a lever in back of the breech is then pulled back and turned up, as in Plate 125, the chamber is swung to the left for loading. After loading and capping, the chamber is swung back into firing position by turning down the lever, as in Plate 126.

In addition to the breech-loading and the muzzle-loading guns which used percussion caps to ignite charges of powder, there were other guns which used no gunpowder charge, but depended on the propellent force of the fulminate in a cap to send a projectile to its mark. Such guns were used mainly for indoor target shooting and will be described in the next chapter.

CHAPTER VIII

INDOOR TARGET PISTOLS

ALL of the percussion-cap guns set forth in Chapters VI and VII used the cap solely to ignite a gunpowder charge which was the propellent in the barrel.

In this chapter a few short-range pistols and rifles that use no gunpowder will be described. The propellent in these guns is simply the fulminate in the cap. Pistols of this type, which dispensed with a gunpowder charge, are called saloon pistols. In the days when they were fired indoors at targets the word saloon referred not to the corner grog shop, but to a large elaborate reception room. The English "saloon" is synonymous with the French "salon". These small-calibre guns were designed for use in rooms in homes. Their successors, the target duellers, which fired heavy bullets with charges of gunpowder, were designed for possible use in duelling but chiefly for practice in public shooting galleries.

Some saloon pistols were muzzle-loading; some were breech-loading. A German muzzle-loading pistol of very simple construction but with a finely carved stock is shown in Plate 127. The barrel takes a round pellet of ·17 calibre, with no powder charge. The fulminate in a cap placed on a nipple which is screwed into the centre of the barrel breech provides propellent force sufficient to permit hitting a large bull's-eye at twenty or thirty feet. The striker is a solid steel block with no protruding spur for cocking. To cock the hammer a separate tool is employed. Its end is thrust in a hole in the striking block, and the tool is pulled back. The illustration shows the tool in use.

It is not completely impossible that the original gun had a spurred hammer and that the owner became tired of seeing it snapped by untutored guests. These so-and-so's would be frustrated when handed a gun they could not snap without a separate tool which the owner carefully did not supply.

A scarce early form of French saloon pistol is shown in Plates 128 and 129. In Plate 128 a breechblock pivoted to the rear of the barrel is shown swung open so a cap may be placed on the nipple on one side of the block and a pellet inserted on the other side. Pressure on the trigger guard permits opening of the gun. An external cocking lever operates an internal striker having a wide flat circular nose.

A peculiar saloon pistol, equipped with set triggers, by the famous Austrian maker Contriner, is pictured in Plate 130. A lever on the side of this pistol is shown turned partly down. The part of the lever back of the screw which holds it is irregularly shaped so as to push an inner striker back along a slot against spring pressure. The lever when pushed fully down cocks the gun and also uncovers a cavity into which a ball is dropped, followed by a copper cap. The cap does not go on a nipple; it is pressed in a hole as a cartridge is pressed in a breech chamber. Only when the lever is locked alongside the barrel will the gun fire.

The pistol in Plate 131 has a separate holder for the cap. This holder, which is inserted in the breech has a spider in it which supports the nipple on which the cap is placed. As may be seen in the photograph, there is a small bar fastened to the holder to lock the holder in place when it is inserted in the barrel.

Pistols were more frequently made for indoor target practice than were long guns. An American shoulder gun that uses no propellent other than fulminate in a cap is the lower of the two guns in Plate 132. This was made by William H. Forker, of Meadville, Pennsylvania. The cap is placed on a nipple fixed in the centre of the barrel only six inches from the muzzle. The striker is a long rod which is cocked by depressing the trigger guard.

The upper gun in Plate 132 is a German *Zimmerstutzen* which fires a percussion cap in the form of a very small rimmed cartridge which is inserted in a special holder shown below the gun. Perhaps this should be called a cartridge gun, but no powder is used. Like the other gun in the picture, it has a long striking rod, but in this gun the rod is attached to a hammer of conventional form. The gun is pretentious though it is incapable of accurate shooting at a range of more than a few feet. The gun is of Schuetzen pattern and is equipped with set triggers. Nothing more than a plain open sight is warranted, but instead there is a peep sight adjustable both for elevation and windage.

A rare Remington pistol is shown in Plate 133. This is a feeble pocket pistol; it cannot properly be called a saloon pistol. True, it fires a cap and not a cartridge, but it was not designed for target shooting. Joseph Rider patented this firearm September 13, 1859, United States patent 25,470. The barrel is counterbored at the breech, to permit loading in it a metal breech pin which is combined with a cap tube. Projecting from the breech pin there is a lever which drops into a notch in the stock and thereby prevents the breech pin from falling from the counterbore. The notch is wide enough to permit short longitudinal movement of the pin. To prepare the pistol for shooting the hammer is cocked, the breech pin is withdrawn, a ball of about ·17 calibre is inserted in the barrel breech, a cap is placed on the nipplelike cap tube within the breech pin and the breech pin is returned to the counterbore. When the trigger is pulled the pin is driven forward until the cap tube bears against the front of the counterbore and the cap is exploded.

CHAPTER IX

TAPE, DISK, AND CAP MAGAZINE GUNS

ALL the guns described in Chapters VI and VII were primed by putting caps on nipples, one at a time and by hand. The task was time-consuming and consequently slowed the rate of fire. Often a man, fumbling in the cold with numbed fingers, was exasperated by the time that fled while he tried to fix a little cap on a little nipple.

From the 1500's on many gunmakers attempted to increase rate of fire with repeating guns. As long as they had to depend for ignition on sparks produced by flint rubbing on steel, just that long a truly successful repeater was out of the question. With the coming of percussion ignition, and in particular the copper cap, successful repeaters were just around the corner, and one of the two methods of getting increased rate of fire was at hand. This method involved multiple charges and was first used in percussion-cap pepperboxes and revolvers. An Allen double-action pepperbox could not discharge a large number of shots in a minute, but its rate of fire was high because it could get four, five, or six shots away as fast as the trigger could be pulled. Then, with fixed ammunition came a host of repeaters, Colts, Spencers, Winchesters, Mausers, and the like, and finally machine guns.

The other of the two methods that increased rate of fire involved the use of automatic primers. Automatic primers eliminated the time lost in priming by hand—at least until the primer magazine was emptied. Automatic primers were used on both muzzle-loading and breech-loading guns. When used on cartridge-loaded capping breechloaders they greatly increased rate of fire, but they were all quickly discarded when guns firing fixed ammunition were ready.

Some of the primer magazines, both American and European, fed copper caps to the nipples. Still others developed on both sides of the Atlantic fed fulminate in strips of tape. Some American inventions had the fulminate enclosed in individual disks. Other American inventions had fulminate pellets in magazines reminiscent of the magazines on the early European detonators.

A study, without a practical test, of either the Christian Sharps American disk primer or the Heurteloup European tape primer, if made by anyone who has never heard of either primer, will convince that student that neither primer could work. But, a hundred years ago, both primers were in use and functioning highly satisfactorily.

Let's look first at guns having automatic primers which fed ordinary copper caps to the nipple.

Of obsolete American long guns the most renowned type is the Kentucky, the most renowned make is the Sharps. No other single-shot breechloader in the Civil War was produced and used in such large numbers. After that war the Sharps won added fame in the West where the buffalo hunters preferred it, and in the East where it was first choice of United States teams who shot in the international rifle matches. The first Sharps rifles were primed with automatically fed copper caps. Only on the first model was there a magazine for conventional copper caps. All subsequent models, up to the time Sharps took up fixed ammunition, were equipped with automatic magazines for either tape or disk primers, first one and then the other. The gun in Plate 134 is a first model Sharps. Illustrations of tape-primer, and then disk-primer, models will come later in this chapter, in their separate places.

Christian Sharps (1811–1874) obtained United States patent 5763, dated September 12, 1848, for a "Breech-Loading and Self-Capping Rifle-Gun". The finished product, a modification of the patent design, was manufactured in Mill Creek, Pennsylvania, by a gunmaker named Nippes, whose first name is a matter of controversy. The lid of the large nearly round brass-cap magazine shows clearly on the first model Sharps in Plate 134. Under the lid is a wheel, notched to hold caps at its edge. (The lid is pushed up and the wheel lifted out of its recess when the capping device is to be re-armed.) To load the gun, the breech, which has a nipple at its top, is dropped by pushing the long lever under the trigger guard fully forward. When the breech is down the wheel in the cap magazine turns, as a result of spring pressure, so that when the long lever is pulled back the nipple will pick up a cap.

Alonzo Perry obtained United States patent 12,244 of January 16, 1855, for a gun with a tubular magazine containing caps and running straight through the stock from the butt to the nipple on the cartridge chamber. Perry had a factory in Newark, New Jersey, where he produced several types of firearms, some with automatic cappers, and some without. He manufactured rifles, shotguns, carbines, and oddities that collectors call cane guns. It is generally believed that one variety of Perry carbines was manufactured in the South for the Confederacy, but there is some question as to the location of the factory—perhaps Tallahassee—and more question as to Perry's connection with it. No Perry carbines were adopted by the United States Army but they were purchased in sizeable numbers by sundry states for their troops.

A pure Perry pistol is shown in Plate 135. When the long double-curved trigger guard of this breech-loading pistol is lowered—the guard will not go to the vertical—the mouth of a swinging chamber, or what Perry called a "vibrating breech", comes up so a combustible cartridge may be loaded in it. When the cartridge is pushed home its powder end is torn open by a cone projecting from the base of the chamber. This cone, which is hollow and open at both ends, has one end running up and into the powder charge, and the other end connecting with the vent in the nipple.

A coiled spring in the cap magazine keeps the caps pressed forward, and when the trigger guard is fully down, forces one cap on the nipple. When the trigger guard is brought up and the hammer is cocked, the chamber is tightly in place. When the gun is fired the flame from the cap passes through the nipple and on through the cone, igniting the powder charge at the centre. More and more experimenters in this day are coming to believe the old-timers had the right idea in attempting to get the gunpowder ignited at the front, not the rear, of the charge.

I described this Perry pistol as "pure", because unfortunately many are tainted. Probably most of the Perry pistols in existence were made by cutting about twenty inches off the barrel of what is commonly called a Perry cane gun. That cane gun is much like a Perry pistol, except in length of barrel and in not having a cap magazine. Whether or not the gun was made to handle an automatic capper in the butt may be seen at a glance. Other slight differences between a genuine Perry pistol and an altered cane gun, such as the absence of a pierced cone in the chamber and the fact the trigger guard lever will swing the chamber to the vertical, are not readily detected on an altered gun.

Perry's concern with a "vibrating breech", and with a tubular magazine in the breech of a gun stock, went back at least to 1849. On December 11th of that year he obtained patent 6945 for a gun with a "vibrating breech" and not one, but four, tubular magazines, but then the magazines were to hold combustible cartridges, not copper caps. The four magazines, called tubes in the patent, were "attached together about a common axis . . . on which they all turn, that each of the tubes may, in succession, be brought in line with the hole or bore" in the "vibrating breech". The 1849 gun was to have "pills of fulminating-priming" automatically fed with the turning of the "vibrating breech". Perry's 1855 guns were successes, his 1849, failures. I wonder if an 1849 now exists.

An almost unknown type of Brown Bess, one with a tubular-cap magazine in the butt, is pictured in Plate 136. Though the magazine itself is much like the magazine in a Perry, the method of getting a cap on the nipple is altogether different. The self-capper on this Brown Bess was patented in England in 1842, British 9285, by Alexander Rousseau, who was then in business in the Strand in London. The mouth of the tube containing the caps is movable. The action of cocking the hammer swings the tube sideways to put a cap on the nipple. When the gun is fired the tube swings back as the hammer goes down.

Westley Richards obtained a patent in 1838 for a self-capper which was applied both to pistols and to long guns. Plate 137 shows such a primer on a carbine. Placing a cap on the nipple is an automatic action only in a limited sense. The action is performed mechanically but only after the magazine is pulled back and the knob pressed down with the fingers. The cap magazine lies alongside the barrel and is charged by the insertion at its forward end of a tube containing caps. After the nipple is capped, as a result of the knob being drawn back and depressed, the cap magazine "will instantly fly back into its quiescent position" when pressure on the knob is released.

Self-cappers of varying types and uncertain worth were produced by dozens of British makers. The last examples of many of these are gone beyond recovery. Two that were given trials are shown in the next two photographs. Plate 138 is of a Blanch gun with a lock reported to be a Ritchie self-capper. The capper does not conform to Ritchie's specification, British patent 12,648 of 1849, but finished products often vary greatly from patent descriptions. Another lock I know little about is depicted in Plate 139. The gun was catalogued in an English collection as having a Della Noce automatic capper. The Della Noce capper was tried briefly on a few French military rifles. It was patented in France in 1854. (French Patents—Series 2, volume 39, page 44, plate 7.)

Tape primers were made in far fewer types than were cap primers, but many more guns were equipped with the tape primers.

The best known and the most successful tape primer was invented by an American dentist, Dr. Edward Maynard, one more man in the roster of inventors whose primary interests were in professional fields having no relation to their inventions.

Dr. Maynard was born April 26, 1813, in Madison, New York, and died May 4, 1891, in Washington, D.C. He attended to the dental needs of several presidents, received various honorary degrees, and was awarded medals by European royalty. He made far-reaching discoveries in the medical field and had to his credit a little known invention in the firearms field that may have been more important than his tape primer with which we are now concerned. That little known invention covered a method of seating a long bullet in a cartridge so the axis of the bullet would coincide with the axis of the cartridge.

Guns that used Maynard primers will be described in this chapter, a few at length, the rest briefly or not at all. About the primers, and the special lock needed to feed the primers, let it suffice here to say that Dr. Maynard's 1845 patent claimed "Making primers . . . in a continuous series" and "The mode of . . . measuring out the primers by the movement of the lock". Illustrations and fuller descriptions of the primers, as well as of Maynard cartridges, will be found in Chapter XII. Maynard primers were fitted to primary U.S. martial arms and secondary U.S. martial arms, as well as to nonmilitary guns, long and short. Examples of Maynard, Jenks, Burnside, and Merrill martial arms which were not equipped with Maynard tape-primer locks were described in Chapter VII. All four were sometimes equipped with Maynard tape primers, but of these only one, the Maynard, will be shown here.

It should be mentioned that Maynard tape-primer locks are of two kinds. One feeds the individual primers by means of "fingers", the other by means of a "feeding wheel".

Many gun hobbyists have probably noticed that Maynard guns equipped with tape primers are scarcer than Maynard guns not so equipped. The common disuse may be a result—I am speculating—of a contract Maynard made with the United States Government, a contract which may have prevented his use of his primer on some of his own guns. Dr. Maynard turned over his "entire right, title, and interest" to the government for a final total of at least $75,000.

Maynard firearms were made by Maynard Arms Co., Washington, Maynard Gun Co., Chicopee Falls, and by Massachusetts Arms Co., Chicopee Falls.

Throughout the Civil War Maynard arms used outside-primed metallic cartridges. In later years outside priming, both copper cap and tape, was abandoned, and fixed ammunition employed. From about 1873 to 1882 an unconventional "heavy-head" centre-fire cartridge was used; from then on into the 1890's the cartridge was a conventional centre-fire. We are not concerned here with Maynard guns that used fixed ammunition but it is of interest to know that Maynard single-shots, whose construction was not materially changed from first to last, from the 1850's to the 1890's, were popular with shooters up to the time repeaters were being persistently demanded.

Various experimental outside-primed cartridges were tried out in the early Maynards. Finally, one primary type of cartridge, along with one variation of that type, was agreed upon. One peculiarity of the early Maynard sporting rifle in Plate 140 is that it was designed to fire either the primary type or the variation, whereas the Maynard military carbine made without a tape primer, the one in Plate 112, was designed for the primary type only, though use of the variation was possible. The fact that both guns were not designed to take the variation will be apparent to the collector who is familiar with the deviating cartridge, and who examines the fulcrum screw that holds the barrel in the frame. This pin on the Maynard which is not equipped with a tape-primer lock has a kerf in its head, to permit the use of a screw-driver, if a tool be needed to take the barrel out of the frame. The fulcrum screw on the gun which is equipped with the tape-primer lock has no kerf in its head. Instead, there is a hole through which a nail, or some similar implement, may be thrust to turn the pin if any tool be needed. (At least in theory, tools were not needed to take down a Maynard rifle.) However, the principal purpose of the hole through the head of the pin was to prevent loss of a cartridge. The unusual cartridge described in Chapter XII has a leather strap which was attached to the wide rim of the cartridge at one end, and to a hook at the other end. The point of the hook went through the eye of the fulcrum screw.

A man who shot these early Maynard guns could carry with him a supply of loaded cartridges, which would usually be of the conventional type with a wide circular rim, or he could reload fired cartridges with powder and ball as he went along.

Dr. Maynard's patent of December 6, 1859, 26,364, has a drawing of a cartridge complete with strap and hook, which he refers to as a "metallic cup". The patent says the cup ". . . may be connected to the perforated head of the fulcrum-screw by means of a strap or a chain, to be used with loose ammunition; or any number of flange-bottomed metallic cups of the proper size may be charged with powder and projectiles and be carried to the field by the soldier or sportsman for ready and rapid firing. Each of the aforesaid metallic cups must have a small aperture formed in the centre of its bottom to receive the priming-fire, which passes through the central perforation in the abutment of the breech-piece; and I have ascertained by practical experience that the filling of the small apertures in the bottoms of the aforesaid metallic cups with some greasy composition renders them, when charged, perfectly water-proof, while it does not in the slightest degree impede the entrance of the priming-fire".

The 1845 patent, 4208, was for a tape-primer lock which was at that time applied to muzzle-loading muskets. The 1859 patent, 26,364, was for an improved breech-loading gun to use the lock. Other patents having to do with firearms were issued to Dr. Maynard in 1851, 1856, 1860, 1863, 1865, 1867, 1869, and 1873.

The Maynard tape-primer lock was a late arrival at London's Crystal Palace Exposition in 1851, but still, of firearms exhibits, it ran second in interest only to Colt's revolver, according to a report in the January 29, 1853, issue of the *Scientific American*. Certainly, Colt's revolver was far out in front in public interest at this first of what we now call World's Fairs, but the unofficial second place given by the *Scientific American* to the Maynard primer may be credited to zeal. After all, the double-action British revolver by Adams and the pin-fire French pepperbox by Lefaucheux were on exhibition, too.

Two outstanding books on firearms by American writers were published in the 1860's, *Hints to Riflemen* by H. W. S. Cleveland, and *The Crack Shot* by Edward C. Barber. All well-known guns of the period, single-shots and repeaters, were described at length and their worth evaluated. Both writers endorsed the Maynard as having no superior.

There were several reasons why sportsmen held in high esteem Maynard guns of the type shown in Plate 140. Reloading the cartridges, with the assurance the bullet would always be exactly positioned, was a simple procedure. The gun was astonishingly accurate—even though it was a two-piece gun—and the bullets had uncommon striking power. The gun was light in weight and easy to carry or transport.

The Maynard pictured here, which is marked, "Maynard Arms Co., Washington", and which is stamped with only three patent dates, 1845, 1851, and 1856, may be quickly taken apart without tools, after the underneath lever is lowered to put the barrel in loading position. Maynard guns were regularly made so that a barrel of one calibre could be substituted without difficulty for a barrel of another calibre. This particular gun has three interchangeable barrels, with a leather holster to hold them. The barrels, two rifled and one smooth, each twenty inches long, are calibres ·35 and ·50 for ball, and ·55 for shot. Guns like this may sometimes be found in wood cases which contain, in addition to the three barrels, several cartridge cases having leather straps and metal hooks attached, as well as a powder flask, mould, and other tools, including the special bullet seater.

The Maynard rifle shown has a stock only one inch thick, and may be packed, in a valise, for instance, in a space 20 in. by 6 in. by 1 in.

A Maynard lock having the "finger", or "spring" form of tape feeder is shown in Plate 141. The gun is an 1855 model U.S. rifle musket.

An 1855 model U.S. pistol-carbine having a lock of the same design as that on the 1855 model musket is shown in Plate 142. The pistol lock is smaller and carries a tape with fewer primers. The pistol becomes a shoulder gun when the detachable stock is connected to it.

A Maynard lock having the "cog" or "feeding wheel" form of tape feeder is shown in Plates 143 and 144. The revolver was made by Massachusetts Arms Co. Two unusual features of this revolver, beyond the fact that it could be fired either with caps or with tape primers, are that it has but one nipple and that the cylinder is turned by hand after releasing it by pressing up on the stud in front of the trigger.

Well over 100,000 Sharps rifles and carbines equipped with automatic primers were manufactured. Probably the number of first model Sharps, which had copper-cap magazine primers (described earlier in this chapter) was well under 1000. There might have been a total of 10,000 Sharps that made use of the Maynard primer invention. All the rest had disk primers. The Maynard primers on Sharps were themselves, in outward appearance, of three types, but they were basically all the same and all of the "finger" type. The earliest of the Maynard primer Sharps is known as model #2. One of these second models is pictured in Plate 145. The facts about the place, or places, of manufacture of the second model Sharps are not clear to me. The March 8, 1851, issue of the *Scientific American* states these guns were being manufactured by Butterfield & Nippes, Kensington, Philadelphia. However, of the few examples of this model now in existence, some—and perhaps all except those quite unmarked—are marked "Maynard Gun Co., Chicopee Falls, Mass."

Second of the Sharps to use Maynard primers was the 1851 model shown in Plate 146. This is often called the "box lock" model, because it has a centre hammer, rather than a side hammer such as was used both on earlier and later models.

At this point it becomes increasingly difficult to be sure where some Sharps rifles were made. Guns marked "Sharps Rifle Manufacturing Co., Hartford, Conn.," may have been made by Robbins & Lawrence under contract. Probably all marked "C. Sharps & Co., Philadelphia" were made in Philadelphia.

Christian Sharps applied his disk-primer invention, described along with other disk primers later in this chapter, to his 1852 and 1853 models. His 1855 model, in Plate 147, again had the Maynard primer. The greater part, 5000 or more, of the 1855 models were military carbines shipped to England, and the odds are that most 1855 models in firearms collections will have British proof marks.

Another Maynard primer-equipped gun, Plate 148, of which the major output went to Great Britain, is the Greene carbine. (The Greene rifle, of widely different construction, was described in Chapter VII.) Nearly all Greene carbines, United States patent 11,157 of June 27, 1854, manufactured by Massachusetts Arms Co., Chicopee Falls, were shipped to England for use by the British cavalry, but they proved to be extremely difficult to load on horseback unless the horse stood still. Many of the 2000 exported Greene carbines came back to the United States, some recently. Pressing the forward of the two triggers to be seen in the illustration permits opening the breech for loading.

A Symmes carbine, United States patent 22,094 of November 16, 1858, is shown in Plate 149. It will be noticed its Maynard primer lock is different in appearance. No two makes of guns have Maynard locks quite alike. The Symmes is opened for loading by depressing an underneath lever.

An 1842 model U.S. martial pistol with a Maynard primer lock is pictured in Plate 150. The same unusually shaped lock is to be found on small numbers of early U.S. martial shoulder arms converted from flint. As far as Maynard locks on flint conversions are concerned, this is the "first type" Maynard lock. The "second type" is that shown on the previously illustrated 1855 rifle-musket.

All the tape-primer guns mentioned above were production models. The tape-primer pistol in Plate 151 was probably not a production model. The pistol is a true Philadelphia Deringer. It is a pistol made by Henry Deringer, not an imitation such as most collectors spell D-e-r-r-i-n-g-e-r.

The invention in Plate 152 is generally called a Ward primer. That designation is a little misleading. The tape primer used is, as Mr. Ward stated in his patent, a "Maynard primer". The Ward patent, United States patent 15,262 of July 1, 1856, covers a "Priming-Cock", or "Magazine-Hammer". The hammer is thick with a movable lid on the side and a recess under the lid in which a roll of Maynard primers is carried. The act of cocking the hammer feeds a single primer over the vent in the nipple. When the hammer falls the protruding portion of the tape is cut off and the primer detonated. The gun in the illustration is one converted from a U.S. contract musket to use the Ward invention.

One startling difference between the Maynard "tape primer" and the earlier Heurteloup "continuous priming" is that the Maynard invention had individual primers separated on the tape, whereas the Heurteloup invention employed a pewter tube filled from end to end with detonating powder. Baron Heurteloup, Dr. Maynard, and J. N. Ward all made use of a hammer having at the tip of its striking end a cutting edge which struck the tape or tubing a tiny fraction of a second before the flat part of the hammer nose hit the priming. The cutting edge struck the Maynard tape between the rounded lumps of fulminate. The cutting edge struck right through the fulminate-filled Heurteloup tube. Fulminate being at that time highly sensitive to rough treatment, one would fully expect such a blow to detonate, or at least slowly burn all the fulminate in the tube. However, Charles Louis Stanislas, Baron Heurteloup, a French subject living in England, discovered that fulminate made of chlorate of potash by itself, or in a mixture of 48 parts chlorate of potash to one part only of sulphur and one of charcoal, would not ignite when placed in tubes of soft metal, lead or pewter, and cut through. Commonly used mixtures, which had much higher proportions of sulphur and charcoal, were apt to ignite.

Baron Heurteloup was granted several British patents, and one American patent. His 1834 and 1839 British patents contained improper claims and careless wording. On January 7, 1842, he filed a "Disclaimer and Memorandum of Alterations" in which he withdrew the improper claims and corrected minor faults, such as the one referring to the priming as "continual", instead of "continuous".

The drawings of the Heurteloup invention, British patent 7980 of the year 1842, take up three sheets in a book whose pages measure approximately 26 by 19 inches.

Here are two illustrations of a gun equipped with a Heurteloup lock. The first, Plate 153, shows the position immediately after firing. The second, Plate 154, shows more clearly the part along which the fulminate-filled tube travels. Instead of the tube being coiled, as is the tape in a Maynard lock, it lies flat in a channel running through the stock under the barrel about a foot past the feed roller. Cocking the hammer moves a short segment under a nipple. When the underhammer drives up, the segment is cut off by the blade on the nose of the hammer, and then detonated by the flat part of the nose.

Now to guns using disk primers, and back to Sharps.

The theorist might argue it is impossible to cut through a fulminate-filled tube with a single hard blow without igniting all the fulminate. He would almost surely say it was a fantastic idea to believe gunpowder could be exploded by throwing a flat fulminate-filled disk in the air and having it caught in mid-air by a hammer which would then crush it on a nipple. Christian Sharps had the disk-throwing idea, and it was a good one.

Just how the Sharps disk primer operated can be seen in Illustration J, which is a reproduction of page 73 of *The Gun Collectors Letter*, issue 15.

An arrow points from A in figure 1 in this illustration to a sliding part which Sharps called a "driver". Cocking the hammer and thereby drawing the driver fully back, as in figure 1, causes a fulminate-filled disk to be forced to the top of the primer magazine.

Figure 2 shows the hammer falling and the driver being carried forward and pushing a disk out toward the nipple.

Figure 3 shows the forward movement of the driver stopped because a lug on the driver has turned a corner in the channel in the side of the hammer. The disk is flying free.

Figure 4 shows the hammer after it has caught the flying disk and detonated it on the nipple.

As Mr. Sharps pointed out, in his United States patent 9308 of October 5, 1852, it was necessary that the driver first push, then throw the disk with just the right force to ensure the disk would neither fall short nor overshoot the mark.

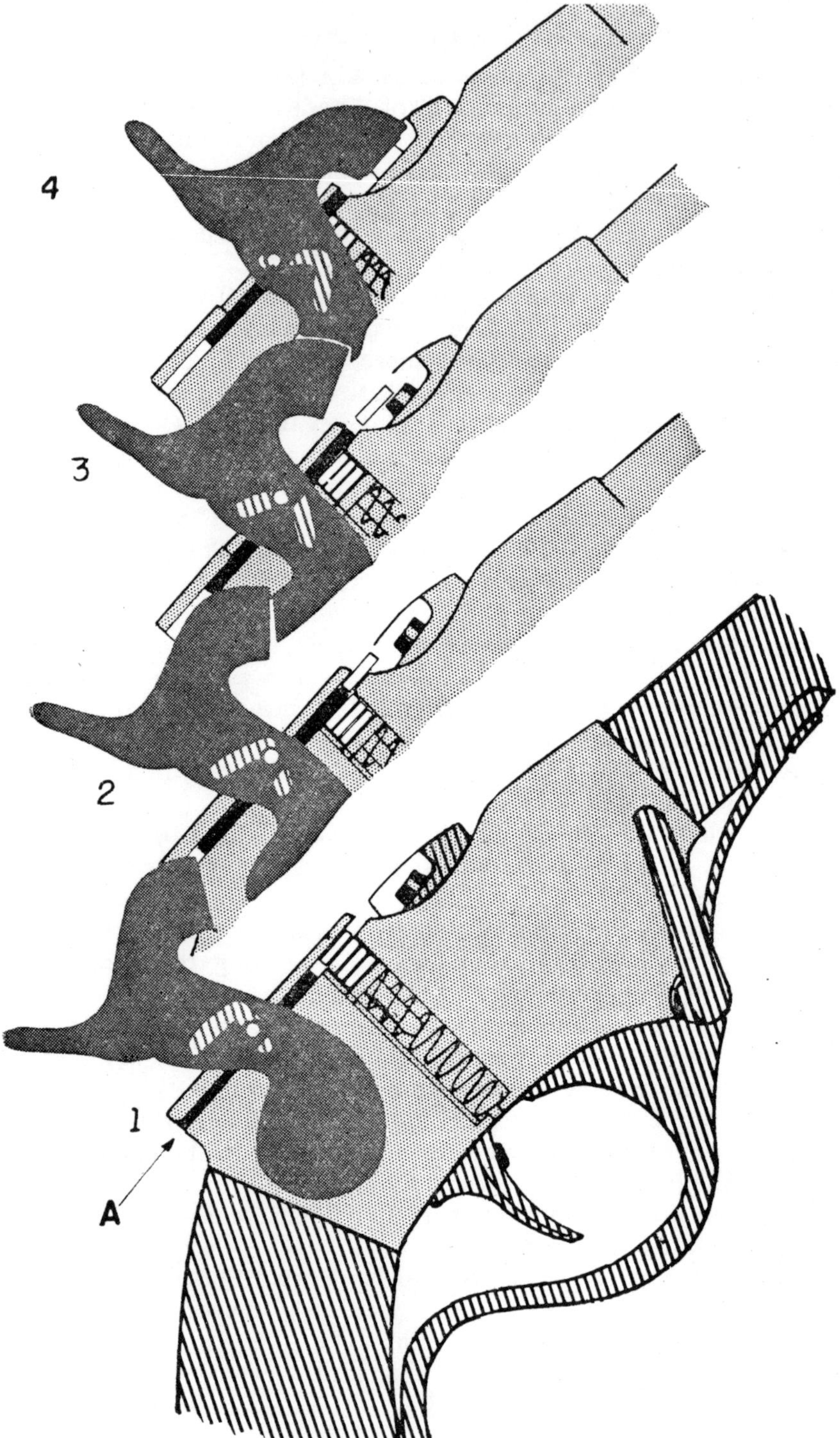

ILLUSTRATION J. Operation of Sharps disk primer

The unique construction of the disks is described, as are other forms of primers and primings, in Chapter XII.

A collector who studies both the functioning of a Sharps disk-primer lock and the construction of the disks, and who keeps in mind that the locks were in use well over one hundred years ago, will concede that Christian Sharps's invention was extraordinarily ingenious.

Earlier in this chapter it was pointed out that of the hundred thousand and more Sharps made with automatic primers, only about ten thousand altogether used tape or cap primers. More than ninety thousand had Sharps disk primers.

Two models that were almost alike were the 1852 and the 1853. These were of the slanting-breech type.

Two others that were almost alike were the 1859 and the 1863 models. These were of the straight-breech type.

An example of an 1853 model is pictured in Plate 155. This gun, as well as all the rest of the slanting-breech Sharps, is without the Lawrence cutoff which is found on the 1859 and 1863 models. This cutoff permitted the disengaging of the primer feed to allow the use of copper caps. The 1859 and 1863 models, which used the improvement patented by Richard Lawrence April 12, 1859, United States patent 23,590, are frequently but erroneously called Lawrence Primer Sharps. Strictly speaking, they are Sharps having Sharps primers with the Lawrence cutoff.

A straight-breech 1859 or 1863 Sharps like the one in Plate 156 is seldom seen, even in specialized collections of American carbines. The gun is fitted with a coffee mill in the butt. The government's plan—how well it was carried out I have no idea—was to have each cavalry company which was outfitted with Sharps carbines supplied with one "coffee-mill" Sharps. The coffee beans were poured in the mill through an opening underneath the stock. The ground coffee came out the side of the butt opposite the crank.

Plate 157 shows a Sharps pistol which, like all the Sharps long guns previously described, fires a combustible cartridge. This pistol, like the 1859 and the 1863 Sharps long guns, has a Sharps disk-primer lock with the Lawrence cutoff. The pistol is much scarcer than the 1859 and 1863 model long guns, considerably scarcer than any of the 1851, 1852, 1853, or 1855 models, but probably not as scarce as either the first or second model rifles.

Two other Sharps disk-primer rifles that are scarcer than Sharps pistols are shown in Plate 158. They are known to some as "pistol-rifles" and to others as "officer's models". They are different from all other Sharps firearms in that they fire outside-primed metallic, not combustible, cartridges. The upper gun was made to take a cartridge having a tiny vent in the centre of the base and a cord or wire loop attached to the edge of the base. The lower gun took a cartridge having a flange at the edge of the base, rather than the loop. The flange and the loop were intended solely to make easier the extraction of fired cases.

At the left in Plate 159 is a Sharps pistol: neither the barrel breech nor the breechblock is cut away. In the centre is a Sharps pistol-rifle: the breech bolt has been furrowed to give room for a loop. At the right is another pistol-rifle: the barrel breech has been mortised for the flange of a "mule-ear" cartridge.

The possibility is remote that any Sharps pistols were made from pistol-rifles. I have neither seen nor heard of any pistol that was cut away to take a special cartridge, nor of any pistol-rifle that was not so cut away.

Firearms with Butterfield disk primers are highly prized by discerning collectors. The total of such guns in collections—pistols, revolvers, and long guns—probably will run little over one hundred, and may fall short of that figure.

The "New and useful Improvement in Self-Priming Locks for Fire-Arms" was patented June 14, 1859, United States patent 24,372, by Jesse S. Butterfield and Simeon Marshall. The fulminate-filled disks were called pellets in the 1852 Sharps patent; they were called wafer-primers in the 1859 Butterfield patent. The sliding part called a "driver" by Sharps was called a "carrier or conductor" by Butterfield. One advantage of the Butterfield invention was that the carrier would cover "the vent when the hammer is raised for firing, thus protecting the vent from rain-drops when used in stormy weather". The one claim in the Sharps patent was for "throwing" the priming over the nipple. The Butterfield specification spoke of "conducting" the priming but made no claim regarding the method of getting the wafer-primer from the tubular "charger" to the touch hole.

It should be noted that the 1859 Butterfield patent covers improvements to the Butterfield lock patented December 11, 1855. Either patent date may appear on a firearm having a Butterfield primer.

The best-known Butterfields are the military revolvers like the one at the top in Plate 160. These are usually marked with the 1855 patent date and the Butterfield name, but some are unmarked. The revolver at the bottom is larger and heavier, and is the only one of its size known to exist. The upper gun is about 13½ inches overall and weighs about 2½ pounds. The lower gun is about 14½ inches overall and weighs about five pounds.

The Butterfields most sought after are derringers like those shown in Plate 161. They fit into a collection devoted to rarities, a collection specializing in derringers, a collection of oddities, or a collection designed to be of general interest.

Two interesting American muskets equipped with Butterfield primers are pictured in Plate 163. The upper gun was originally a Wickham flintlock dated 1832. The lower is an experimental breechloader which has a brass cartridge, on the style of a reloadable Maynard cartridge, attached to the breech.

The Butterfield primer was patented in England by Joseph Lemuel Chester of Philadelphia, Pennsylvania, British 2050 of 1858, and was applied to small numbers of Enfield rifles. An Enfield with a Chester lock is shown in Plate 162.

Jacob Rupertus took out two patents in 1859 for automatic primers, 23,711 on April 19th, and 23,952 on May 10th. In 23,711 he said he preferred to use priming in the form of "lozenge-like caps"; in 23,952 he referred to "caps or pellets or other priming". In both cases patent drawings clearly show disks, or wafers, in tubular magazines. Though the patent for the second type followed the first by less than a month the construction of the second type is markedly different.

The disk in a Butterfield is "conducted" to the nipple in a "carrier"; in a Sharps it is thrown by a "driver"; in a Rupertus it is deposited in a cavity in the hammer nose and carried forward in that hammer nose to be crushed against the nipple.

A revolver marked on the barrel with the name of the Philadelphia maker, Jacob Rupertus, and on the lock plate with the April 19, 1859, date is shown in Plate 164. This gun has the magazine for primers in the butt.

A Johnson 1842 model U.S. martial pistol fitted with the May 10, 1859, type of Rupertus automatic primer is reproduced in Plate 165. This gun has the magazine for primers contained in the hammer.

Compared to the number of Sharps primers produced, the number of Butterfield primers was small, and of Rupertus primers inappreciable. Another primer produced in insignificant quantity was the Gedney. In Plate 166 there is another Johnson pistol, this one fitted with an automatic primer believed to be a Gedney. It has no identifying markings, and it does not look quite like the patent model—which is now in the Smithsonian Institution—but its construction does closely conform to the specification in Mr. Gedney's United States patent 23,241 of March 15, 1859. It would seem that a "continuous priming", similar to that used in Heurteloup guns, would work in this pistol, and Mr. Gedney stated in his patent, "the priming is a cylinder of fulminate", and he spoke of "the piece of priming which has been severed from that in the magazine" by a blow of the hammer.

There were several other automatic primers that did not get beyond the experimental stage. Mostly, these unsuccessful automatic primers were designed to supply priming in the form of pills, but several failures were disk-primer inventions.

William H. Bell took out at least three patents for automatic primers, two in 1859—the first dated January 18th—for mechanisms having the priming magazines contained in the hammers. Colonel Gluckman states in *United States Muskets, Rifles and Carbines:* "There is a notation of a Washington contract of January 25, 1859, with W. B. Bell" (probably the same as W. H. Bell) "for application of his primer to 3000 arms at compensation of $2000. No data is available and it is not believed that the system was adopted".

The 1859 Bell inventions were not radically different from other self-primers of the period, but his 1860 invention, United States patent 27,518 of March 20, 1860, was undeniably different. The model submitted by Mr. Bell when he made his patent application is shown in Plate 167. His specification included, "The main invention which I have developed is adapting the stem on which the cylinder revolves to containing or supplying the wafer continuously to the cap-nipples of revolving fire-arms". A point weighing against adoption of this invention was the fact the barrel must be taken off to re-arm the primer magazine.

The only Colt revolver I recall having seen equipped with a disk primer is the 1860 Army, serial 4340, in Plate 168. Unfortunately, I have no information as to where, when, or by whom the primer was fitted to the revolver, and I am not sure as to who invented the primer. It may have been Rupertus.

In the United States, manual priming with pills, as in the punch-lock guns mentioned in Chapter IV, was successful, but most attempts to use fulminate pills in magazines for automatic priming did not turn out well.

Two inventions that did not get far are shown in Plate 169.

The piece at the top is an Edwards revolver. This was patented by David Edwards, United States patent 1134, on April 25, 1839.

The pill magazine was a minor feature. The invention dealt primarily with a complex and dubious system of revolving and indexing the cylinder.

The piece at the bottom in Plate 169 is incredible. It was patented July 9, 1850, United States patent 7496, by O. B. Percival and A. Smith. It represents what was probably the next to the last attempt to construct a gun that could be loaded with a bullet, then charged with gunpowder, and then primed, all with one movement. The pistol shown is the patent model. Only one production model, in the collection of William Locke, is believed to exist, and there may never have been more than one other. Under the barrel there are two cylindrical magazines, shown in firing position. The forward magazine has within it several tubes to hold bullets. The rear magazine is filled with gunpowder, except for a small space in which is a tube holding "percussion-seed". When the two magazines are turned up and around the barrel through a half circle, the bullet, the gunpowder, and the fulminate all fall in place.

The percussion Percival & Smith creation seems to be more untrustworthy than the flintlock, and even wheel lock, repeaters that loaded ball, powder, and priming in one operation, and which were put out by dozens of gunmakers from the early 1600's on.

One more invention that practically died a-borning was the Wright vertical-turret revolver, Plate 170. The fulminate pills were contained in a boss on the side of the turret and fed automatically to the touch holes when the turret was revolved. To fire the gun, the curved trigger under the turret was drawn back, after the straight trigger—back of the hammer—was pressed down. The curved trigger rotated the turret, cocked the hammer, and pressed a stop in a chamber mouth to index the turret cylinder. The straight trigger permitted movement of the curved trigger so the latter would withdraw the cylinder stop and then proceed with its other just described duties. Finally, the thumb trigger, if pressed down when the curved trigger was fully retracted, released the hammer. Mr. Wright obtained his United States patent, 11,917, on November 7, 1854.

The three futile inventions described in the last three paragraphs were produced in numbers exceedingly small, whereas the Jennings invention was put in volume production. Its importance lies largely in the fact the Jennings hatched the Volcanic, the Volcanic hatched the Henry, and the Henry hatched the Winchester. From the first Winchester rifle, the 1866 model, the Winchester line has grown, until in this year of imperfect grace, if a man needs a gun that will knock over a small predatory animal at three hundred yards, or drop a charging African buffalo at twenty paces, there is a Winchester rifle capable of doing the job. Whether the man behind the gun can do his part is quite another thing.

It should be acknowledged that the Lewis Jennings invention, patented December 25, 1849, United States patent 6973, was similar to the too complicated Walter Hunt invention, patented August 21, 1848, United States patent 6663, of which the only specimen produced was probably the one believed to be the patent model, now in Winchester's firearms collection. The Jennings was of better construction and more nearly satisfactory as a tubular magazine rifle, but it is perhaps improper to call the Jennings an improvement on the Hunt. Improvement implies subsequency, but despite the later date of the Jennings patent it is not certain, as will be shown, that the Jennings rifle was a later invention. Walter Hunt, born Martinsburg, New York, 1796, died New York City, 1859, deserves more than three sentences. The man was a prolific inventor, but highly unsuccessful in his ability to capitalize on his inventions. Hunt was described by the Smithsonian Institution as having "invented a greater number and diversity of original ideas than any other man of his time". The unvarnished facts of his inventions are well established, but I think the reports of some related episodes may have been coloured. At least, the tales do not all agree. Hunt was surely the original inventor of the safety pin. It is said he invented it on the spur of the moment, and immediately sold his rights in the invention for $400. He invented the foot-operated gong that became popular with stage lines, and later on trolleys, to warn pedestrians. He invented and patented the self-closing inkwell that may still be seen in some post offices, and the fountain pen that was improved and made popular years later by Lewis Waterman. His was the first patent to use the word "fountain pen". Hunt patented the paper collar, which eventually sold millions a year, but which had small sales until his patent had expired, apparently because he made immoderate royalty demands.

Hunt did not patent all his inventions. About 1832 he constructed but did not patent a sewing machine with an eye-pointed needle that sewed a lock stitch rather than the unsatisfactory chain stitch of an earlier invention. One story is that Hunt did not apply for a patent because he did not wish to chance putting the country's seamstresses out of work. In any event, George A. Arrowsmith, a New York metal-worker, with whom Hunt was early associated, applied for a patent for Hunt's sewing machine in 1853, but the application was disallowed on the ground of abandonment.

Hunt's application for a patent for the peculiar cartridge to be used in both the Hunt rifle and the Jennings rifle was made in 1847, a few months before his 1847 application for the repeating rifle patent, and was granted a few weeks sooner than his rifle patent. The Hunt cartridge patent was 5701, dated August 10, 1848. The Hunt rifle patent was dated August 21, 1848. The Jennings rifle patent was dated December 25, 1849. All three patents were assigned to George A. Arrowsmith. Though the dates the United States patents were granted is clear, it cannot be said with certainty that Hunt worked out his invention before Jennings had completed his. In 1847, Britain granted a patent for an invention that embodied both the 1848 Hunt cartridge and the 1849 Jennings rifle. This patent was issued to one Stephen Taylor who made the statement, routine in such cases, that the application was ". . . a communication from a foreigner residing abroad . . ." As Mr. Hall wrote, in *Forerunners of the First Winchester*, it is probable that Taylor was acting for Arrowsmith, to whom both Hunt and Jennings may have even then assigned their rights.

Hunt called his cartridge a "loaded ball", which the 1850 issue of *Annual of Scientific Discovery and Useful Arts* described as: "A hollow cone of lead, or rather a bullet elongated on one side in a hollow cylinder to about one inch in length, is filled with powder, and the end covered with a thin piece of cork, through the centre of which is a small hole, to admit fire from the priming". It should be noticed that though there is a basic similarity in the appearance of Hunt and Volcanic cartridges, there is a fundamental difference in construction. Though each is a "loaded ball" containing a propellent charge of gunpowder, the Hunt cartridge contains no priming, whereas the Volcanic cartridge does contain priming.

Jennings rifles which used pill-lock magazines were manufactured both as single-shots and repeaters. A Jennings repeater, circa 1851, is shown, full length, in Plate 171. The flat pill reservoir may be seen above and in back of the hammer. This particular rifle is marked "Robbins & Lawrence Makers Windsor, Vt. C. P. Dixon Agent New York Patented 1849". The Jennings name does not appear on the gun. It seems that by 1851 both Jennings and Hunt, as well as Arrowsmith, were out of the picture, and Robbins & Lawrence were manufacturing the gun for a financier named Palmer, for whom Dixon was sales agent.

The procedure recommended by Dixon for operating the rifle required pushing forward the ring lever with the forefinger while at the same time drawing back the hammer with the thumb, then pulling back the ring lever. When the operation was completed a cartridge would have been taken from the magazine, elevated and thrust in the chamber, and priming dropped into a touch hole in a breech pin which moved forward until the vent was in position to receive the hammer blow. Firing required a final, harder pull of the ring. A thorough understanding of how the mechanism works may come, possibly, with study of Plates 172 and 174.

It would not do to conclude this account of automatic primers without mentioning the Porter rifle. As most collectors know, the Porter was a moderately successful rifle of the vertical-turret type. Many of these guns—let's say half—had turrets with a separate nipple for each chamber. For these "nipple guns" (Porter's name for them) Porter directed, "Use Colt's metal lined cap, which fits the nipple well". The remaining half had no nipples, only tiny touch holes drilled in the flat surface of the turret. Such guns are nearly always called "pill lock Porters" by collectors, but Porter himself called them "cap box guns", and in regard to them, said, "The cap box contains a spiral spring, which by means of the follower plate, continues to place a cap under the hammer as often as the gun is cocked", and "The caps should be of a size to fit the groove, so as not to fall in side ways and are placed mouth upwards".

Clearly the "pill lock Porters" did not make use of pills like any that collectors would be apt to visualize. In the circumstances, because of custom, it seems best that I continue to call the guns pill locks, though I do not know quite what the primers looked like.

For the record it should be mentioned that the Porter patent model—presently at the Smithsonian Institution—is much different from the gun that was put on the market. It is believed no second abnormality like the patent model was ever constructed. I referred to the impractical 1850 invention of Percival and Smith as probably the next to the last attempt to construct a gun that loaded ball, powder, and priming all at once. The Porter patent model, United States patent 8210, of July 8, 1851, may well have been the final try. This model had a "cylindrical vessel" to contain bullets, gunpowder, and copper caps. One lever movement cocked the hammer, stripped a detonated cap from a nipple and replaced it with a fresh cap, and loaded with powder and ball. The "cylindrical vessel" was intended to contain powder for thirty shots—and that powder would probably all explode at the first shot.

In the production model—a fine example is shown in Plate 173—it was only now and then that all chambers went off simultaneously. However, multiple discharges did occur, sometimes with fatal results to the shooter, since a fully loaded turret always had a bullet pointing at the shooter. As the guns were expensive and unwieldy, and their use fraught with danger, it is surprising that so many were bought and even more surprising that so many survived and are now to be found in collections.

CHAPTER X

GUNS FIRING SELF-PRIMED NON-RELOADABLE CARTRIDGES

THE previous Chapter (pp. 128–30) described a Jennings rifle, the gun generally considered as first of three forerunners of the renowned 1873 model Winchester which fired the 44/40 cartridge. This chapter discusses the two other forerunners, and brings us up to that Winchester rifle that began the modern era, at whose threshold this volume ends.

Mention will be made in this chapter not only of cartridges that, once fired, cannot possibly be reloaded, but also of cartridges—borderline cases such as rim-fires, inside-primed centre-fires, lip-fires—that can probably, under favourable conditions and with special tools, be reloaded by experts.

A few gunmakers, all with but a single aim, created a few peculiar types of revolvers that had a brief existence just before modern centre-fire cartridges were developed. Those revolvers which fired now obsolete cartridges, some reloadable and some non-reloadable, will have the next chapter devoted to themselves.

The German needle gun, with its self-primed combustible cartridge, probably influenced the course of world events more than any other firearm in history—after the Forsyth invention, that is. Edward Crabb called it "the great granddaddy of all bolt action rifles . . . the magic wand with which the various Germanic states were united to form Germany under the Hohenzollern dynasty". This needle gun was developed by a man, Johann Nikolaus von Dreyse, who had served an apprenticeship under that inventive genius, Pauly. Dreyse worked for Pauly in Paris from 1808 to 1814. Dreyse probably returned to Germany when Pauly went to England.

The 1841 model was the first of the Dreyse military breech-loading needle guns. Though the Dreyse rifle was used by the German armed forces before 1848, it was not adopted as the official rifle for the German army until then. It was the first military breech-loading, bolt-action rifle ever made to chamber a cartridge that was a complete unit containing projectile, charge, and primer. (With "military" omitted, that statement is untrue.)

A prophetic passage in the royal pronouncement made when the gun was officially adopted referred to the invention as "a special dispensation of Providence for the strengthening of our National resources" and went on to express the hope "that the system may be kept secret until the great part it is destined to play in history may couple it with the glory of Prussian arms and the extension of Empire". It is remarkable how well the secret was kept, and how ridiculous were some of the printed reports about the gun. The *London Athenaeum* for September, 1850, asserted that ". . . the barrel is slightly rifled, but the grooves are perfectly straight, and not spiral, as is the case in our guns. By this means, much of the force of the powder, which is usually expended in giving the ball a rotary motion, is saved, and the ball is consequently thrown to a much greater distance. Indeed, it is said that with half the charge used in a percussion musket, it will carry the ball to the mark at a distance of 900 yards. The fire is communicated from the side of the barrel, instead of the breech . . ." That last ambiguous sentence was developed in the article—but not its meaning. If straight rifling has advantages such as the writer claimed, it is strange we have gone on to quicker and quicker spiral rifling. The Dreyse needle-gun rifling actually spiralled one turn in 42 inches. The article concluded with the statement that needle guns "were successfully used in quieting the late insurrection in Baden".

The needle gun was later highly successful in Germany's short war with Denmark in 1864, and spectacularly successful in her Seven Weeks' War with Austria in 1886. Denmark and Austria had muzzle-loading rifles—and no chance against Germany's breech-loaders. In the battle of Sadova the Prussian casualties were 10,000 against 40,000 Austrian. All Europe was quivering, and muzzle-loaders were done.

Probably the only way to give a clear idea of the impact the Dreyse rifle had on European governments in the 1860's is to quote from contemporary writers. The following fragments are from unsigned articles in 1866 issues of *Chambers Journal:* ". . . the arm, the fame of which is ringing throughout the world, and causing a degree of excitement which almost amounts to a panic in those countries which are unprovided with it"; and ". . . one universal cry from every civilized nation for the arming of their troops in like manner";

and "How a man feels, or ought to feel, who has invented an instrument which enables a greater number of his fellow-creatures to be maimed and killed, than could be accomplished by any other means, is a matter which none are more competent to discuss than German metaphysicians . . ." One writer seemed to believe the gun should not get all the credit, for he wrote: "The Prussian soldier has long been trained to fire his regulation number of balls as though they were objects to be deposited in an assigned position, and not merely to be got rid of with the least possible trouble to himself." That statement's truth was amply demonstrated in the Franco-Prussian War—by the time that war came along the French, who lost it, had superior weapons—but that truth has been forgotten or at least disregarded in recent years.

The Dreyse rifle, Plate 175, employs a long needlelike firing pin which is driven through the base of a combustible cartridge and on through the powder to detonate a primer resting at the base of the bullet. On this first type of military breechloaders the bolt handle works the same as in modern bolt-action guns, in that it is raised and pulled back, and then, after a cartridge is dropped in the receiver, pressed forward and down—but this action on the Dreyse does not complete preparation for firing. On the gun shown it is necessary to draw back a thumb piece before opening the bolt, and to push back this piece after closing the bolt.

The Dreyse breech-loading needle gun evolved from a muzzle-loading needle gun. Dreyse may or may not have been first with a true muzzle-loading needle gun. He is generally credited with inventing one, sometime between 1827 and 1829. His first model was loaded with powder poured down the barrel, then with a round ball having a cavity containing fulminate covered with thin paper. In order to ensure that, while being rammed down the barrel, the ball would not turn, and that the cavity would be centred in the bore in front of the needle, the ball was held by a hollow cardboard cylinder.

The use of loose powder in needle guns was abandoned after a year or so. After that the muzzle-loading needle guns were loaded with self-contained combustible cartridges similar to those fired in breech-loading needle guns.

It has been asserted that the needle gun was invented by an Englishman, Abraham Adolph Moser, and that the patent granted to Moser in 1831, British 6196, was for a needle-fire cartridge. However, the patent was granted to Moser "in consequence of a communication made to him by a foreigner residing abroad". The foreigner was probably Dreyse. Furthermore, the patent was not for a self-contained cartridge. It was for ignition of a charge of gunpowder poured down the barrel, by a needle striking fulminate in wadding at the base of a bullet rammed on top of the powder. Only the method of guiding the ball in its travel down the barrel was different from the first Dreyse method used in his muzzle-loading needle guns.

After mid-century many makers of sporting guns, both in and out of Germany, produced quantities of breech-loading needle-fire long guns, mostly shotguns. The difference in these guns lay principally in the various systems used to retract the needles. Often the needles were automatically cocked as the barrel breeches were swung open.

A gun with a long firing pin is not necessarily a needle gun. A true needle gun has a needle that penetrates a cartridge until it hits priming which lies inside the cartridge.

Needle-fire rifles and shotguns are plentiful; needle-fire pistols are much scarcer; needle-fire revolvers are rarely found.

Dreyse marketed needle-fire rifles, shotguns, pistols, and revolvers. I believe no other maker produced needle-fire revolvers.

One form of needle-fire double shotgun produced by Dreyse is pictured in Plate 176. Under the barrel breech there is a lever which when turned moves the breech forward and up to permit loading. Some models had the lever under the triggers.

Two Dreyse revolvers are shown in Plate 177. In both guns a far-forward position of the cylinder is required to provide room for the mechanism that drives the needle deep in a chamber and then withdraws it after detonating the fulminate. The partly wood-covered lever on the top gun, from the Frank Horner collection, serves to cock the striker, also to revolve the cylinder. This lever must be held close against the grip when the trigger is pulled. The smaller revolver, from the writer's collection, is conventionally double-action in that both the turning of the cylinder and the firing of the cartridge require no more than a pull on the trigger.

Plate 178 shows a muzzle-loading needle-fire pistol made by Dreyse & Collenbusch. Turning the lever on the side of the pistol up and back, and then returning it to its first position, retracts the needle and makes the gun ready to fire. The metal piece sticking down just in back of the trigger protects the spring by preventing the trigger's being pulled too far back.

The only American military needle gun was the Schroeder, patented December 23, 1856, United States 16,288. An example of this extremely rare gun is found in Plate 179. It fires a cartridge similar to the cartridge used in the regulation Dreyse army rifle, and it has a lever on the side which turns back through a half circle as does the lever on the muzzle-loading pistol mentioned in the preceding paragraph. This long gun is a breechloader and its lever serves to slide the barrel forward for loading.

That the bolt-action breech-loading rifle invented by Alphonse Antoine Chassepot and used by French troops in the Franco-Prussian War is a true needle gun is an open question, though it is so called. (It is not illustrated here.) The needle is no more than a long striker which does not penetrate the cartridge as does the needle on a Dreyse or a Schroeder. It merely pierces the base of the cartridge and there detonates a percussion cap which has two holes in it to permit the ignited fulminate to pass through to fire the gunpowder. Admittedly, the cap inside the cartridge is reversed and has its opening at the base of the cartridge and consequently the cap itself is penetrated a short distance by the striker.

A needle that passed more deeply into the cartridge was used in the British Needham rifles and shotguns. That needle did not go through the powder charge, but it did penetrate a perforated zinc cup and two thick wads before driving into a reversed percussion cap, a cap whose open end faced rearward as did the cap in the Chassepot cartridge. The Needham in Plate 180 is one put out in the early 1850's to fire a combustible cartridge. The picture shows the gun in position for loading, a rear-pivoted block having been raised and the needle striker cocked by lifting a broad finger piece.

A needle gun which used a cartridge differing hardly at all from the Needham cartridge, except in having its percussion cap placed with its open end forward, is the Chatauvillard in Plate 182. A British patent, 12,613, was granted in the year 1849. Instead of the patent being issued to an Englishman at the behest of "a foreigner, living abroad", this patent was issued directly to "Louis Alfred De Chatauvillard, of Rue Saint Lazare, in the Republic of France". (The specification was signed by Chatauvillard in Brussels and witnessed by T. W. Waller, the British chargé d'affaires. The British consul in Antwerp certified the authenticity of the De Chatauvillard signature. Then William Ritchie signed an affidavit in England that he believed that Waller was the chargé d'affaires at Brussels, and that he believed Waller's signature was in Waller's handwriting. Unaccountably, in the several mentions of De Chatauvillard's address, the street and the country are given, but never the city.) The Chatauvillard gun is opened for loading by raising a bascule something like that used on a Pauly gun. It will be remembered the striker on a Pauly gun is cocked by an external cocking lever. The striker on the Chatauvillard is cocked by the bascule as that is raised to open the gun. The Chatauvillard is a hammerless gun.

A particularly rare and beautiful gun is the muzzle-loader seen in Plate 181. This double-barrel shotgun was made by J. G. Picker in Leipzig for someone who wanted a truly elaborate gun. Replacement needles were carried in a trap in the butt. Several are shown under the gun. The paper cartridges which were rammed down the barrels were held in place by turning a short underneath lever so that metal barbs would prevent a cartridge working forward in one barrel if the other barrel was used for several shots in succession. Shooters were aware that repeated firings from one barrel with the charge in the other barrel held in reserve might cause that charge to shift forward, with possibly ruinous results if the reserve charge was fired.

Most pin-fire cartridges are reloadable without difficulty by anyone with the necessary tools, and therefore guns firing such cartridges do not come within the scope of this chapter. Of the several types of tools that were available some years ago for reloading ordinary pin-fire cartridges, one type will be shown in the final chapter. A rare gun that fired a peculiar and probably non-reloadable pin-fire cartridge is shown in Plate 183. Beyond question this gun has a properly descriptive name, *Mousqueton des Cent Gardes*. Examples are scarce indeed. This musketoon was used in the early 1850's to arm Louis Napoleon's personal guardsmen, who numbered one hundred when the guard was formed. The number finally reached 300. The Musketoon of the Hundred Guardsmen was probably the only military gun that fired any sort of pin-fire cartridge. It was also the first military small-bore, only ·36 calibre at a time calibres over ·50 were usual. The cartridge, which had a paper case and a brass head, was unusual in that there were two pins, one opposite the other. The fixed pin at the top was used to pull out a fired cartridge. The other, the firing pin, was underneath and was driven into the fulminate when the breechblock slammed up after the trigger was pulled. The cartridge was pushed in the barrel chamber when the breechblock was down, and it was held in place by a small movable stud backed by a light spring. The cartridge head was in full view at the instant the trigger was pulled. Of course, the guardsman knew the breechblock would be interposed between his eye and the cartridge when the firing pin was struck, but what he saw was not conducive to his peace of mind.

A revolver which is sometimes mistakenly included in the brief list of revolvers which successfully evaded the Rollin White patent, revolvers which will be described in the next chapter, is the Allen & Wheelock lip-fire in Plate 184. This centre hammer, and rather scarce revolver in ·44 Army calibres, fires a peculiar lip cartridge, in which the fulminate is concentrated in a small prominence on the cartridge rim. The chambers are bored through as in rim-fire revolvers, and the gun was therefore an infringement rather than an evasion of the Rollin White patent controlled by Smith & Wesson. A small cut to hold the lip of the cartridge was made in the rear of the cylinder at the edge of each chamber mouth. Obviously, in loading it was necessary to place each cartridge so the lip would fit into the cut prepared for it. The cartridge was patented, United States 30,109, dated September 25, 1860, by the second of the two famous men to bear the name Ethan Allen.

On the question of reloading such cartridges as lip-fires and rim-fires (the lip-fire is no more than a variation of a rim-fire) which are commonly considered non-reloadable, it may be well to note that American Indians along in the 1870's were able to reload rim-fire, and inside-primed centre-fire cartridges, using crude and primitive tools. They drilled holes in the centre of the cartridge heads and inserted musket caps.

There is a further point of interest about the cartridges that are generally considered to be forerunners of the modern rim-fires. Those cartridges, the early Flobert "bulleted breech caps", were fired by a hammer that had on its nose a narrow crossbar rather than a pointed striker. This bar struck completely across the head of the cartridge.

Inside-primed centre-fire cartridges were developed after rim-fires were in common use, but they had a short life, and, unlike the rim-fires, their manufacture was discontinued soon after modern centre-fires were developed. Many varieties of inside-primed centre-fires are in cartridge collections. Externally, many have flat, smooth heads and are hardly distinguishable from rim-fires, save by men with specialized knowledge. A revolver made to shoot an inside-primed centre-fire cartridge is shown in Plate 185. This was made in France by Perrin. A few of these rather scarce revolvers were bought both by the North and the South in the Civil War. The fact the cartridge was centre-fire and not rim-fire was not generally recognized by gun collectors for many years.

Long before the Civil War, and before the existence of inside-primed centre-fire cartridges, a French gun known as the "fusil

Robert" was for a time considered a possible weapon for armed forces in the United States but it was finally rejected. It was issued in small numbers to the military of Belgium and France. The gun is also known as the Demondion. It was patented in England in 1831, British patent 6137, by "Augustus Demondion, of Old Fish-Street Hill, in the city of London, on consequence of a communication made to him by a certain foreigner residing abroad". The *Mechanics' Magazine Journal* about that time said the foreigner was Le Page, and it cannot now be determined with certainty that the London publication's statement was in error. There is some evidence that one or another of the Le Page gunmakers was responsible for the patenting in England of a gun which copied the Robert gun. However, it is now generally considered that Demondion was acting for the Parisian gunmaker Robert, not for Le Page.

Another magazine, the *London Journal*, disapproved the form of the patent, saying, "The Patentee appears to presume that the English nation have but an imperfect idea of the construction of a musket; and has, under this impression, given us in detail figures drawn at the full size of every part or individual piece of which a musket is constructed, as well as of many of the tools by which they are to be manufactured. These, with a very copious description of the drawings, comprehending forty-nine shaded and coloured figures, the explanation of which occupies many skins of parchment, constitute the specification of the invention . . ." When I saw the patent drawings I too was surprised that it had been thought necessary to illustrate a musket butt, for instance, full-size.

Examples of Robert long guns are more apt to be found in collections than are pistols. Two views of a Robert pistol are given in Plates 186 and 187. On the barrel "Pistolet Robert Bte. à Paris" appears in gold. Gold lettering on the breechblock reveals that Robert received the *Académie de L'Industrie* gold medal for his invention at the 1834 Paris exposition.

When the breechblock is fully raised, as in Plate 186, the mainspring will be compressed and a cartridge may be pushed in the barrel breech. The unusual cartridge is combustible and has extending straight back from it a tube of thin copper filled with fulminate. This tube is at the edge of the cartridge base and vertical to the base. When the cartridge is chambered, the tube is in line with the bottom of the barrel bore, and when the breech is closed the tube will lie under a fixed anvil. The rear portion of the mainspring itself acts as a hammer, and when the hinged block is pressed firmly down the hammer will be cocked. Pressing the trigger will then cause the hammer to fly up and crush the priming.

France was early awake to the fact that muzzle-loaders and capping breechloaders would surely give way to breechloaders firing self-contained cartridges, and her inventors designed many guns to shoot fixed ammunition. A study of Bartlett and Gallatin's *Digest of Cartridge Patents*, which purports to list all cartridge patents issued in the United States, England, and France up to given dates in 1877 and 1878, indicates that France was the leader in the number of self-contained cartridges invented—but it should be kept in mind that not all French cartridge patents are actually listed in that volume. Until about the time of the Civil War, France would incorporate a cartridge specification in a patent for a firearm, and would require no separate patent for the cartridge.

A French transitional revolver, the Michallon, which is really no more than a pepperbox with a barrel screwed on a centre-pin, is shown in Plate 188. This fires a self-contained cartridge patented in 1844—French patent 76, Series 2, volume 1, page 107, plate 25. The gun was certainly not purposely made to circumvent the Rollin White patent—it was much too early—but had it been made in the 1860's it would properly belong in the next chapter, which is devoted to the curious revolvers which did lawfully circumvent that patent. The cartridge had some resemblance to a Moore teat-fire. The revolver was sold to me as a pill lock, for which I submit it can be easily mistaken. I must now admit that I mistakenly illustrated it in *Pepperbox Firearms* as a pill lock.

Plate 189 shows a horizontal-turret pistol invented by Heinrich Genhart, of Belgium, and patented in the United States January 27, 1857, patent 16,447. Many collectors have been misled into accepting a Genhart as a pill-lock weapon, just as I was misled about the Michallon. I have seen several of these guns, both long and short, but it is not easy to find one for sale. They are unusual in construction and method of operation, and they chamber peculiar front-loading cartridges. Pressing down a lever on the left of the frame cocks an underhammer and moves the barrel forward until its breech end is drawn out of a chamber mouth and the turret is free to be turned. The turret was indexed by pins pressed into its underface. When a small button at the top edge of the frame was held down the pins were withdrawn and the turret could be manually revolved. When the side lever was pressed back the barrel breech entered a chamber mouth, to form a tight joint and prevent gas escape.

An empty Genhart turret could be replaced with a loaded spare quickly and with few motions. Six shots could not be fired as quickly from a Genhart, whose turret had ten chambers, as could six shots from a six-shot revolver, but sixty shots could be fired at a faster rate, using spare loaded turrets.

Genhart guns are scarce but the cartridges are much scarcer. The cartridges are metal and nearly conical. At the powder end they "are pierced . . . in the line of the longitudinal axis to receive a small metal tube, one end of which extends within the powder, and the other end to about an equal extent outside the cartridges". The tube was filled with detonating powder.

In stating there were three forerunners of the 1873 Winchester I am doing as others have done; I am arbitrarily excluding the Hunt rifle and the 1866 Winchester. The Hunt rifle—of which probably no example exists except the patent model now in the Winchester collection in New Haven—fired the same sort of cartridge as the Jennings rifle. The 1866 Winchester rifle fired the same sort of cartridge as the Henry rifle. The Jennings, the Volcanic, and the Henry include all types of evolution in ignition to be found in the forerunners of the 1873 Winchester.

An example of a Volcanic rifle, with Volcanic cartridges above it, is given in Plate 190. This gun, like the earlier Jennings and the later Henry, has a magazine under the barrel, as have many models of Winchesters. Each succeeding forerunner displayed improvements in methods of charging the tubular magazine and of carrying cartridges from the magazine to the barrel chamber, and improvements in those particulars continued with the Winchesters themselves.

The Volcanics were manufactured first by Smith & Wesson in Norwich, then by Volcanic Repeating Arms Company in New Haven, and last by New Haven Arms company in New Haven. From start to finish was about six years, 1854 to 1860. Nearly all the Volcanic shoulder arms were made in the final two years by New Haven Arms Company. The production before 1858 by Smith & Wesson and the Volcanic Repeating Arms Company was largely confined to pistols, the first of them being called Smith & Wesson Magazine Pistols, and not Volcanic pistols. The pistols, some made with iron frames and some with brass, were loaded with from six to ten cartridges, depending on barrel length and calibre; the shoulder arms with from twenty to thirty cartridges.

The Volcanic cartridge was another high point in the development of percussion ignition, and it may be called the next to the last ignition development antecedent to the first modern cartridge, the 44/40, or the ·44 Winchester Centre-Fire, as it is often called.

The Volcanic cartridge is a loaded ball. It is like the Hunt loaded ball except in one cardinal respect. The Hunt cartridge is a lead ball with its hollowed interior filled with gunpowder, but it depends upon separate, outside priming for ignition. The Volcanic cartridge has not only a hollowed interior filled with gunpowder, it contains its own priming. It is of the type of ammunition designated variously as "fixed", or "self-contained", or less fittingly, "self-exploding".

Smith & Wesson obtained United States patent 14,147 on January 22, 1856, for the Volcanic cartridge. The cartridge was already in use when the patent was granted. During its life some changes were made, but basically the cartridge was a Minié ball with a cavity containing gunpowder, which was held in place by two disks—one of cork and one of metal—with fulminate between them.

The cartridge was not combustible, and there was therefore the problem of extracting the disks left in the barrel after the bullet was discharged. An extractor was provided—in fact, several types were issued—but it was apt to fail to work satisfactorily. There were many complaints against the gun but most of them, including the outcries about the extractor, arose from faults in the cartridge. The cartridge base was not constructed so as to give an extractor a firm grip, and more important, the cartridge had no rim and was therefore not held firmly in position in the barrel chamber. Being held only by the barrel lands, it might move forward out of reach of the striker.

The powder charge in a Volcanic loaded bullet was small, and the bullet was sadly lacking in both penetration and accuracy.

There was as much nonsense in firearms publicity a hundred years ago as there is today in air-wave commercials. In proof, I quote from *Frank Leslie's Illustrated Newspaper* for October 9, 1858: "A good shot will hit a quarter of a dollar at eighty yards with one of the (Volcanic) pistols".

The home-town paper of the Volcanic Repeating Arms Company, the New Haven *Journal Courier*, in the February 9, 1856, issue, reported—admittedly at second-hand and without assurance—that "an accomplished marksman" had placed 5 out of 9 balls in an 8-inch target at 300 yards, with a Volcanic pistol. The Winchester Repeating Arms Company some time ago stated the chances of anyone's getting such a score were not as good as one in seven thousand.

There was one truth in 1858 about Volcanic pistols that was far from truth in 1958. Joseph Merwin, New York agent for the New Haven Arms Company, then offered the four sizes of Volcanic pistols, with engraved frames, at retail prices from $12.00 to $18.00 each.

Cartridges of the Volcanic type were patented in England and France in 1854. A pistol that bears no maker's name but which fired a fully self-contained cartridge of the Volcanic type—a cartridge patented in France in 1854 by Gaupillat—is shown in Plate 191. (It should be kept in mind that the Volcanic pistol was in use in the United States as early as 1854, though the patent for the Volcanic loaded bullet was not granted to Smith & Wesson until 1856.)

A Volcanic pistol has a tubular magazine under the barrel. The European pistol in Plate 191—the example shown has Belgian proof marks and is commonly called a "gravity feed" pistol—has its magazine over the barrel. In operation the hammer is put at half cock and left there until the cartridge is inserted in the chamber, a proceeding that requires more thought and attention than is necessary to get a cartridge chambered in a Volcanic, where one lever movement down and back suffices. The illustration shows the hammer half-cocked and the chamber block as a result raised until the chamber is in line with the magazine. Now the muzzle is pointed up, so that gravity will cause a cartridge to slide down to the chamber. Next, a very small rammer, operated with the thumb and forefinger, pushes the cartridge home. The hammer is now brought to full cock, and the chamber block slams down, violently and with considerable noise, and the cartridge is in line with the barrel, ready for firing.

The lever-action Henry rifle, Plate 192, the last of the forerunners of the modern lever-action Winchester rifle, was in many respects like the Volcanic rifle. In one most important respect—the cartridge for which it was chambered—it was different, and greatly improved. (The meaning of "modern" is often problematical. I contend the 1873 Winchester is modern because that model was in production in 1873 and was not discontinued until 1924, and because it is still in wide use. Neither the gun nor its cartridge, the first modern centre-fire, is obsolete.)

The Henry had several of the deficiencies of the Volcanic. Except at short range it was unsatisfactory in accuracy. Some of its parts were not sturdy. Its tubular magazine under the barrel was partially open for its entire length, and care was necessary to prevent its becoming clogged with dirt or other debris. Loading of the magazine was from the front, so that the first cartridge loaded was the first fired. The lever-action Winchesters incorporated needed improvements. They were sturdy and reliable; their magazines were closed throughout their length and loaded from the rear, so the last cartridge loaded was the first fired.

Despite its unsatisfactory features the Henry was a far better gun than many others issued to troops, before and since. At close quarters it could create havoc in the ranks of men who faced it. The Henry was not officially approved by the United States Government but its use was sanctioned by the Federal government in the case of several companies, and one or two regiments, of state troops during the Civil War. There were several engagements where small bodies of men armed with Henry rifles were able to rout forces numerically greatly superior. A remark that has been attributed to many Confederate leaders was to the effect that they did not fear our Springfields, but they wanted nothing to do with troops armed with "the guns that were loaded on Sunday and shot all week".

The vast superiority of the Henry over the Volcanic lay in the fact that the Henry fired a self-contained cartridge that was both metal-cased and rimmed, and therefore unlikely to cause difficulty in extraction. The cartridge was less apt to misfire, and it was more powerful. Still, it was far too weak, imperfect, and inferior to meet today's standards. The cartridge was not only rimmed, it was rim-fire. That second fact necessitated the use of thin copper in the case. It had to be thin so that the striker would indent the rim sufficiently to detonate the fulminate. The thinness of the case in turn limited the amount of gunpowder and the weight of the bullet, and consequently the effectiveness of the gun. All these drawbacks were overcome when the 44/40 cartridge was developed. In that cartridge a light thin cap was put in the centre of the cartridge head and, within reason, there was no limit to the thickness of the cartridge shell, nor to how much powder, or how heavy a bullet, was loaded in it. The 44/40 cartridge of today is better than it was in 1873, thanks largely to metallurgists and chemists, but it is basically unchanged.

CHAPTER XI

SMITH & WESSON EVASIONS

SOME ten or a dozen types of revolvers of decidedly unusual construction, revolvers which in some cases fired cartridges of unmistakably radical form, came into being in the last years before the 1873 Winchester 44/40 rifle and its new cartridge opened the era of modern firearms.

These revolvers did not represent an attempt at progress. They were designed for but one purpose, to avoid infringement of a patent that had been granted Rollin White, of Hartford, Connecticut. An understanding of why gunmakers contrived these strange revolvers requires some slight knowledge of the patent, of its sale, and of the litigation it gave rise to.

Rollin White was granted United States patents 12,648 and 12,649 on April 3, 1855, for what he claimed were "new and useful Improvements in Repeating Fire-Arms". The set form, "new and useful improvements", was most inappropriate. For one thing the complicated invention embodied a device which would bring about unpleasant results if it did not work, and perhaps disastrous results if it did work. The invention was never put in production. As far as I can discover, only one model was built and tested. In the test the operator tied the gun to a tree, fastened a cord to the trigger and went round a corner before pulling the cord. All shots went off in unison, as feared by the audience, but not as intended by the inventor.

No one would have had the slightest interest in Mr. White's incredible revolver, had it not been for one claim in the specification for patent 12,648. This stated the invention included, "extending the chambers through the rear of the cylinder for the purpose of loading them at the breech from behind".

The right to manufacture a revolver with chambers bored

through was vitally important to Smith & Wesson, who had invented a metallic self-primed cartridge and were about ready to market a revolver to shoot this new cartridge. The cartridge was to be loaded from the rear in a cylinder having its chambers bored through.

Smith & Wesson must have felt they would have some chance of showing the White invention was quite useless, and they must have believed they would be on firm ground in showing that a bored-through cylinder was nothing new. The fact is, a revolver with such a cylinder was patented by Hertog & Devos in Belgium in 1853; a pepperbox-revolver, with barrels bored through and loaded from the rear, invented by Lefaucheux in 1845, was well known and had been exhibited at the Crystal Palace in 1851; and finally, George Leonard in his 1850 patent referred to barrels "drilled and bored entirely through".

However, Messrs. Smith and Wesson realized that if they demolished the Rollin White claim, they would gain no exclusive rights, but they would open the door to any competitor who wished to manufacture revolvers with bored-through cylinders. Accordingly, Smith & Wesson entered into an agreement with Rollin White to let them manufacture under his patent on a royalty basis. They could see there would be tests in court of the validity of the patent claims, and they could but hope against hope the vital claim would be upheld. Mr. White agreed to defend his patent claims against infringement.

Soon after Smith & Wesson brought out their revolver other manufacturers began producing revolvers that were clearly infringements, or would be if the Rollin White patent claims were upheld. Smith & Wesson brought an action at law, climaxed by a November, 1863, verdict of the Massachusetts Circuit Court in their favour. Anyone who wishes to read the voluminous evidence and to ascertain the process of reasoning which resulted in a decision that "the thing which constituted the subject matter of the patent" did not exist before Rollin White made it, is referred to Case 17535, Smith & Wesson *vs.* Allen, "Federal Cases Circuit & District Courts, 1789–1880".

The defendants appealed to the United States Supreme Court. Less than two months before the patent expired by limitation the Supreme Court gave its judgment. The minutes of the court for February 8, 1869, state that the decree of the Massachusetts Circuit Court was affirmed, "the court being equally divided in opinion, upon the question of affirming or reversing the decree".

Within a week after the patent expired, a bill designed to permit a 7-year extension of White's 14-year rights was passed by both Houses of Congress, without debate. President Grant returned the bill to the Senate without approval and accompanied it with a letter which said, ". . . the government suffered inconvenience and embarrassment enough during the war in consequence of the inability of manufacturers to use this patent . . ." The letter went on: "The validity of the patent has been questioned for many years, and it is understood that it was only affirmed by the Supreme Court by a tie vote, four of the justices voting affirmatively and an equal number negatively". One sentence read, ". . . justice to the government and to the public forbids this patent from being renewed". The bill was not passed over the veto.

Even before the Circuit Court, in 1863, ruled the Rollin White patent valid, some inventors had been working to produce revolvers that would fire self-primed metallic cartridges from cylinders that were not bored entirely through. As soon as the court's ruling was announced the problem of making such revolvers was attacked in earnest.

In the period from 1859 through 1866 there were thirty or more United States patents issued for revolvers designed to circumvent the White patent. All of these designs avoided infringement, but many did not get past the experimental stage.

We are concerned here only with the Smith & Wesson evasions that were manufactured for sale. Of these, some made use of the regular rim-fire cartridges; others used cartridges of unconventional design, loaded from the front of the cylinder. None had a cylinder bored all the way through. A cartridge for a Thuer conversion of a Colt revolver will be described on pages 154–5, along with the tools used for reloading. The other cartridge types, all and sundry, which were fired in the other revolvers that legally circumvented the Rollin White patent will be briefly described in the next chapter.

The first of the successful evasions to be put on the market was at the same time the first revolver to use front-loading self-contained metallic cartridges. Three revolvers that all fired this special ammunition, called cup-primer cartridges, are shown in Plate 193.

The topmost of the three revolvers is the little known hinged-frame Plant, manufactured by and marked on the barrel, "Plant's Mfg. Co., New Haven, Ct." The patent for it was issued July 12, 1859, to Willard C. Ellis and John N. White, of Springfield, Massachusetts, United States 24,726. The middle of the three revolvers is the solid-frame Plant Army. The hinged-frame revolver is marked with no date other than the 1859 patent date. The solid-frame revolver bears the 1859 date and the date of a July 21, 1863, patent, United States 39,318, also issued to Ellis and White. There are several differences in these two revolvers, but the important patented feature is in both. This was the constructing of the cylinder chamber, without boring it entirely through, so that a small round opening was formed at the rear to permit the tip of the hammer to pass through and strike within the hollowed base of the cartridge. This construction left at the rear of the chamber an annular ring, or shoulder, which served adequately as a recoil shield.

A further use for this rear opening in the chamber was discovered by Henry Reynolds, who invented an ejecting rod, patented May 10, 1864, United States patent 42,688. This ejector, which fastened to the frame back of the cylinder, and was pushed through the opening to force out fired shells, may be seen on the solid-frame revolver illustrated, but was not used on the earlier model.

The earlier, hinged-frame model has a fixed ejecting rod. This is anchored under the barrel, and removal of waste cases requires taking the cylinder out of the frame so a chamber may be pushed over the rod.

The early cartridges had a narrow flange projecting outward at right angles at the bullet end. This flange was "simply to give a hold for removing the exploded shell" as explained in the 1859 patent. With the invention of the movable Reynolds ejecting rod the flange became unnecessary and will often not be present on a cap-primer cartridge in a cartridge collection.

The hinged-frame Plant illustrated has a rounded frame, and the solid-frame a flat frame. This latter model is also known with rounded frame.

The cup-primer revolvers manufactured under the Plant patent are found in various sizes and calibres, marked with names of numerous manufacturers and sales agents. The revolver at the bottom of Plate 193 is of ·28 calibre and was made by Eagle Arms Company.

Another front-loader made to shoot cup-primer cartridges is the Connecticut Arms Company revolver in Plate 194. Patents for this revolver, sometimes called the Wood revolver, were granted S. W. Wood on March 1, 1864, United States 41,803, and on January 16, 1866, United States 52,105. The cartridges for this revolver are much like the early flanged-mouth Plant cartridges, but the purpose of the flange was not to make extraction easier. The mouth of each chamber on an 1866 model Connecticut Arms revolver has a shallow groove cut in its inner periphery, so that a cartridge with a slightly flared, or flanged, front end, when pressed firmly in, will pass the extreme front edge of the cylinder and be retained by the groove. The difficulty of ejecting a cartridge so held is overcome by a cartridge extractor, which may be seen pivoted to the frame below the cylinder. The device acts as a lever to start expulsion of an exploded shell from the mouth of a chamber.

The files of the Patent Office reveal other firearms patents granted to this same Mr. Wood, who evidently gave a lot of thought to front-loading revolvers. One patent, 44,363, of September 20, 1864, covers a revolver with a barrel that could be turned aside to permit front loading of metallic cartridges, and also to permit expelling the empty cases, without removing the cylinder from the frame. The front-loading cartridges were to be tapered to the rear like the later Thuer cartridges, and to be ejected from the front of the cylinder by blows from the hammer. The circumventing of the Rollin White patent by the Thuer method, which also provided for driving empty cases from the chambers by hammer blows, will be described later.

The front-loading revolvers that probably had the largest sales were those that fired teat cartridges. These revolvers were manufactured first by Moore's Patent Fire-Arms Company, Brooklyn, later by National Arms Company, Brooklyn. The dealers in these revolvers persuaded many men not to buy the newfangled Smith & Wesson revolvers that left the cartridge heads fully exposed at the rear. They argued, speciously but effectively, that the explosive force of the powder acted backward as well as forward, and that energy was wasted and bullet velocity reduced by having the chamber wide open at the rear, with only a weak recoil shield to back the cartridge and protect the shooter.

The teat-cartridge revolvers were made in ·45 calibre as well as ·32, but these large ·45 calibre models are rarely found. A good example is the National shown in Plate 195.

Two of the ·32 calibre revolvers are shown in Plates 196 and 197. The one with the elaborately etched cylinder is a Moore, the other is a National.

Daniel Moore, who had previously manufactured a revolver which, according to the 1863 decision of the Massachusetts Circuit Court, infringed the Rollin White patent, was granted a patent, United States 38,321, April 28, 1863, for these teat-cartridge revolvers that were not infringements, but were legal evasions.

The Moore 1863 patent covered the formation of the rear of the cylinder so as partially to close the chambers, preventing the use of a rear-loading cartridge but permitting the use of a front-loading cartridge having fulminate contained in a teat in the base. The patent claim included a swinging gate at the front of the cylinder. This gate, when closed, as in Plate 196, keeps the cartridges in place in the cylinder. The later models had this gate fitted with an extension to the rear which served to start ejection of the cartridge. In Plate 197 this combination of gate and ejector is shown open with a cartridge case partly ejected.

The name of David Williamson will often be found on these teat-cartridge revolvers. Mr. Williamson obtained patents, which he assigned to Moore's Patent Fire-Arms Company, covering improvements in the shape of both cartridges and chambers. The original Moore cartridges had flat bases with round teats. The Williamson improvements had hemispherical, domed bases with flattened teats.

The first successful revolver designed to use a conventional rim-fire cartridge without infringing the Rollin White patent—or the Smith & Wesson patent, if you prefer—was the Slocum Patent Side-Loading Revolver shown in Plate 198.

The Slocum, once loaded, was a good pocket revolver, safe, strong, and sure-fire. Testimonials of the period mentioned the "ease and certainty in loading, either in the dark or light" and the fact that the gun did not require being taken apart for loading or unloading. A dexterous and practised operator can load the gun very quickly, but a man who is "all thumbs" considers the procedure complicated.

Frank Slocum obtained his patent for this revolver April 14, 1863, United States patent 38,204. The invention permits the loading of rim-fire cartridges sideways into a cylinder which is not open at its rear end, except for a slot for the hammer nose. Rounded troughs, open at the front only, are cut in the cylinder and fitted with sliding tubes which function as chambers for the cartridges. Loading requires the hammer be brought to half cock, with a tube in line with a "stationary piston" which also serves as an ejecting rod. When a small catch at the rear of the cylinder is turned out of a groove in the tube, or chamber, the tube is pushed forward over the piston, a cartridge dropped sideways in the trough and the tube drawn back. The operation can be completed in less time than it can be explained.

Plate 198 shows a Slocum just after a tube has been pushed forward over the piston and a cartridge dropped sideways in a trough.

A discharged shell will fall out when the revolver is turned partly over with the tube pushed forward over the "piston".

Papers sent to me by John Hintlian tell of an early popularity contest, held at the Northwestern Fair of the Sanitary Commission and Soldiers Home in Chicago in 1865, which awarded the winner a gold-mounted, engraved and inlaid Slocum revolver. That revolver, now in the collection of the Smithsonian Institution, is pictured here in Plate 199 with the tube, or chamber, drawn back over the cartridge.

The contest was to pick "the best General". The *Chicago Evening Journal* in the issue of May 22, 1865, after describing the two Slocums on exhibit as "probably the richest pistols ever made", went on to say: "The one in full gold will be in charge of a handsome young lady at the Fair to be given to the General having the greatest number of votes, each vote representing a sum of money". The *Brooklyn Daily Eagle*, on June 24, 1865, in telling about the contest at Chicago, said: "The voting was variable, Sherman being ahead until the eleventh hour, when Sheridan's friends made a sudden dash in imitation of their favorite's tactics, and carried off the prize. The final vote stood: Sherman 447; Sheridan 879".

The *Chicago Merchants' Circular* of May 19, 1865, ended its account of these luxury Slocums with: "In these dangerous times, when so many have lately been assaulted in our streets after nightfall, it would be well if our citizens generally carry this efficient protection".

Times change. Beauty queens now dominate popularity contests. The papers no longer urge citizens to carry guns. And, of course, our streets are now free of violence(?)

The Slocum Patent Side-Loading Revolver was probably made in ·32 calibre only.

Another evasion that also used regular rim-fire cartridges, the Pond Separate-Chambers Revolver, was made in both ·22 and ·32 calibres, seven-shot and six-shot respectively. An example of the ·32 is shown in Plate 200. It is marked on the top flat of the octagon barrel, "L. W. Pond, Worcester, Mass. Pat'd Sept 8, 1863" and on the flat next to the left, "Pat'd Nov. 8, 1864". The 1863 United States patent, 39,869, was granted to John H. Vickers, and the 1864 United States patent, 44,953, to Freeman W. Hood. The 1863 patent pertains to a cylinder having chambers of sufficient diameter to enclose "lining-thimbles" which themselves held rim-fire cartridges. The thimbles were tubes "with a proper internal calibre to receive the cylindrical portions of the cartridges, and of an external circumference equal to that of the flanges of the cartridges". One of these hollow thimbles, with a cartridge pressed in up to its rim, is an easy fit in a chamber. The 1864 patent related to the ejector which was made integral with the centre pin. This ejecting rod—it was called a stem—may be turned through 90 degrees. It is shown turned down, in shooting position, in the illustration. In this position the chambers cannot be loaded or unloaded. When a spring-catch is pressed, the stem may be turned up to the left, and then, when it is lined up with a chamber, the cylindrical thimble may be drawn forward out of the chamber and over the stem. A cartridge may be dropped into the chamber and the thimble pushed back over it. If a fired shell is in the thimble when drawn out of the chamber, it will be knocked away by the stem. The cylinder is, of course, not bored through, but its rear edge is pierced with notches through which the hammer nose gets through to strike a cartridge rim. There are other notches, so small they will hardly show in the photograph, located midway between the larger notches. It is only when the hammer nose rests in one of these very small notches that the stem will line up with a chamber and permit either loading or unloading.

The knob seen protruding from the butt is the end of a short screw driver. Some Ponds have this; others do not.

The man who had trouble loading a Slocum Side-Loading Revolver probably had more trouble loading a Pond Separate-Chambers Revolver.

The scarcest of the Smith & Wesson evasions that got past the patent model stage are the Crispin revolvers. Probably only few were made. I have seen just two, both unmarked. Chapel's *The Gun Collector's Handbook of Values* reports one with frame stamped "Smith Arms Co., New York City. Crispin's Pat. Oct. 3, 1865".

An unmarked Crispin is shown in Plate 201. Mr. Silas Crispin was granted a patent for his revolver on October 3, 1865, United States 50,224. Almost two months earlier Mr. Crispin received a patent for the peculiar cartridge to be fired in his revolver. That cartridge, though not the most fantastic ever invented, certainly does rank among the oddest ever put in production. A specimen of a Crispin cartridge will be briefly described in Chapter XII.

The Crispin revolver has a hinged frame and a two-part cylinder, both sections of which revolve. When the gun is opened with the barrel tipped down the cylinder comes apart into two right circular divisions, one being connected to the swinging barrel and the other to the frame. Each section has its own centre pin. The rear section has chamber borings that match those in the front section, except that they are not bored through. When the gun is loaded, by inserting the ball ends of the cartridges in the front section of the cylinder and closing the gun, the cartridges have their bases seated in the rear section of the cylinder, and the cartridges then act as dowel pins. With the chambers so loaded, with the fulminate-filled rims at the junctions of the two cylinder sections, the front section of necessity turns with the rear section. The gun is single-action, with the usual ratchet for revolving the cylinder. In the gun illustrated the hammer nose is long, to reach the hooplike rim. Sometimes a firing pin, rather than a long hammer nose, was employed. Crispin suggested the use of such an "igniting rod" and Sawyer reported the existence of a Crispin revolver so equipped.

One advantage in the Crispin was that no mechanical ejector was needed for removal of fired cartridges. When the gun was opened the cartridges could easily be withdrawn with the fingers.

An example of what is probably the only revolver that used a pin-fire cartridge and was still able to avoid infringement of the Rollin White patent is shown in Plate 202.

Prosper Polain, of Brussels, Belgium, patented his invention in the United States, March 27, 1866, patent 53,548. He obtained a patent in France too, and perhaps in other countries.

The Polain invention combined the main feature of the Slocum revolver—side-loading—with the main feature of the Pond—the "lining thimble". What Pond called "lining thimbles" were called "cartridge-tubes or small barrels" by Polain. In the Pond revolver these tubes are separate entities; in the Polain they are grouped in a circle and fastened at the front to a metal disk. In both guns these cylindrical, open-end tubes act as containers for conventional metallic cartridges and they are inserted into cylinder chambers, which are not bored through, by being pushed back into those chambers. The metal disk in the Polain revolver, to which these tubes are secured, is free to revolve with the cylinder, and it has holes in it corresponding to the front openings in the tubes. Looking either at the actual gun, or at the photograph in Plate 202, it is not at once apparent what is so unusual about the cylinder.

It will be noticed there are large grooves, shaped like pointed bullets, in the side of the cylinder. These grooves are not troughs; they are lengthwise openings cut right through the cylinder wall, wide enough to accept 12 mm. cartridges. The cartridge-tubes, with slots in their rear ends for the cartridge pins, are visible through these large cylinder openings. The raised disk to which these tubes are attached may be seen just in front of the cylinder itself.

By moving a lever, which may be seen turned down under the

barrel breech, the entire barrel assemply may be drawn forward, along with the disk and the cartridge-tubes. When loading a cartridge through the side of the cylinder it is necessary to guide the cartridge pin forward into its slot in the cartridge-tube.

There is an ejecting rod under the barrel. Extraction of a fired case is made easier by the fact the cartridge pin is caught at the point of the long opening in the side of the chamber when the tubes are drawn forward.

The Polains were the last of the evasions, except for the Thuer Colts.

A Thuer Colt is a Colt revolver that has been converted from a percussion-cap weapon to a cartridge gun by the installation of a special cylinder, invented by F. Alexander Thuer, and patented by him September 15, 1868, United States patent 82,258.

The cartridge used is front-loading, tapering down slightly from the bullet to the primer end, and is loaded with the loading lever in the usual way. It is metallic, rimless, centre-fire, and reloadable. The Thuer Colt revolver is not only the last of the Smith & Wesson evasions; it is the first Colt revolver to use metallic cartridges, and the first American revolver to use all-metal, self-primed, reloadable cartridges.

The Polain revolvers used self-primed metallic cartridges that were readily reloadable, but, though patented and sold in this country, it is believed none was manufactured here. The example shown bears Belgium proof marks.

A fine example of an 1862 model Colt equipped with a Thuer cylinder is shown in Plate 203.

The usual method of producing one of these patented cylinders was to turn down the rear of a percussion cylinder far enough to expose the ends of the chambers but not deep enough to interfere with normal operation of the ratchet, and fit an intricate ring, equipped with both a firing pin and an ejecting lever in place of the turned-off portion. This ring, or annular plate, is capable of lateral movement, independent of the cylinder. When it is turned to the right the firing pin will be driven by the hammer against the cartridge head in line with the barrel when the trigger is pulled. When the ring is turned to the left, snapping the hammer will cause the ejecting lever to give a sharp blow to a fired case in the chamber second to the right of the hammer. The striking end of this small ejecting lever is recessed in the centre to prevent contact of the lever with the primer, so a loaded cartridge may be ejected safely.

Under the illustration of the Thuer Colt a complete set of Thuer cartridge reloading tools is shown. These are the subject of Mr. Thuer's United States patent 98,529, of January 4, 1870. The tool at the right is the shell holder. It has a saddle-shaped base so it may be placed partly around the centre pin and back against the recoil shield when the cylinder is removed. It has a short mandrel and a longer socket, protruding from the base. Just to the left is a small threaded "capping-plug" that is screwed into the concave face of the plunger on the loading lever. Next to the left is the capping-guide. Farthest to the left is the ball-guide. Underneath is a punch, to be used for knocking out used primers, or for pushing out loaded cartridges from the socket of the shell holder. In use, with the shell holder in position (the short mandrel in line with the rammer and an empty shell placed on that short mandrel) a primer is placed in the head of the capping-guide, which has been inverted over the end of the shell. When the ramming lever is lowered, the capping-plug seats the primer. After priming a supply of shells, the capping-plug is unscrewed. A shell, charged with powder, is placed in the socket of the shell holder, which has been turned so the socket will come in line with the rammer. The ball-guide is placed over the powder-loaded shell and a ball placed in it. The ball is rammed home when the loading lever is pulled down.

To permit proper use of the Thuer cartridge-loading apparatus, it was necessary to tap a small hole in the concave face of the rammer. No change whatever was required in a Colt percussion revolver to enable it to fire Thuer cartridges, other than the removal of the percussion-cap cylinder and the substitution of a proper Thuer cylinder. However, it was customary to deepen the groove on the right side of the barrel lug, to permit loading and ejecting of Thuer cartridges without removing the barrel.

CHAPTER XII

EARLY PRIMINGS, CAPS, AND CARTRIDGES

IN the early days of the 19th century when sportsmen spoke of "primings" they were referring to fulminate in the form of loose powder, or fulminate in pellet form, or to what they called "patches". When they spoke of "primers" they were not referring to metal caps, neither those placed on nipples of muzzle-loaders nor those now placed in the heads of centre-fire cartridges; they were talking of tube primers.

Patches consisted of morsels of fulminate with thin paper covers. They resembled caps for modern toy pistols. They were fragile and impermanent, and, like the locks that fired them, few have survived. A half dozen are shown in Plate 204. Patch-lock pistols, as well as a box containing a number of strikers, some with patch primings affixed were described in Chapter III.

Below the patches in Plate 204 there are fulminate "pills". These are believed to have been for a Billinghurst gun (Chapter IV) and, as can be seen, they vary considerably in size. Patch locks seem to have been unknown in America, but pill locks—known at first in America as punch locks—long remained popular, notably in the western part of New York State, where the fulminate pills were sold as "percussion powder". A tin box of such priming, made in Waterville, New York, is shown in Plate 205.

It would seem that a man priming a gun like a Billinghurst would have a problem in deciding how many of these pills of different sizes would be needed.

Uniformity in size would be needed if pills were to be supplied automatically, one at a time, from a magazine. Plate 206 shows a bottle of pills along with three chargers such as were used in the Egg detonator described in Chapter V.

Pills consisted of fulminate and a binder, and were varnished—

unless they were waxed. Varnished pills were hard and durable, but wax-coated pills "suffered from agglomeration", to quote an early writer.

Varieties of tube primers—we leave early "primings" and get on to early "primers"—are shown in Plate 207. These different styles of tube primers are alike in having fulminate contained in a thin copper wrapping forming a cylinder which is hardly thicker than a pencil lead. To be ready for detonation, a tube's open end was pressed in a vent leading to the powder chamber. Usually, in Manton guns for instance, the tube lay on an anvil and was crushed when the descending hammer struck it midway between the ends. The tubes were often plain cylinders with both ends open, and, when detonated, spurted flame out from the side of the lock as well as in to the powder. This sudden spitting of flame could be disconcerting to anyone standing alongside. As the illustration shows, some primers had one end closed. At the left are two of the primers patented by Clayton—see page 88 of the 10th edition of Hawker's *Instructions to Young Sportsmen.* The second of these shows the underside, with the hook for securing it. Third is a Charles Lancaster primer—see page 87 of the 9th edition of Hawker's famous book. Fourth is a tube with a block at the end—provenience unknown. Fifth is a tube with a hook to fasten under the anvil. A tube like this was used on the lock of a rare Tower seven-barrel detonator. Sixth is a tube for a stanchion gun. Tube locks worked particularly well on those huge guns which were carried on punts and often loaded with two ounces of powder and a pound of shot. Users of those guns steadfastly maintained the copper cap was less reliable than the tube primer in igniting the powder in a gun on a boat in wet weather. Seventh is a tube for a duck gun designed to be fired from the shoulder. Eighth is a tube for a Manton or similar fowling piece.

At the top in Plate 208 are four more tube primers. At the right in that group is a Westley Richards primer, commonly called a mushroom primer. It is different from the tube primers in the previous picture in that it was designed to be thrust into a nipple with a very wide vent, and to be detonated by being struck on its flanged end. The flanges helped to retain the tube in the nipple. Westley Richards made guns to use his special primers, equipped with hammers and nipples that at a glance are not to be distinguished from those on a regular side-hammer cap lock. A Westley Richards gun and a Wilkinson gun, both designed to make use of mushroom primers, are described in Chapter V.

Farthest to the left in the group of four is another Manton tube primer. Next it is another form of mushroom primer, and third is another Lancaster type.

In the centre of this same illustration is a charger loaded with the later disk primers. At the right there are some twenty of these wafers, emptied from a charger. These remarkable disks were used in several models of the famous Sharps rifles described in Chapter IX. In that chapter it was also told how these disks were catapulted through the air. Now, it should be explained what the disks are like. These amazing primers are tiny, only about $\frac{1}{8}$ inch across, but each is made of two circular halves, with each half having an edge turned up at a right angle. Pressed together over fulminate the two parts are not easy to separate. Would anyone but Christian Sharps dream that such a primer not only could be built to sell at a low price but also could be thrown into space toward an anvil, intercepted in mid-air by a hammer and then be carried by that hammer to the anvil and there crushed?

At the left in this Plate 208 is a roll of Maynard tape primers, made under Dr. Maynard's United States patent 4208 of September 22, 1845. The roll is made of two narrow strips of paper cemented together and enclosing small mounds of fulminating mixture, which are well separated one from another. The individual primers are fed out either by a curved spring or by what Maynard called "a feeding wheel". Firearms equipped with Maynard magazine locks were pictured in Chapter IX. A circular put out by Maynard to list the advantages of his patent primer is shown in Illustration K.

A row of metal caps, some ribbed and some plain, and of various sizes, is shown at the bottom of Plate 208. After the conventional pistol and rifle caps there is one of the top-hat variety used on many muskets. The domed affair next to the top hat is definitely a percussion cap but I do not know what gun used it. I have been assured it was made for a Russian gun. Farthest to the right is one of the patented caps designed for the Samuel & Charles Smith gun described in Chapter VI. All by itself at the left of the row is a cap made for use in pin-fire cartridges.

There was a time, in the not too long ago, when we referred to the igniting agents used in centre-fire cartridges, not as primers, but as caps, which is all they were. That was when centre-fire was "central fire". See the box top at the right in Plate 209.

Present-day primers often have built in anvils, but many do not. Many cartridges still being manufactured use the Berdan-type primers, which do not contain the anvils. Such primers rest against

CIRCULAR.

In answer to the very numerous inquiries made at the War Department and elsewhere, respecting the Maynard Primer, the undersigned, its inventor, offers the following statement of some of its advantages over the Percussion Cap for military use.

EDWARD MAYNARD,
Washington, D. C.

CAPS.	PRIMERS.
Copper for 1,000,000 Caps costs six hundred dollars.	Paper for 1,000,000 Primers costs six dollars.
Caps cost one dollar per thousand.	Primers cost from 10 to 20 cents per thousand.
One machine will make fifty thousand Caps per day.	One machine of equal cost will make fifteen hundred thousand Primers per day.
The Cap gun has to be primed by hand every time it is loaded.	The Primer gun primes itself.
The Cap gun often goes off at half-cock, and even when the hammer is down, if it gets a blow by falling or otherwise.	The Primer gun is not primed except when cocked.
The act of priming the Cap gun is the most difficult one the soldier has to perform in battle.	The Primer gun primes itself.
The Caps, being carried in a pocket separate from the gun, are liable to be separated permanently from it, rendering it useless.	The Primers are carried in the gun and cannot be accidentally separated from it.
Nearly as much time is required *in battle* to prime the cap gun as to load it: and if the weather be cold, or the time be night, *more* time will be required.	With the Primer gun, all this time is saved.
In drilling raw recruits, a great deal of time is required to teach them to use the cap.	With the Primer gun, all this time is saved.
The Lock for the Cap gun is the cheapest; but—	The Primers cost so much less than the Caps that the saving on five hundred will pay the difference in the cost of the Locks.

ILLUSTRATION K. Maynard circular

anvils embodied in the cartridge heads. The Berdan primers, at the left in Plate 209, are like the caps on their right except that they are shallower and wider, and in this instance have extra strength. Boxes of such primers as those shown—of "extra strength for candle practice only"—are rarely seen in collections. Candle practice was a form of target practice in vogue in the United States Army around 1880. The bull's-eye was a candle flame. The cartridge was a primed empty case. A few pertinent excerpts from the 7th revised edition (1879) of *Manual for Rifle Practice* by General George W. Wingate, may be of interest. "Candle practice should be frequently indulged in, this portion of the drill being always interesting to the men . . . A series of candles should be placed in sockets placed opposite to each bull's eye used for aiming drills, and the men drawn up in front of them in a single rank, and dressed so that the muzzles of their pieces when at an 'aim' will be three feet from the lights . . . each candle extinguished counting one and a miss zero, the aggregate score of each man being announced at the close of the firing". It was stated that special primers should be used because regular primers would not extinguish the flame at a distance of three feet with certainty. A man who did not extinguish five candles in his allotted ten shots was barred from the next regular target practice.

In his circular, Illustration K, Dr. Maynard stated in regard to caps: "The act of priming the Cap gun is the most difficult one the soldier has to perform in battle". Actually, anyone, in battle or not, was apt to have difficulty picking up a cap and pressing it on a nipple, without dropping it. Its smallness made a cap nearly impossible to handle with heavy gloves. Many shooters found cappers very useful. Cappers are magazines, usually holding fifty or more caps which are forced by a spring to an open slot. The cap in the slot is pressed over the nipple, and is left on the nipple when the capper is pulled away. In Plate 210 two brass cappers are on the left, one round and one straight. On the right is an all-leather capper, probably home-made. This springless capper is almost identical with one patented September 24, 1872, by Claudius Verniaud and William Spencer, United States patent 131,642, except that the patented article is of rubber and metal. Cappers were usually suspended by a cord dangling from the neck or coat. Also in this picture is a tool made of wire and having a hook on the end for pulling fired caps from the nipple.

Pellets used in pill-lock guns, and primers used in tube-lock guns, were also small and troublesome to handle without special chargers.

Two magazines for pellet primings are at the right in Plate 211. At the left is a tube dispenser. All are British.

As to the cartridges now to be considered in this chapter, it should be said that, unlike the guns in preceding chapters, no limitation is placed in respect of modernity. Basic types of percussion cartridges are illustrated, but varieties within a species are given little or no attention. (There are no less than 28 *varieties* of the calibre 40 *species* of the centre-fire *genus* of the metallic *family* of the fixed ammunition *order* of the ball-cartridge *class*.)

This cartridge section is written more for the dabbler than for the ardent collector. I have accumulated more than a few cartridges but I have not been a true cartridge collector. I have been more interested in learning that cartridge cases have been made of paper, of paper and brass foil, of paper and sheet tin, of linen, of silk, of wool, of gutta percha, of zinc, of tin, of iron, of lead, and of animal tissue, as well as of plain brass or copper, than I have been to discover that a 40/90 Sharps straight case is $3\frac{1}{4}$ inches long whereas a 40/90 Sharps necked case is $2\frac{5}{8}$ inches long.

Of course, the enthusiast who gets intensely interested in such things as differences in case lengths and in head stamps, which are of importance in making identifications, is a real hobbyist.

It may not be amiss for me to suggest to the man who has no hobby, and particularly to the man who says his work is his hobby, that he consider the collecting of cartridges. A collection of cartridges may enhance in value nearly as much as a collection of firearms, and buying cartridges puts less strain on the pocketbook. A gun may run into hundreds of dollars, sometimes thousands, but specimens of many cartridges, some long obsolete, can at this time be bought at prices from 10¢ to $1.00 each. Only an outstanding rarity will be tagged over $5.00. There is no telling what prices will be ten years from now. I can remember when Colt Dragoons went begging at $10.00 each.

Muzzle-loading percussion firearms, particularly hunting guns, were commonly charged with powder poured down the barrel from a horn or flask. A martial muzzle-loader was often charged with powder emptied from a cartridge. The cartridges used with those percussion firearms were about the same sort used with earlier guns. They were simply wrapped and tied paper containers, each one holding a charge of gunpowder and a bullet, or sometimes a bullet and several buckshot. Cartridges of that nature, which contained gunpowder and projectile only, were used long before percussion ignition was known.

The approved method of tearing open such cartridges may best be given by quoting from British and American military instructions. The British *Instructions for Light Infantry and Riflemen*, dated 1813, contains this: ". . . the right hand then seizes the cartridge with the three first fingers and draws it from the pouch; the cartridge is brought to the mouth, and placed between the two first right double teeth, and the end twisted off . . ." The British instructions are explicit as to which teeth to use, but as far as loading is concerned, the directions merely say: "the cartridge is put into the barrel" and "The cartridge will be forced down (with the ramrod) with both hands . . ." The American regulations for the same year state: "The right hand opens the cartridge box, seizes the cartridge, shuts the case of the cartridge box. Bite the top of the cartridge off" and "The cartridge is then emptied into the muzzle and the empty paper pushed in with the finger". The American recruit was given considerable leeway in choosing which fingers as well as which teeth to use. By 1836 the American regulations provided that the cartridge be seized with "a thumb and the next two fingers" and placed "between the teeth" but they no longer mentioned closing the cartridge box after the cartridge was extracted.

In Plate 212 the paper cartridge at the left is for a British muzzle-loading Enfield. The Enfield cartridge was not wholly to blame for the 1857 uprising in India but it was the spark that set off the massacres. Probably the best reporting of the facts is in Volume Four of Churchill's *A History of the English-Speaking Peoples*, published by Dodd, Mead & Company, where Sir Winston writes:

> In the year of the centenary of Plassey rumours began to flow that the cartridges for the new Enfield rifle were greased with the fat of pigs and cows, animals which Moslem and Hindu respectively were forbidden to eat. The cartridges had to be bitten before they could be inserted in the muzzle. Thus sepoys of both religions would be defiled. There was some truth in the story, for beef fat had been used in the London arsenal at Woolwich, though it was never used at the Indian factory at Dum-Dum, and as soon as the complaints began no tainted missiles were issued. Nevertheless the tale ran through the regiments in the Spring of 1857 and there was much unrest. In April some cavalry troopers at Meerut were court-martialled and imprisoned for refusing to touch the cartridges, and on May 9 they were publicly stripped of their uniforms. An Indian officer told his superiors that the sepoys were planning to break open the jail and

release the prisoners. His warning was disbelieved. Next night three regiments mutinied, captured the prison, killed their British officers, and marched on Delhi.

An American paper cartridge for a muzzle-loading 1855 model Springfield musket is next to the Enfield cartridge. In the photograph the Enfield cartridge is placed with the bullet at the bottom, and the Springfield with the bullet at the top. The Enfield cartridge was built up of three pieces of paper rolled on a cartridge former; the Springfield of two pieces. Earlier paper cartridges were formed from single sheets. The other cartridges in the illustration were designed expressly for Colt cap-and-ball revolvers and are known as combustible cartridges. The smaller is ·36 calibre with its envelope made of animal tissue. Specifically, the tissue is the outer membrane of either pig intestines or cattle intestines. The larger, at the right, is ·44 calibre with its envelope made of paper. Combustible cartridges such as these commonly had their envelopes chemically treated to ensure speedy and complete burning.

The cartridge that is second from the right in Plate 213 is the famous Sharps linen, of which more than 16,000,000 were purchased for use in Sharps breechloaders in the Civil War. This cartridge with its linen envelope is a successor to a similar Sharps cartridge which had a paper envelope. The nitrated linen envelopes were highly inflammable but they did not always burn fast enough to exclude the possibility of burning residue remaining in the chamber when the gun was opened for reloading. The powder end of the linen envelope was covered with very thin paper, through which the flame coming from the nipple would pass instantly.

All the cartridges in Plates 212 and 213 were fired by separate priming, and all could be fired by ignition from a copper cap set on a nipple. However, in the case of the Sharps the flame passing through the nipple usually came either from a Sharps pellet primer or a Maynard tape primer, both of which have been described.

Immediately to left and right of the Sharps cartridge in Plate 213 are two other external ignition cartridges for breechloaders. The one at the right has a case made of brass foil and paper. It has a tiny hole in the centre of the base, to permit the flame from a percussion cap to reach the powder charge, and was one of several types used in Smith carbines. The other of the two, next to the Sharps at the left, is for a Renette & Gastinne shotgun and was described along with the gun in Chapter VII.

The cartridge at the extreme left is a paper covered Eley shot cartridge, designed for muzzle-loading shotguns.

The four cartridges in Plate 214 are alike in that they all have brass cases and tiny flash holes in their bases. They were designed, left to right, for the Requa-Billinghurst volley gun, the Burnside carbine, the Gallager carbine, the Maynard rifle. The first one hardly rightly belongs in the picture, as it is for a Civil War machine gun, but it is commonly found in collections of rifle and pistol ammunition. The Burnside cartridge was patented, along with the carbine, March 25, 1856, United States patent 14,491, by Ambrose Burnside, who became a general commanding the Army of the Potomac in the War Between the States. The Burnside cartridge pictured has the improvement, patented April 10, 1860, by G. P. Foster, United States patent 27,791. The improvement is a chamber for grease, located in the bead around the mouth of the case. Most of the Gallager carbines used a cartridge having a brass-foil-and-paper case. The all-metal Gallager cartridge as pictured here is seldom found. The Maynard cartridge, when it had developed into the wide-rimmed version shown here, was an excellent product, and a considerable improvement over the cartridge Dr. Maynard patented June 17, 1856, United States patent 15,141. That earliest of the Maynard cartridges would look quite like the one illustrated here except that it would be completely without a rim. The patent states the cartridge was ". . . a cylindrical-shaped shell . . . having a centrally perforated bottom" which ". . . should be removed from the chamber of the gun" after discharge. How the extraction was to be accomplished was not stated. The idea of a large flange, in the form of a circular perforated disk soldered to the tubular cartridge case, came later. The flange, which could be grasped with the fingers to extract the case, was not always a round rim. Sometimes the flange was only a flat ear projecting from the base of the cartridge. It is not known who first had the idea of using a projecting flange to facilitate cartridge extraction. Some models of both Sharps and Maynard rifles in the late 1850's used cartridges now known as "Mule Ear" and "Flop Ear". Of course, well before 1850 the pin-fire cartridge had a projecting pin which served as an extractor as well as a firing pin.

The Maynard cartridge in Plate 214 is what was referred to in Chapter IX as the primary type. Three examples of the variation, or deviating type, are shown in Plate 215. These are of the three different calibres needed for the three barrels supplied with the gun illustrated in that chapter.

Before the days of modern, self-contained, centre-fire cartridges, there were no other cartridges with as great popularity as the wide-rimmed Maynards, which were easy to reload and could be reloaded many times. The wide rim did more than aid extraction; it assured accurate fit of the cartridge in the chamber. An objection to a cartridge without a rim was that its position in the barrel varied according to the exact size of the cartridge and of the chamber; a poor fit might result in a bullet not centred, or even a misfire.

Four early self-contained cartridges are pictured in Plate 216. Each conforms to the definition of fixed ammunition, in that the projectile, the propellent, and the primer are all in one container, but only the one at the left, a Pauly pistol cartridge, is reloadable. The Pauly cartridge, the very first self-contained, centre-fire, reloadable cartridge was described at length in Chapter II.

What appears to be simply a bullet in Plate 216 is an early form of fixed ammunition. Cartridges of this general type were produced in the mid 1850's both in this country and in Europe. The particular one shown here was made for the American Volcanic rifles and pistols. Instead of being solid the lead projectile shown has a cavity holding a charge of gunpowder, and in back of this propellent a large primer holding fulminate in its centre. Repeaters used these hollow-bullet cartridges. In America they were carried in a magazine under the barrel; in France in a magazine over the barrel. The guns are described in Chapter X.

The two cartridges at the right in Plate 216 are two types used in needle guns. The long one is for a French Chassepot, the other is for a German sporting rifle. The famous German military rifle which fired this type of fixed ammunition is described in Chapter X. Needle cartridges usually have paper coverings, like the two shown, but wool, linen, and other fabrics were used at least experimentally. A major difference between the French and German versions illustrated was in the location in the cartridge of the fulminate. In the French cartridge the priming was placed just inside the base and could be detonated by a short firing pin. In the German cartridge the priming was placed in a hollow in the sabot at the base of the bullet and could be detonated only by a long firing pin or needle, which had to be driven entirely through the powder charge before it could reach the fulminate. The steel needles could not long withstand the intense heat of the powder explosions and required frequent replacement. In early Dreyse cartridges the bullet was round, but for the 1854 and later models of the military rifle the bullet was elongated and rather egg-shaped. The cardboard wad in back of the bullet, in which the fulminate was placed, had slits in the sides so it would quickly drop away from the bullet after the bullet was out of the muzzle. The reason the Germans placed the fulminate ahead of the powder was because they subscribed to the theory that more power was developed when gunpowder was ignited at the front of the charge, to burn backward. The front ignition was never used by any other military power, and it was discarded by Germany soon after the Franco-Prussian war. However, in the November 1956 issue of *Guns*, Elmer Keith reported tests were made a few years ago at Frankford Arsenal with front ignition in ·50 calibre machine-gun rounds and that velocities were raised from 2800 f.p.s. to 3000 f.p.s. In these tests the flash from the primer was carried through a tube so the forward part of the charge would be ignited first.

In Plate 217 are four early and rare cartridges that have casings of different materials but are alike in that in each the flame from the percussion cap reached the powder charge through a small hole in the centre of the cartridge head. The first of the four is an empty case made for a Pottet pistol. It is entirely of brass, and in that respect differs from the Pottet cartridge cases for long arms, which were composites of metal and paper. As in the earlier Pauly pistol cartridge, Plate 216, there is an extractor groove near the head. The Pottet extractor is, like the Pauly tool shown in Chapter II, a two-pronged implement. It differs from the Pauly tool in having the two tines in a plane at right angles to the handle. From the side it looks like a small hoe.

Next in Plate 217 is a rubber-case cartridge of the type used in the earliest of the Smith carbines. This cartridge was patented by Gilbert Smith in 1857, United States patent 17,702.

At the right of the rubber cartridge is "a ball for fire-arms, with a cavity to contain the charge of powder for propelling said ball, in which cavity the powder is secured by means of a cap inclosing the back end of the same". The quotation is from the claim in the patent granted Walter Hunt, August 10, 1848, United States patent 5701, for his invention of what he called a "rocket-ball". Fastened to the open end of the "rocket-ball" was a small metal cap encircling a cork disk perforated in the centre. This flash hole in the disk was sealed on the inside by thin tissue which would retain the powder in the cavity but which would be instantly penetrated and consumed by the fire from the priming. The Hunt cartridge was used in Jennings rifles, one of which is mentioned in Chapter IX. It looks much like the Volcanic cartridge, *q.v.*, but it uses external priming whereas the Volcanic contains its own priming.

On the right, Plate 217, is a cartridge for the Marston pistol shown in Chapter VII. This Marston cartridge has a combustible paper casing with a thick disk of stiff noncombustible leather in its base. The edges of the leather are greased, and as successive shots are fired the barrel is cleaned as the leather from one cartridge is driven through the barrel ahead of the bullet from the next cartridge. The cartridge was patented May 18, 1852, United States patent 8956, by William W. Marston and Frederick Goodell, and the leather breech-piece of the cartridge was stated to serve the purposes of "a foundation for its own cartridge, a protection to the breech pin, a wad for the next cartridge in succession, and of a swab, to clean out the soilage caused in the barrel by the antecedent explosion".

No other type of metallic self-exploding cartridge, except perhaps the rim-fire in ·22 calibre only, has been manufactured continuously for as many years as the pin-fire was manufactured. I am by no means sure the pin-fire cartridge is not still being made in Europe. There are still many pin-fire pistols, revolvers and shotguns in good shooting condition, and at least until quite recently supplies of pin-fire cartridges were available. The cartridge at the left in Plate 218 is the type of pin-fire patented by Houillier in France in 1846.* A blow on the end of the projecting pin will fire this cartridge by driving the point of the pin into the mouth of a small percussion cap and crushing the priming in the cap.

It has been generally forgotten that pin-fire cartridges are easily reloadable with proper tools. One simple form of such tool, sometimes found in cased sets made for pin-fire pistols, is not at a glance distinguishable from thin-nose pliers. The nose of the thin pincers is fitted to permit grasping, and inserting inside the head of the cartridge, of a tiny percussion cap. There is also a slot where the two parts join in which the pin may be seized for extraction.

A more elaborate tool is shown in Plates 219 and 220. It is not unlikely there are many tools like this one in the possession of people who have often said, "I wonder what that is for?" The illustrations are side and top views of a brass tool, about 3½ inches overall, made by James Dixon & Sons, Sheffield, for a 10-gauge shell. There is a small hole in the centre of the base of this tool to accept a cartridge pin, which is a short length of stiff wire. When the turnscrew in the side of the base is tightened such a pin may be quickly

* French Patents—Series 2, volume 7, page 196, plate 37.

withdrawn from a cartridge. The dome-shaped top of the cylinder may be pushed down about one quarter inch against spring pressure. To prime a cartridge, a percussion cap is placed sideways in an oblong opening in the very top of this movable dome. The cap rests on the concave end of a fixed rod that will protrude through the opening when the surrounding dome is pushed down. A fresh pin is started with the fingers into the cartridge case and the cartridge case is then pressed down firmly over the tool. The outer end of the pin will engage in a slot in the long thin spring which is attached to the base of the tool, and when this spring is pushed inward it will lock the pin and cap into position.

The other cartridges in Plate 218 were made for special guns. The largest is a Crispin cartridge used in one model of a Smith carbine. Similar Crispin cartridges in smaller calibres were used in the Crispin revolvers which circumvented the Smith & Wesson patent and which were described in Chapter XI. Mr. Crispin in his United States patent 49,237 of August 8, 1865, claimed a cartridge "with the fulminate placed within a projecting annular recess or rim, which is formed at a point between the ends of the cartridge-case". The cartridge could be used only in a gun with a divided chamber. It provided an efficient gas check and the empty case was easily removed with the fingers, but its construction, with that fulminate-filled belt around its mid-section, invited premature explosion.

The third and fourth cartridges in Plate 218 were also made for use in revolvers which successfully evaded the Smith & Wesson patent. The third cartridge is for a Plant front-loader, and to distinguish it from an ordinary rim-fire the inventors stated such cartridges "were made without the laterally projecting flanges commonly provided, but have flanges projecting in a rearward direction or parallel with the bores of the chambers to contain the fulminate priming". Nowadays a collector calls them "hollow-base" or "cup-primer" cartridges. The fourth cartridge is for a Moore front-loader. This has a round, rather than flat teat. The explosion resulted from the hammer crushing the fulminate-filled teat against the anvil formed by the side of the opening through which the teat protruded. The revolvers that used flat teat cartridges only required a little more care in loading, to be sure each cartridge was turned properly so it would be fully chambered.

The smallest cartridge in Plate 222 is called a lip-fire. It has the fulminate concentrated in a small prominence on the rim, and was made for use in some models of Allen & Wheelock revolvers.

Cartridges of this type, of larger calibre, were used in the Allen & Wheelock revolver described in Chapter X.

Next in Plate 222 is the famous rim-fire known as the ·44 Henry Flat. This is a development of the early small calibre rim-fire cartridges, the ·22's, of which millions are still fired every year. The ·22's themselves developed from the bulleted breech caps invented by Flobert of France.

Centre-fire cartridges were invented long before rim-fires, but just about all guns manufactured in the United States in the 1850's and 1860's to fire self-contained metallic cartridges were rim-fire arms. In the manufacture of a rim-fire cartridge the fulminate placed in the base was whirled by centrifugal force into the rim. That the fulminate would be distributed evenly around the rim was not always assured. The unconsidered spot on a cartridge rim where a hammer might strike was as uncertain as the hole in which a roulette ball might drop. If the hammer chanced to fall where there was no priming there would be a misfire. The larger the calibre, the greater the circumference of the rim, and the greater the risk of that bane of the old-time shooter's life. The previously mentioned lip-fire cartridge was a form of rim-fire, but it could not be chambered so any part of the rim other than the lip would come under the hammer. The long-before invented centre-fire system did not come into its own until the 1870's, but in the 1860's many men were working on the idea of improved metallic cartridges which would have the fulminate located in a small area inside the centre of the head and held in place by some form of anvil against which it could be crushed. Scores, perhaps hundreds, of schemes were devised for locking a perforated anvil in position so the fulminate would be detonated by a blow from a hammer or firing pin striking the centre of the cartridge head. Outwardly, some of these inside-primed cartridges look just like rim-fires. At the right of the ·44 Henry Flat is an inside-primed cartridge for a converted Civil War musket. The two partial cannelures near the rim mark this one as inside-primed, not rim-fire. Those indentations provide internal supports to hold a cup or disk anvil close to the inside of the cartridge head.

The last of the four cartridges in Plate 222 was made in France for a centre-fire cartridge revolver, the Perrin, of which a small number were used in the Civil War. One of the revolvers is described in Chapter X. This inside-primed cartridge has the smooth head we nowadays expect to find only on a rim-fire.

Of the eight cartridges in Plates 218 and 222 the pin-fire is the only one it is feasible for an amateur to reload.

An English reloadable, outside-primed centre-fire cartridge was developed by Colonel Boxer and was approved for use in the Snider rifle on October 11, 1866. This ·577 Snider cartridge, at the left in Plate 221, was the first such cartridge to be officially adopted by any government for its armed forces. The case, made of thin brass covered with brown paper, cemented and rolled into a cylinder, is fitted into a cup riveted to an iron base. The centre-fire primer is a simple percussion cap which rests against a small, shouldered anvil. The cylinder was secured to the base by pressure of a rolled papier-mâché wad which was squeezed with great force against the sides. These Snider cartridges were complex creations and though definitely reloadable with proper tools, they could not be satisfactorily reloaded in the field as could 1865 Maynard cartridges, for instance. After a charge of powder was emptied into the Boxer case a layer of cotton was placed over it before the bullet was inserted. The bullet was unusual and perhaps warrants brief description here. The Mark I Snider cartridge fired a bullet that was hollow both in the nose and at the base. The hollow at the base was filled with a baked clay plug which expanded the bullet into the grooves of the rifling when the Snider was fired. The Snider rifle using this cartridge was of large calibre and its rifling had a slow twist. Only a long bullet would follow a true course without tumbling. The hollowing of the nose permitted giving the bullet necessary length and correct centre of gravity without undue weight.

The long cartridge next to the Snider is a later Boxer cartridge developed for the Martini-Henry rifle. Kipling implied that the British Tommy sometimes called the Martini-Henry rifle a "cross-eyed old bitch",* but certainly it was more often called simply the "Martin 'Enry". The cartridge is of the bottle-neck variety and its thin coiled brass casing is not covered with paper. Otherwise, except for the bullet, the construction is practically the same as that of the Snider. The bullet is of ·45 calibre, rather than the ·577 of the Snider, and is solid except for a very slight hollow in its base. Further, the bullet is lubricated by a wad of beeswax placed just behind it, whereas the Snider bullet was lubricated by wax packed in three of its four cannelures.

To the right of the Martin-Henry cartridge is a tapered front-loading cartridge designed for Thuer Colts. These cartridges, to-

* When 'arf of your bullets fly wide in the ditch,
Don't call your Martini a cross-eyed old bitch;
She's human as you are—you treat her as sich,
An' she'll fight for the young British Soldier.
—*The Young British Soldier*

gether with reloading tools, are described in the preceding chapter.

With the production of the one-piece drawn-brass cartridge on the far right in Plate 221 the modern centre-fire cartridge arrived. This is the 44/40, first used in the Winchester 1873 model rifles and the Colt Frontier Six Shooters. In making it, a brass disk was forced through a series of dies until a cartridge case with thin walls but heavy head was drawn. The head was formed with an outside pocket to contain a primer, but it was left thick enough to withstand a strong hammer blow and so ensure the crushing of the fulminate, and thereby the prevention of misfires. There have been many refinements and improvements, particularly in powder and in primers, but the cartridge of today is basically unchanged from the cartridge of eighty years ago.

Will this year's cartridge in this year's rifle give more accuracy at long range than could be had from a breechloader, or even a muzzle-loader, of seventy or eighty years ago? Perhaps, a little, but not much. In the 1876 International Shooting Match, J. K. Millner, of the Irish team, made fifteen consecutive bull's-eyes at 1,000 yards, firing a muzzle-loading Rigby rifle, the first time this possible was ever fired. The Americans, with Sharps and Remington breechloaders, won that match by an extremely small margin, with the Irish second. To win the 1880 match the American team's breechloaders scored 221 bull's-eyes, 41 centres, 7 inners, 1 outer, and no miss. Six men each fired fifteen shots at 800, at 900, and at 1,000 yards.

The purpose of Plate 223 is to show how greatly cartridges may differ in size. Of the three small cartridges the first is a pin-fire made for a watch charm pistol. Next is a rim-fire made for the German indoor target rifle shown in Plate 132. The third of the little cartridges is a 2·7 mm. Kolibri. This cartridge, made for a German autoloading pistol, is $\frac{7}{16}$ inch long and is the smallest calibre centre-fire cartridge. The largest and most powerful cartridge commercially produced for big game shooting is shown below the three small cartridges. It is ·600 calibre, fires a 900-grain bullet, and develops a muzzle energy of 7600 foot pounds.

Some gunmakers and some cartridge manufacturers supplied empty and unprimed cartridges to be loaded by shooters when and as they saw fit.

Metal inserts to contain a powder charge and to be chambered in a breech-loading gun were known in the 16th century. The chamber insert at top left in Plate 224 differs from those earliest cartridges only in that it has a nipple for percussion-cap ignition. The early ones had simple vents to admit the flame of match- or friction-ignition. The small insert at the right is an auxiliary chamber for a Williamson Derringer. That single-shot pistol was constructed so one of these inserts, loaded and capped, could be substituted for the ·41 rim-fire cartridge it normally fired. The two cartridges directly under the Williamson auxiliary chamber are Roper shotgun shells. They are of steel and without the elasticity of thin brass cases, but they are sturdy, not apt to misfire, and were popular for many years. They could, of course, be loaded and reloaded many times. The upper of the two Roper shells has a conventional nipple for a percussion cap with a single flash hole in the centre; the lower has a solid nipple with two flash holes, one at either side. The two shells at the left of the Ropers are 10-gauge and of brass. The upper has a nipple formed in the case. There are three flash holes, one in the centre of the nipple and one at either side of it. The lower has a solid movable anvil with two flash holes alongside. The anvil was made movable, so a rod could be inserted in the shell to push out the anvil and remove the fired cap.

As brevity is my intention,
I purposely omit to mention
Many more matters which you'll find
In shooting books, if you're inclin'd.

Remarks on Shooting
W. Watt, London, 1835

BIBLIOGRAPHY

BIBLIOGRAPHY

THIS is a Bibliography of Publications I have found to contain material germane to percussion guns and their accessories, such as are illustrated in this book.

No newspapers, novels, popular magazines, dealer or manufacturer catalogues, auction catalogues, or exposition catalogues, are listed, though such publications on odd occasions do contain worthwhile information.

Every periodical named is technical and each usually has dissertative material in various issues. The periodicals are in two classes: (1) periodicals currently being published; (2) periodicals which I believe have ceased publication. Probably in only a few large public libraries will complete files be found of those periodicals discontinued many years ago. Rarely in other than a few private libraries will there be files of a few periodicals whose publication ceased after disappointingly brief runs.

Books listed with a single asterisk (*) are old works that have been reprinted without revision in recent years. Books listed with two asterisks (* *) are either old works that were reprinted in revised and usually enlarged editions years ago, or modern works that have been issued in revised editions printed recently.

CURRENTLY PUBLISHED PERIODICALS

The American Arms Collector. Towson, Md.

The American Rifleman. Washington, D.C.

Antiques. New York, N.Y.

Arms & Armour Society, The Journal of the. London.

Army Historical Research, The Journal of the Society for. Sheffield.

The Connoisseur, London.

Franklin Institute, The Journal of the. Philadelphia, Pa.

Gun & Ammo Collector—Dealer—Shooter. East Ellsworth, Wis.

The Gun Digest. Chicago, Ill.

The Gun Report. Aledo, Ill.

Guns. Skokie, Ill.

Guns & Ammo. Los Angeles, Cal.

Hobbies. Chicago, Ill.
Muzzle Blasts. Portsmouth, Ohio.
Ordnance (Formerly *Army Ordnance*). Washington, D.C.
Patent Specifications. (England, France, Germany, United States, *et al.*)
Scientific American. New York, N.Y.

OTHER PERIODICALS

Annual of Scientific Discovery and Useful Arts. Boston, Mass. Publication ceased 1871.
Antique Arms Journal. Chicago, Ill. Publication ceased 1953.
Arms and the Man. New York and Washington. Publication ceased 1923.
The Arms Collector. East Syracuse, N.Y. Publication ceased 1939.
Great Guns. Dearborn, Mich. Publication ceased 1956.
Gun and Cartridge Record. Chagrin Falls, Ohio. Publication ceased 1954.
The Gun Collector. Whitewater, Wis. Publication ceased 1957.
The Gun Report. Akron, Ohio. Publication ceased 1942.
Guns. Bellport, N.Y. Publication ceased 1948.
London Journal of the Arts and Sciences. London. Publication ceased 1866.
Magazine of Antique Firearms. Athens, Tenn. Publication ceased 1912.
The Marksman. London. Publication ceased 1950.
Mechanics' Magazine. London. Publication ceased 1844.
The Rifle. Boston, Mass. Publication ceased 1888.
Shooting and Fishing. New York, N.Y. Publication ceased 1906.
The Texas Gun Collector. Dallas, Tex. Publication ceased 1956.

BOOKS

ABELS, ROBERT. *Early American Firearms*. Cleveland, Ohio, 1950.
AMBER, JOHN (Compiler). *Ten Rare Gun Catalogues 1860–1899*. New York, N.Y., 1952.
A GENTLEMAN OF PHILADELPHIA COUNTY. *The American Shooter's Manual*. Philadelphia, Pa., 1827.*
BARBER, EDWARD. *The Crack Shot*. New York, N.Y., 1868.
BARTLETT, W. A., and GALLATIN, D. B. *Digest of Cartridges*. Washington, D.C., 1878.
BENTON, JAMES G. *Ordnance Memoranda No. 22*. Washington, D.C., 1878.
BLANCH, H. J. *A Century of Guns*. London, 1909.
BOCH, GERHARD. *Moderne Faustfeuerwaffen und Ihr Gebrauch*. Neudamm, Germany, 1911.
BOWMAN, H. W. *Antique Guns*. Greenwich, Conn., 1954.
BUSK, HANS. *The Rifle and How to Use It*. London, 1860.
CARMAN, W. Y. *A History of Firearms*. London, 1955.
CHAPEL, CHARLES. *Gun Collecting*. New York, N.Y., 1939.

CHAPEL, CHARLES. *The Gun Collector's Handbook of Values*. San Leandro, Cal., 1940.* *
CHAPMAN, JOHN. *The Improved American Rifle*. New York, N.Y., 1848.*
CHINN, GEORGE M. *The Machine Gun*. Washington, D.C., 1951.
CHINN, G. M. and HARDIN, B. E. *Encyclopedia of American Hand Arms*. Huntington, W. Va., 1942.
CLEVELAND, H. W. S. *Hints to Riflemen*. New York, N.Y., 1864.*
CLINE, WALTER. *The Muzzle-loading Rifle Then and Now*. Huntington, W. Va., 1942.
DEANE, J. *Deane's Manual of the History and Science of Fire-Arms*. London, 1958.*
DEMMIN, AUGUST. *Die Kriegswaffen*. Leipzig, Germany, 1869.
DEXTER, F. THEODORE. *Thirty-Five Years Scrapbook of Antique Arms*. Topeka, Kan., 1947.
DEXTER, F. THEODORE. *Rare Ancient Arms*. Los Angeles, Cal., 1954.
DEYRUP, F. J. *Arms Makers of the Connecticut Valley*. Northampton, Mass., 1948.
DILLIN, JOHN. *The Kentucky Rifle*. Washington, D.C., 1924.* *
FARROW, E. S. *American Small Arms*. New York, N.Y., 1904.
FFOULKES, CHARLES J. *Inventory and Survey of the Armouries of the Tower of London*. London, 1916.
FREMANTLE, T. F. *The Book of the Rifle*. London, 1901.
FULLER, C. E. *Springfield Shoulder Arms 1795–1865*. New York, N.Y., 1930.
FULLER, C. E. *The Breech-Loader in the Service*. New York, N.Y., 1933.
FULLER, C. E., and STEUART, R. D. *Firearms of the Confederacy*. Huntington, W. Va., 1944.* *
GEORGE, JOHN NIGEL. *English Pistols and Revolvers*. Onslow County, N.C., 1938.
GEORGE, JOHN NIGEL. *English Guns and Rifles*. Plantersville, S.C., 1947.
GLUCKMAN, ARCADI. *United States Martial Pistols and Revolvers*. Buffalo, N.Y., 1939.
GLUCKMAN, ARCADI. *United States Muskets, Rifles and Carbines*. Buffalo, N.Y., 1948.
GRANCSAY, STEPHEN. *American Engraved Powder Horns*. New York, N.Y., 1945.
GRANT, JAMES R. *Single-Shot Rifles*. New York, N.Y., 1947.
GREENER, WILLIAM. *The Gun*. London, 1835.
GREENER, WILLIAM. *The Science of Gunnery*. London, 1841.
GREENER, WILLIAM. *Gunnery in 1858*. London, 1858.
GREENER, WILLIAM WELLINGTON. *The Gun and Its Development*. London, 1881.* *
GREENER, WILLIAM WELLINGTON. *Modern Breech-Loaders*. London, 1871.
HATCHER, JULIAN. *Pistols and Revolvers*. Marshallton, Del., 1927.
HAVEN, C. T., and BELDEN, F. A. *A History of the Colt Revolver*. New York, N.Y., 1940.
HAWKER, PETER. *Instructions to Young Sportsmen*. London, 1814.* *

HELD, ROBERT. *The Age of Firearms*. New York, N.Y., 1957.

HICKS, JAMES E. *U.S. Ordnance*. Mt. Vernon, N.Y., 1938.*

HIME, HENRY. *Gunpowder and Ammunition*. London, 1904.

JACKSON, HERBERT J. *European Hand Firearms of the Sixteenth, Seventeenth, and Eighteenth Centuries*. London, 1923.

JEWITT, LLEWELLYN. *Rifles and Volunteer Rifle Corps*. London, 1860.

JOHNSON, JOHN B. *The Gun and How to Use It*. London, 1860.

JOHNSON, M. M., and HAVEN, C. T. *Ammunition*. New York, N.Y., 1943.

JOHNSON, T. B. *The Shooter's Companion*. London, 1819 and 1823.

KARR, C. L., and KARR, C. B. *Remington Hand Guns*. Harrisburg, Pa., 1947.* *

LACY, R. *The Modern Shooter*. London, 1842.

LATHAM, JOHN. *The Progress of Breech-Loading Small Arms*. London, 1875.

LENZ, E. C. *Muzzle Flashes*. Huntington, W. Va., 1944.

LEWIS, B. R. *Small Arms and Ammunition in the United States Service*. Washington, D.C., 1956.

LOGAN, HERSCHEL C. *Cartridges*. Huntington, W. Va., 1948.

LOGAN, HERSCHEL C. *Hand Cannon to Automatic*. Huntington, W. Va., 1944.

LOW, A. M. *Musket to Machine-Gun*. London, 1942.

MANGEOT, H. *Traité du Fusil de Chasse et des Armes de Précision*. Brussels, Belgium, 1852.

MARKS, EDWARD. *The Evolution of Modern Small Arms and Ammunition*. London, 1898.

METSCHL, JOHN. *The Rudolph J. Nunnemacher Collection of Projectile Arms*. Milwaukee, Wis., 1928.

McHENRY, R. C., and ROPER, W. F. *Smith & Wesson Hand Guns*. Huntington, W. Va., 1945.*

McKEE, T. H. *The Gun Book*. New York, N.Y., 1918.

MORDECAI, ALFRED. *Military Commission to Europe in 1855 and 1856*. Washington, D.C., 1860.

NEAL, W. KEITH. *Spanish Guns and Pistols*. London, 1955.

NORTON, CHARLES B. *American Breech-Loading Small Arms*. New York, N.Y., 1872.

NORTON, CHARLES B. *American Inventions and Improvements in Breech-Loading Small Arms*. Springfield, Mass., 1880.

OMMUNDSEN, H., and ROBINSON, E. H. *Rifles and Ammunition*. London, 1915.

PARSONS, JOHN E. *Catalogue of a Loan Collection of Percussion Colt Revolvers and Conversions, 1836–1873*. New York, N.Y., 1942.

PARSONS, JOHN E. *The First Winchester*. New York, N.Y., 1955.

PARSONS, JOHN E. *Henry Deringer's Pocket Pistol*. New York, N.Y., 1952.

PARSONS, JOHN E. *The Peacemaker and Its Rivals*. New York, N.Y., 1950.

PARSONS, JOHN E. *Smith & Wesson Revolvers*. New York, N.Y., 1957.

PARSONS, JOHN E., and DUMONT, JOHN. *Firearms in the Custer Battle*. Harrisburg, Pa., 1953.

PATERSON, R. M. *Samuel Colt* vs. *Massachusetts Arms Company*. Boston, Mass., 1851.*

PAULIN-DÉSORMEAUX, M. A. O. *Armurerie*. Paris, France, 1852.
PAWLING, J. R. *Dr. Samuel Guthrie*. Watertown, N.Y., 1947.
POLLARD, H. B. C. *The Book of the Pistol and Revolver*. London, 1917.
POLLARD, H. B. C. *A History of Firearms*. London, 1926.
REID, ALEXANDER JOHN FORSYTH. *The Reverend Alexander John Forsyth*. Aberdeen, Scotland, 1909.* *
RILING, RAY. *Guns and Shooting*. New York, N.Y., 1951.
RILING, RAY. *The Powder Flask Book*. New Hope, P.A., 1953.
ROBERTS, NED H. *The Muzzle-Loading Cap Lock Rifle*. Manchester, N.H. 1940.
ROUX, HENRI. *Fusils de Chasse*. Paris, France, 1822.
RUSSELL, C. P. *Guns on the Early Frontiers*. Los Angeles, Cal., 1957.
SATTERLEE, L. D. *A Catalog of Firearms for the Collector*. Detroit, Mich., 1927.
SATTERLEE, L. D. *Fourteen Old Gun Catalogs*. Ann Arbor, Mich., 1941.*
SATTERLEE, L. D. *Ten Old Gun Catalogs*. Ann Arbor, Mich., 1939.*
SAUER, KARL VON. *Waffenlehre*. Munich, Germany, 1866.
SAWYER, CHARLES WINTHROP. *Firearms in American History. Vol. II, The Revolver*. Boston, Mass., 1911.*
SAWYER, CHARLES WINTHROP. *Our Rifles*. Boston, Mass., 1920.*
SAWYER, CHARLES WINTHROP. *United States Single Shot Martial Pistols*. Boston, Mass., 1913.
SCHMIDT, RUDOLPH. *Die Handfeuerwaffen*. Basel, Switzerland, 1875.
SCHMIDT, RUDOLPH. *Die Handfeuerwaffen*. Basel, Switzerland, 1878.
SCHON, JULIAN. *Geschichte der Handfeuerwaffen*. Dresden, Germany, 1858.
SCOFFERN, JOHN. *Projectiles, Weapons of War, and Explosive Compounds*. London, 1845.
SERVEN, JAMES E. *Colt Firearms*. Santa Ana, Cal., 1954.
SHARPE, PHILIP. *The Rifle in America*. New York, N.Y., 1938.* *
SHAW, JOSHUA, *A Sketch or History of the Copper Cap, and Percussion Artillery Primer*. Washington, D.C.(?), 1847.
SHAW, JOSHUA. *Documents Official and Unofficial, Relating to the Claim of Joshua Shaw*. Washington, D.C., 1847.
SHIELDS, JOSEPH W. *From Flintlock to M1*. New York, N.Y., 1954.
SMITH, J. A., and SWANSON, E. *The Antique Pistol Book*. Hoboken, N.J., 1948.
SMITH, W. H. B. *Pistols and Revolvers*. Harrisburg, Pa., 1946.
SMITH, W. H. B. *Rifles*. Harrisburg, Pa., 1948.
SMITH, W. H. B. *Small Arms of the World*. Harrisburg, Pa., 1943.* *
SMITH, W. O. *The Sharps Rifle*. New York, N.Y., 1943.
STELLE, J. P., and HARRISON, W. B. *The Gunsmith's Manual*. New York, N.Y., 1883.*
STOCKBRIDGE, V. D. *Digest of Patents Relating to Breech-Loading and Magazine Small Arms*. Washington, D.C., 1874.
STONE, GEORGE CAMERON. *A Glossary of the Construction, Decoration, and Use of Arms and Armor*. Portland, Me., 1934.

THIERBACH, M. *Die Geschichtliche Entwickelung der Handfeuerwaffen.* Dresden, Germany, 1888.

THIERY, A. *Descriptions des Divers Systèmes à Percussion.* Paris, France, 1839.

TREADWELL, T. J. *Ordnance Memoranda No. 14.* Washington, D.C., 1873.

TRUESDELL, STEPHEN. *The Rifle.* Harrisburg, Pa., 1947.

VAN RENSSELAER, STEPHEN. *American Firearms.* Watkins Glen, N.Y., 1947.

VARIOUS. *Illustrated Catalogue of United States Cartridge Company's Collection of Firearms.* Lowell, Mass., 1902.* *

WHITE, H. P., and MUNHALL, B. D. *Center Fire American and British Pistol and Revolver Cartridges.* Washington, D.C., 1950.

WHITE, H. P., and MUNHALL, B. D. *Center Fire Metric Pistol and Revolver Cartridges.* Washington, D.C., 1948.

WILKINSON, HENRY. *Engines of War.* London, 1841.

WILLIAMSON, HAROLD. *Winchester.* Washington, D.C., 1952.

WINANT, LEWIS. *Firearms Curiosa.* New York, N.Y., 1955.

WINANT, LEWIS. *Pepperbox Firearms.* New York, N.Y., 1952.

WINGATE, GEORGE. *Manual for Rifle Practice.* New York, N.Y., 1879.

* Old books, reprinted since 1900 without revision.

** Old books, reprinted before 1900 in revised editions, Also, books published after 1900 and since reprinted in revised editions.

INDEX

INDEX